THE POSTCOLONIAL POLITICS OF DEVELOPMENT

This collection of essays is the first to chart what a specifically 'postcolonial politics' might look like in the context of global development so as to question development's dominant cultural representations and institutional practices.

The Postcolonial Politics of Development examines recent development policy initiatives in such areas as 'governance', 'human/gender rights', and 'participation' to better understand and contest how knowledge is produced in international development — its cultural assumptions and power implications. It shows how we, development practitioners and westernized elites/intellectuals, are complicit in this knowledge production. Such noble gestures as giving foreign aid or promoting participation and democracy often mask our institutional biases and economic and geopolitical interests, while silencing marginalized groups, on whose behalf we purportedly work.

In developing the argument, the book addresses the following questions:

- how can postcolonialism help us understand the dominant cultural values and politics that frame development theory and practice?
- to what extent are we, intellectuals and development workers, complicit in neocolonial knowledge production?
- how do our institutional practices silence the Third World subaltern, and what postcolonial strategies might we employ for the subaltern to be better heard?
- how might a postcolonial politics open up avenues for democratic dialogue and subaltern agency in development?

Making complex theoretical arguments accessible to development practice, this book will serve as a useful introduction to development scholars, students, policy-makers, and practitioners alike.

Ilan Kapoor is Associate Professor at the Faculty of Environmental Studies, York University, Toronto. His research focuses on postcolonial theory, participatory development, and democracy, and has been published in several academic journals, including *Third World Quarterly* and *Alternatives*. He has worked with many development organizations, including the Canadian International Development Agency.

POSTCOLONIAL POLITICS

Edited by:

Pal Ahluwalia, University of California, San Diego and University of South Australia
Michael Dutton, Goldsmiths, University of London
Leela Gandhi, University of Chicago
Sanjay Seth, Goldsmiths, University of London

'Postcolonial Politics' is a series that publishes books that lie at the intersection of politics and postcolonial theory. That point of intersection once barely existed; its recent emergence is enabled, first, because a new form of 'politics' is beginning to make its appearance. Intellectual concerns that began life as a (yet unnamed) set of theoretical interventions from scholars largely working within the 'New Humanities' have now begun to migrate into the realm of politics. The result is politics with a difference, with a concern for the everyday, the ephemeral, the serendipitous and the unworldly. Second, postcolonial theory has raised a new set of concerns in relation to understandings of the non-West. At first these concerns and these questions found their home in literary studies, but they were also, always, political. Edward Said's binary of 'Europe and its other' introduced us to a 'style of thought' that was as much political as it was cultural, as much about the politics of knowledge as the production of knowledge, and as much about life on the street as about a philosophy of being. A new, broader and more reflexive understanding of politics, and a new style of thinking about the non-Western world, make it possible to 'think' politics through postcolonial theory, and to 'do' postcolonial theory in a fashion which picks up on its political implications.

'Postcolonial Politics' attempts to pick up on these myriad trails and disruptive practices. The series aims to help us read culture politically, read 'difference' concretely, and to problematize our ideas of the modern, the rational, and the scientific by working at the margins of a knowledge system that is still logocentric and Eurocentric. This is where a postcolonial politics hopes to offer new and fresh visions of both the postcolonial and the political.

THE POSTCOLONIAL POLITICS OF DEVELOPMENT

Ilan Kapoor

Routledge
Taylor & Francis Group

LONDON AND NEW YORK

First published 2008
by Routledge
2 Park Square, Milton Park, Abingdon, Oxon, OX14 4RN

Simultaneously published in the USA and Canada
by Routledge
711 Third Avenue, New York, NY 10017

Routledge is an imprint of the Taylor & Francis Group, *an informa
business*

Typeset in Times New Roman by Keyword Group Ltd

British Library Cataloguing in Publication Data
A catalogue record for this book is available from the British Library

Library of Congress Cataloging in Publication Data
Kapoor, Ilan.
The postcolonial politics of development / Ilan Kapoor.
p. cm. – (Postcolonial politics; 1)
Includes bibliographical references and index.
1. Economic assistance. 2. Economic development. 3. Postcolonialism.
4. Economic assistance–Developing countries. 5. Developing countries–
Economic conditions. I. Title
HC60.K344 2008
338.9009172′4–dc22
2007033886

ISBN 13: 978-0-415-77397-3 (hbk)
ISBN 13: 978-0-415-77398-0 (pbk)
ISBN 13: 978-0-203-94614-5 (ebk)

TO THE MEMORY OF MY FATHER
TO MY MOTHER
TO ANISH AND FAMILY
TO ROY AND FAMILY
AND TO KENT, AS ALWAYS

CONTENTS

ACKNOWLEDGEMENTS

My heartfelt thanks to my brother, Anish, for permission to use his beautiful drawing for the cover.

I owe a considerable debt to the following for their insightful comments and critiques on one or more of the essays in this book: Michael Bach, Leesa Fawcett, Cate Mortimer-Sandilands, Kent Murnaghan, Navin Nayak, Vasanthi Srinivasan, and Anna Zalik.

Thanks to my editor, Craig Fowlie, and to the Routledge production staff (especially Stephen Thompson). I am grateful to Natalja Mortensen for her many efforts in seeing this book through the production process. My thanks as well to the Routledge 'Postcolonial Politics' series editors.

For their support and kind invitations, I would like to thank: the York University Consortium on the Global South colloquium series (especially Joelle Reid, Pablo Idahosa, Shubhra Gururani, Ricardo Greenspun, and Peter Vandergeest); the Environment and Culture at York Seminar Series 2006-07 (especially Cate Mortimer-Sandilands and Nick Garside); and the Faculty of Environmental Studies (FES) Samosa Seminar Series 2004-05 (especially Femida Handy).

Over the years, I have benefited immensely from the warmth, friendship, and intellectual solidarity of the following: Harris Ali, Jonathan Barker, Deborah Barndt, Jody Berland, Barbara Brown, Nalini Devdas, Jenny Foster, Bill Found, Beth Franklin, Gail Fraser, Linda Freeman, Liette Gilbert, Roger Keil, Bonnie Kettel, Shahnaz Khan, Stefan Kipfer, Nadia Kostiuk, Ute Lehrer, Linda Libront, David Morley, Ellie Perkins, Barbara Rahder, Anders Sandberg, Joni Seager, Joan Steigerwald, Peter Victor, Gerda Wekerle, and Doug Williams.

I have learned much from my graduate and PhD students and my teaching assistants at FES, some of whom have now become my teaching colleagues. I owe thanks to: Lauren Baker, Pablo Bose, Chandrima Chakraborty, Bruce Erickson, Nick Garside, Andil Gosine, John Greyson, Punam Khosla, Ranjith Kulatilake, Cheryl Lousley, Sherilyn MacGregor, Michael McMahon, Navin Nayak, Rich Oddie, Ryan O'Neill, Allison Sauer, Lucian Vesalon, Adriel Weaver, and Peregrine Wood.

I thank my FES students and colleagues, as well as the FES staff (especially Sharrieffa Sattaur), for their support over the years.

ACKNOWLEDGEMENTS

I have made many dear friendships. Thanks to: Usha Rangan, Leesa Fawcett, Geeta Uppal, Vasanthi Srinivasan, Michael Bach, Cate Mortimer-Sandilands, Joan Steigerwald, Zamil Janmohamed, Sherdil Hussain, Mohamed Khaki, Paul Yee, Jennifer and Kevin Knelman, Cyril Thivollet, Patricia Kohen, Prabha Khosla, Gert ter Voorde, Rosemarie and Wayne Umetsu, Annemarie Cwikowski, Nalini Devdas, Karim Ladak, Rob Gill, Sandra Morrison, Dianne Caldbick, Peter Egyed, Sabine Anderhalt, Rory Crath, and Stelios Stavridis.

I want to say an especially warm thank you to my family: Mum, Anish, Roy, Susanne, Michele, Devon, Benjamin, Alba, and Ishan.

Kent, you are my very best friend. I have been so grateful for your loving support throughout the writing of this manuscript. Thanks for the laughter, too.

I gratefully acknowledge the permission of the following journals and publishers to print here these essays in their revised and edited form:

'Participatory development, complicity and desire', *Third World Quarterly*, 26(8) (2005): 1203-20. Available at: http://www.informaworld.com.

'Hyper-self-reflexive development? Spivak on representing the Third World "Other"', *Third World Quarterly*, 25(4) (2004): 627-47. Available at: http://www. informaworld.com.

'Acting in a tight spot: Homi Bhabha's postcolonial politics', *New Political Science*, 25(4) (2003): 561-77. Available at: http://www.informaworld.com.

'Deliberative democracy or agonistic pluralism? The relevance of the Habermas–Mouffe debate for Third World politics', *Alternatives: Global, Local, Political*, 27(4) (2002): 459-87. Copyright © 2002 by Lynne Rienner Publishers Inc. Used with permission of the publisher.

'Capitalism, culture, agency: dependency versus postcolonial theory', *Third World Quarterly*, 23(4) (2002): 647-64. Available at: http://www.informaworld.com.

I also gratefully acknowledge permission from Anish Kapoor to reproduce a close-up image of the following on the book cover: Anish Kapoor, Untitled, 1987; Gouache and pencil on paper, 40.5 × 56 cm; Collection of the artist; Photo: Gareth Winters, London.

LIST OF ABBREVIATIONS

AusAID	Australian Agency for International Development
BN	basic needs
CEDAW	Convention on the Elimination of All Forms of Discrimination Against Women
CIDA	Canadian International Development Agency
CJM	Coalition for Justice in the Maquiladoras
DAC	Development Assistance Committee (of the OECD)
DANIDA	Danish International Development Agency
DFID	Department for International Development (United Kingdom)
FTZ	free trade zone
G8	Group of Eight countries
GDP	gross domestic product
GNI	gross national income
HIPC	Heavily Indebted Poor Countries
ILO	International Labour Organization
IMF	International Monetary Fund
KKK	Ku Klux Klan
NAFTA	North American Free Trade Agreement
NBA	Narmada Bachao Andolan
NDCP	Netherlands Development Cooperation Programme
NGOs	non-governmental organizations
ODA	Official Development Assistance
OECD	Organization for Economic Co-operation and Development
PD	participatory development
PRA	Participatory Rural Appraisal
PRS	poverty reduction strategy
SIDA	Swedish International Development Cooperation Agency
TI	Transparency International
UNESCO	United Nations Educational, Scientific and Cultural Organization
UNDP	United Nations Development Programme

UNICEF	United Nations Children's Fund
USAID	United States Agency for International Development
WID	women in development

INTRODUCTION

In this book, I use a postcolonial lens to question development's dominant cultural representations and institutional practices. I also explore the possibilities for a transformatory postcolonial politics.

The book examines recent development policy initiatives in such areas as 'good governance', 'human/gender rights', and 'participation' to better understand and contest the production of knowledge in development — its cultural assumptions, power implications, and hegemonic politics. It attempts to show how we, development practitioners and westernized elites/intellectuals, are often complicit in this neocolonial knowledge production. Noble gestures such as giving foreign aid or promoting participation and democracy frequently mask our institutional biases and economic and geopolitical interests, while silencing the subaltern (marginalized groups),[1] on whose behalf we purportedly work. In response, I argue for a radical ethical and political self-reflexivity that is vigilant to our reproduction of neocolonialisms and amenable to public contestation of development priorities. I also underline subaltern political strategies that can (and do) lead to greater democratic dialogue.

The book is a collection of more-or-less self-contained essays that I have written over the last six years.[2] This means that there is no single or overarching argument that runs through it. Rather, the essays roughly build upon one another by asking several questions, inspired by postcolonial thought and focusing on what I see as key development-related issues in the present global conjuncture:

- how can postcolonialism help us understand the dominant cultural values and politics that frame development theory and practice?
- to what extent are we, intellectuals and development workers, complicit in neocolonial knowledge production?
- how do institutional practices silence the Third World subaltern, and what postcolonial strategies might we employ for the subaltern to be better heard?
- how might a postcolonial politics open up avenues for democratic dialogue and subaltern agency in development?

I try to answer these questions by examining the politics of several types of movements and institutions — social/labour movements, governments, universities, development NGOs, global institutions, aid agencies. In addition, I draw on a range of theory — primarily postcolonial theory (Said, and especially Spivak and Bhabha), but also democratic theory (Habermas), poststructuralist thought (Foucault, Derrida), postdevelopment (Escobar, Shiva), and postmarxism (Mouffe, Žižek). Part of my intent here is to try to link theory and practice: this means illustrating theoretical arguments with examples, while simultaneously teasing out the broader theoretical implications of the illustrative material.

If those are the main concerns and sources of the book, I think it also important to outline my understanding of the key concepts that structure the book — 'postcolonialism', 'development', and 'politics' — and the affinities that I build between them.

Postcolonialism: this is a contested field, with porous boundaries and no single or coherent position. Nonetheless, it is a field haunted by the complex connections between domination and subjection/resistance, connections rooted in colonial history but which continue in various guises until today (Moore-Gilbert 1997: 12). A key postcolonial theme, in other words, concerns the process of *decolonization* currently taking place globally, which throws new light on the relationships between hegemon and subaltern, colonizer and colonized, West and Third World.

This focus on decolonization leads to several postcolonial interrogations about history, epistemology, and politics. The challenge, first, is to come to terms with the continuities between past and present, but also with the attendant discontinuities (as is perhaps conveyed by the admittedly ambiguous term 'postcolonial').[3] Prejudice, domination, and inequality persist today, but they often take new and varied forms. For instance, colonialism may have brought about the global unevenness that continues to privilege the First World, but the rise of new global economic forces (transnational corporations, South Korea, Southern China) gives new shape to such unevenness, while also helping to intensify comparative inequality in other regions of the world (namely parts of Sub-Saharan Africa). As a result, the meaning and nature of the links between 'First World' and 'Third World' have changed, at times even making the distinctions between the two terms superfluous.[4]

Decolonization also entails reinterpreting the relationship between colonizer and colonized, that is, seeing it differently by questioning its knowledge/power constructions. So often, the ruse of the colonizer is to turn the gaze on the colonized Other, focusing on issues of culture and character (e.g. blaming the colonial subject's 'underdevelopment' on her/his 'laziness' or inferior 'race' or gender). Postcolonialism turns the gaze back onto the colonizer to better reveal the tactics and representational practices of the dominant. Much effort is thus invested in probing Western knowledge production, critiquing the grand narratives of Euro-North America (about history, progress, modernization, democracy), while valorizing alternative positions and subjugated knowledges (of the Third World, minorities, the subaltern).

Finally, decolonization has an unmistakable political intent, aimed at disrupting hegemonic power in all its forms. Partly, this involves bringing attention to subaltern counter-discourses and acts of insurgency. And partly it means explor-ing the more complex transnational cultural practices — hybridity, creolization, border politics — most often being evolved by those on the margins (the displaced, migrants, exiles, women, minorities) to challenge fixed or closed representations and institutions.

Development. I use the term as a short form for 'discourse of development', that is, the dominant representations and institutional practices that structure the relationships between West and Third World.

I say 'dominant' because, of course, there are several alternative (or counter) development discourses, and no single logic to any: for instance, development in its hegemonic form (favouring capitalist growth and top-down decision-making) may be decidedly exploitative, but it may also be enabling, for example by provid-ing jobs and income to a few marginalized groups or pushing them to resist their exploitation. In other words, development discourse is a contested terrain; it may be hegemonic, but it has no single or stable foundations or directions.

I say 'institutional practices' because discourse is always bound up with insti-tutions. Hence, 'development', in the sense that I mean it in this book, covers such activities as development policy-making and programming by a range of organi-zations (civil society, market, state in both the North and South), the production of knowledge in the academy (especially in development studies and related disciplines), and aid funding (by transnational, bilateral, or multilateral agencies and financial institutions).

Placing 'development' alongside 'postcolonialism' turns out to be a productive exercise. It leads me, first, to examine ways of decolonizing development. My intent is to probe development's relative amnesia about (neo)colonialism; to ques-tion its deep-seated loyalties to notions of scientific progress and universal economic prescriptions; and to interrogate its belief in disinterested knowledge and 'pure' gestures (e.g. objective policy-making, uncontaminated foreign aid, transparent participation, gender neutrality). My intent is also to unsettle the more liberal tendencies in development towards unproblematically supporting notions of 'community' or 'tradition'; and equally the tendencies in critical development studies (i.e. postdevelopment thinkers such as Escobar and Shiva) towards roman-ticizing the subaltern and social movements. The latter stand, it should be noted, is indicative of postcolonialism's unrelenting vigilance to essentializing gestures which, as Chapter 3 will argue, so often mask the consolidation of privilege and position. Postdevelopment is undoubtedly a ground-breaking critique of main-stream development, but postcolonialism helps us understand that it is not immune to its own reproduction of power.

Which leads me back to postcolonialism itself. By placing it alongside devel-opment, I have come to better appreciate its vulnerabilities. As several of my chapters will indicate, its culturalist biases tend to underappreciate the economic dimensions of development.[5] Postcolonial discourse may well include material and institutional practices, but it often forgets to adequately emphasize them. This is evident, as we shall see, not just in its relative lack of treatment of such issues as poverty or distribution, but in the comparative neglect of such considerations as the role socioeconomic position can play in subaltern agency.

Politics: I use the word 'politics' in two related senses: (i) it is about collective or public action, which can take multiple forms, i.e. electoral politics, deliberative democracy, revolutionary struggle, local resistance, and so on; and (ii) it is about the power relationships (competing, collaborative, agonistic, hegemonic) between different claims, positions, subjects.

The 'postcolonial politics of development', accordingly, refers to the play between hegemonic development, which often attempts to hide or impose its claims, and the contestation of these claims by a range of groups, which often attempt to resist, publicly interrogate, or deflect these claims. I thus take the word 'of' in the title as implying both a joining and a disruption: it refers to the politics proper to (hegemonic) development, a set of actions and power relationships that the postcolonial helps illuminate; and simultaneously to the unravelling of this hegemony, which can be (and is) initiated at least in part by both postcolonial critics and subaltern groups.

Yet, just as hegemonic politics is always already unravelling, so is postcolonial resistance; it is, as I hope to show, an impossible politics, replete with dangers and the prospect of reproducing neocolonialism in various forms. I will nonetheless argue that a self-reflexive and democratic postcolonial politics is conducive to a more just development. By better establishing an ethical and dialogical relationship with the subaltern, by being ever-vigilant to the disguises of power, by clearing discursive spaces for bottom-up and insurgent subaltern action, a postcolonial politics may better be able to strive towards an always unfinished yet democratic development.

A final note on the structure of the book: it has three main sections. Part I comprises two chapters that provide some of the key insights of postcolonialism, with a view to underlining and questioning the cultural assumptions and politics of development. Part II brings together three chapters analyzing how Western cultural/institutional representations of, and benevolence towards, the Third World can conceal a range of complicities (professional, institutional, socioeconomic, gendered, geopolitical, psychoanalytic), which silence the subaltern. While not uncritical of postcolonialism itself, the chapters also sketch postcolonial strategies for making development more accountable. Part III is made up of three chapters outlining a postcolonial politics that attempts to answer to Third World/subaltern exigencies, while being both democratic and contestatory.

Part I

POSTCOLONIAL INSIGHTS?

1

CAPITALISM, CULTURE, AGENCY
Dependency versus postcolonial theory

The dependency school seems to have lost favour among current scholars of social science and Third World politics, while postcolonial theory — in spite of, or perhaps because of, growing out of literary studies — appears to be on the rise. This trend is at least partly due to the fresh and exciting perspective that postcolonial theory brings relative to (or retrospective to) dependency, much like the latter did in the mid-1960s/early 1970s in relation to 'modernization'. But the contemporaneity and novelty of the one need not blind us to the continuing importance of the other. In fact, I want to suggest that reading dependency alongside and against postcolonial theory can help reinvigorate and re-validate some of the insights of the former, while at the same time supporting the latter's ascendancy.

Dependency and postcolonial theory cover some similar territory and share important common concerns — a suspicion of Western liberal modernity, a historical-global analysis, and a critical politics. Yet at the same time, as Christine Sylvester points out, 'One field [development studies, of which dependency is part] begins where the other refuses to look' (1999: 704). Dependency chooses a structuralist and socioeconomic perspective, seeing imperialism as tied to the unfolding of capitalism, whereas postcolonial theory favours a poststructuralist and cultural perspective, linking imperialism and agency to discourse and the politics of representation. Dependency's politics is premised on state and class control of capitalist development; postcolonial theory's on the subaltern subversion of orientalist discourses.

I shall not attempt, in this chapter, to reconcile or synthesize these differences. Rather, believing (and showing) them to be irreducible, I shall stage a mutual critique between the two by bringing their tensions — economy/capitalism versus culture/representation, structuralist versus poststructuralist politics — to productive crisis. Reading one against the other will help draw out the strengths and persuasiveness, but equally the limits, vulnerabilities, and blind spots, of both. Accordingly, after outlining the main arguments of, and similarities between, dependency and postcolonial theory, the chapter will stage their mutual critique. The fault lines of this mutual critique will be drawn principally around the status, if any, each gives to the issues of capitalism, culture, and agency.

3

Some brief programme notes on the characters in this staged mutual critique: I shall rely mainly, although not exclusively, on a close reading of the work of Frank and Cardoso/Faletto to treat dependency, and that of Said, Spivak, and Bhabha to treat postcolonial theory. While not representative of the entirety of their respective schools of thought, the writing of these theorists provides a sense of the variety, refinement, and even divergences within each school. Moreover, I shall 'stage' the mutual critique more in one direction than in the other: postcolonial theorists *have* commented on dependency and Marxist theory (albeit mostly on the latter); while the *dependentistas*, unable to enjoy this chronological advantage, cannot have (and have not) commented on postcolonial theory. I will attempt to redress this disadvantage by leaning on contemporary critics of postcolonial theory (e.g. Ahmad, Dirlik, O'Hanlon & Washbrook, Parry), whose mainly Marxist arguments conform at least in spirit to those of the *dependentistas*,[1] and who will serve, so to speak, as understudies.

Dependency

Andre Gunder Frank's insights derive primarily from his critique of modernization's 'dual society' thesis. This thesis holds that the 'modern' and 'traditional' sectors of developing societies are independent. The former sector is modern because of its exposure to the outside capitalist world. The latter is 'underdeveloped' because it has lacked such exposure; but it can be modernized through the diffusion of 'capital, institutions, values' (Frank 1969: 4). Based primarily on research on Chile and Brazil (1967, 1969), Frank argues that, on the contrary, 'underdevelopment is not due to the survival of archaic institutions and the existence of capital shortage . . . [but] is generated by the very same historical process which also [generates] economic development: the development of capitalism itself' (1969: 9). Far from being separate, the modern and traditional sectors are 'fully . . . integrated parts of the imperialist system' (1969: 221). Latin America may have been '*un*developed' in pre-colonial times, but it is '*under*developed' as soon as capitalism arrives on its shores. And it is this self-same underdevelopment that makes possible Europe's modernization (1969: 4). Frank concludes that 'Economic development and underdevelopment are the opposite faces of the same coin' (1967: 9).

For Frank, imperialism is primarily about the appropriation of 'economic surplus', a process that begins when Brazil and Chile are colonized and that ends up integrating even the most isolated areas into the global capitalist system: 'a whole chain of constellations of metropoles and satellites [or 'peripheries'] relates all parts of the whole system from its metropolitan center in Europe or the United States to the farthest outpost in the Latin American countryside' (1969: 6; cf. 226; 1967: 6-7, 10, 16). National development in the colonial and post-colonial periphery is thus severely constrained: the periphery is 'condemned to underdevelopment' (1967: 11).

Frank has little faith in the national bourgeoisie playing a progressive role even after political independence, believing it to be nothing more than a collaborator in imperialism. He writes that the

> national bourgeoisie, where it can be said to exist, and indeed the entire national metropolis and capitalist system on which it thrives, are necessarily so inextricably linked into the imperialist system and the exploitative metropolis-periphery relationship it imposes on them that it cannot possibly escape from and can only extend and deepen the resulting underdevelopment.
>
> (Frank 1969: 228-9; cf. 1967: xv, 118; 1972)

The only way forward, according to him, is socialism, to be arrived at through revolutionary 'class struggle' and even 'guerrilla warfare' (1969: 371-2, 402).

Like Frank, Fernando Henrique Cardoso and Enzo Faletto adopt a 'historical' and 'structural' approach to dependency, viewing capitalism as a 'world system' (1971: x, xxi, 23). But their approach differs from Frank's in being 'dialectical'. They analyze dependency as a complex outcome of global capitalist relations: 'We do not see dependency and imperialism as external and internal sides of a single coin, with the internal aspects reduced to the condition of "epiphenomenal"' (1971: xv; cf. ix, 22, 173). Based on a number of Latin American case studies, they specify the varied and complex ways in which imperialism and capitalism manifest themselves, concluding that dependency is the result not of the 'abstract "logic of capital accumulation" but . . . of particular relationships and struggles between social classes and groups at the international as well as at the local level' (1971: xvii; cf. xiii, 173). This conclusion leads them to resist a 'theory of dependent capitalism' in favour of specific 'situations of dependency' (1971: xxiii).

Unlike Frank, who pays scant attention to social analysis, Cardoso and Faletto focus their study on how local social groups and practices reproduce and/or resist imperialism (in the post-colonial period).[2] They delineate two main dependency situations, one in which there is a relatively strong local state that allows for more national control of development, the other, an 'enclave situation', in which foreign interests dominate, thereby allowing for less national control. For Cardoso and Faletto, the type of local dependency is dictated by the specific nature of alliances among and between local and foreign classes, groups, and ideologies (labour, peasantry, national or collaborating bourgeoisie, state bureaucracy, landed/traditional oligarchies, the army, ethnic groups, nationalism, populism, multinational corporations, international financial systems, foreign states, etc.) (1971: xvi-xx, 17-18, 27, 174). For example, at times the ruling bourgeoisie may ally itself with foreign multinational corporate interests, while at other times it may seek an alliance with local classes/groups to better insulate itself from these foreign corporate interests. Of note here is Cardoso and Faletto's articulation of what they call a 'new dependency', ushered in by the rise of mainly US multinational corporate power in Latin America after World War II (1971: xvii, xxii).

Cardoso and Faletto's dialectical approach suggests various degrees of dependency, so that given the appropriate sociopolitical alignments, dependent relations can generate some growth and do not necessarily have to induce underdevelopment: 'in spite of structural "determination," there is room for alternatives in history' (1971: xi). Cardoso thus speaks of 'associated-dependent development' (1973), and appears to be distinguishing himself from Frank when he writes that 'it is possible to expect *development* and *dependency*' (1972: 94, italics in original). But despite the possibility of some growth, he and Faletto end up in agreement with Frank when they advocate that Latin America's dependency ties ultimately need to be broken by constructing 'paths toward socialism' (1971: xxiv; cf. 19). What such paths entail remains vague, although other *dependentistas* such as Celso Furtado (1970) suggest a move to more autonomous development through regional (Latin American) cooperation.

Postcolonial theory

In contrast to dependency, which relies on social science methodology and 'field' research, postcolonial theory emerges out of literary studies, disclosing its arguments based primarily (although not exclusively) on literary sources. Edward Said's work (1978, 1993) builds on an analysis of Western novels (e.g. Austen, Conrad, Chateaubriand, de Nerval, Flaubert), travel/anthropological writing (Burton, de Sacy, Renan), opera (Verdi), and media (mainly in the US) to link Western imperialism with Western culture. This linkage produces what Said calls 'Orientalism'. Orientalism is the systematic 'body of theory and practice' that constructs or represents the Orient (1978: 6; cf. 1993: xxiii; 1985: 248). By 'theory', Said means the Western imperial 'episteme' — the West's intellectual and cultural production, including research, writing, ideas, arguments, images; and by 'practice' he denotes the accompanying sociocultural institutions and structures — the colonial administration, universities, museums, media, etc. (1978: 3, 5, 332).

While Said distinguishes between British and French imperial Orientalism, as well as between colonial and post-colonial Western Orientalism, he argues that there is general continuity in the way West and East are depicted (1978: 3-4, 201ff.). Westerners tend to be characterized as 'rational, peaceful, liberal, logical . . . without natural suspicion' (1978: 49) and Easterners as irrational, degenerate, primitive, mystical, suspicious, sexually depraved, and so on (1993: xi; 1978: 49, 172, 187-8, 190). What is important for him is that these representations are not neutral; drawing on Foucauldian discourse theory, he shows how they are laden with a 'will to power', a will 'to control, manipulate, even to incorporate, what is a manifestly different . . . world' (1978: 12). In this sense, Orientalism is the 'enormously systematic discipline by which European culture [has been] able to manage — and even produce — the Orient politically, sociologically, militarily, ideologically, scientifically, and imaginatively during the post-Enlightenment period' (1978: 3).

Although Said does later recognize it (1993: xii),[3] 'Orientalism' tends to be an overly unifying and monolithic concept, at least as it is portrayed in his book *Orientalism*: it depicts colonial discourse as all-powerful and the colonial subject as its mere effect. This tendency is evident in the following statement: 'because of Orientalism, the Orient was not (and is not) a free subject of thought or action' (1978: 3).[4] And it is partly in response to this tendency that Gayatri Chakravorty Spivak and Homi Bhabha make their respective interventions. While accepting the general idea of Orientalism, which Spivak indicates as the '"worlding" of what is today called "the Third World"' (1985a: 247), both theorists show it to be ruptured and hybrid, Bhabha suggests that Said himself hints at, but leaves 'underdeveloped', this idea in *Orientalism* (1994: 73; cf. Young, R. 1990: 141-2). In fact, Bhabha makes 'hybridity' the keystone to his subsequent elaborations.

Hybridity describes the way in which colonial/imperial discourse is inherently unstable, 'split' in its 'enunciation', so that 'in the very practice of domination the language of the master becomes hybrid' (Bhabha 1994: 33). Bhabha illustrates this instability through an analysis of the 'colonial stereotype', which he considers an instance of the deployment of imperial authority. Applying a poststructuralist (in particular, a Lacanian[5] psychoanalytic) lens to various colonial texts, Bhabha shows how these stereotypes — the 'noble savage', the 'wily oriental' — are meant to be accepted as 'fixed' and 'natural'; yet they are endlessly and anxiously repeated and reconfirmed by the colonizer. Often the stereotypes are also contradictory: the colonial subject, Bhabha writes, is 'savage (cannibal) and yet the most obedient and dignified of servants (the bearer of food); he is the embodiment of rampant sexuality and yet innocent as a child; he is mystical, primitive, simple-minded and yet the most worldly and accomplished liar' (1994: 82; cf. 66, 85ff., 111). Such repetition, such 'double inscription', for Bhabha, betray the slipperiness and ambivalence of colonial discourse and authority (1994: 108).

Discursive instability has two important implications. First, it makes for agency. While critical of imperialism's discursive violence, Spivak speaks of an 'enabling violence' (1996: 19; cf. 1988b: 198) and of the persistent transformation of 'conditions of impossibility into possibility' (1988b: 201). Similarly, Bhabha sees discourse as both 'incitement and interdiction' (1994: 72), its doubleness empowering: 'The ambivalence at the source of traditional discourses on authority enables a form of subversion, founded on the undecidability that turns the discursive conditions of dominance into the grounds of intervention' (1994: 112).

Bhabha conveys this subversive intervention by way of a number of colonizer–colonized encounters.[6] For example, in the essay, 'Of Mimicry and Man', he writes about the colonizer's attempt to promote a civilizing mission by creating 'mimic men', that is, recognizable and docile colonial subjects who are '*almost the same, but not quite*' (1994: 86, italics in original). But this ambivalence

7

('same'/'not quite') is exploitable: mimicry is easily camouflaged as mockery, with the colonial subject consequently subverting or refusing to simply repeat the master's lessons. Rather than producing a controlled imitation or a managed response from the native, the civilizing mission elicits an answer back, a menacing look, a distorted and disturbing echo.

Bhabha provides contemporary illustrations of agency as well. He singles out, for example, the British group, Women Against Fundamentalism, for using the Rushdie affair, not to endorse or defend either Western liberalism or Islamic conservatism, but to draw attention to women's issues (household inequality, education, prostitution), thereby 'reconjugating, recontextualizing, translating the event into the politics of communities and public institutions' (1995a: 114). Bhabha's point, in these or other colonizer–colonized and migrant–metropolitan encounters, is to demonstrate that agency is a kind of cultural and 'psychological guerrilla warfare' (Moore-Gilbert 1997: 130). It involves estranging, contaminating, or misreading the master discourse, at times imposing suppressed knowledges and at others making unanticipated, slight alterations, with the overall effect of denying or subverting dominant authority.

It should be noted that such agency is emergent only from within the master discourse, a situation that Spivak describes as saying an 'impossible "no" to a structure, which one critiques, yet inhabits intimately' (1990c: 228). This means that there is unavoidable collusion and complicity between the colonizer and colonized (Spivak 1985b: 9; 1988b: 180). Not surprisingly, Bhabha repeatedly refers to subaltern agency as a form of 'negotiation' (1994: 25, 38, 185, 191). It also means that the agent cannot hearken back to pre-colonial, pre-orientalist discourse in search of an 'authentic' identity or out of 'nostalgia for lost origins' (Spivak 1988a: 291). According to both theorists, colonial discourse has forever marked colonized and ex-colonized societies (and for that matter colonial and ex-colonial powers), so that it is impossible to recuperate any identity uncontaminated by it. They thus warn of the dangers of direct opposition to dominant power, arguing that the result is often reverse Orientalism and racism or substitution of one power for another. Referring to Spivak, Bart Moore-Gilbert explains that 'directly counter-hegemonic discourse is more liable to cancellation or even reappropriation by the dominant than a "tangential", or "wild", guerrilla mode of engagement. For this reason, too, she advocates the modes of "negotiation" and "critique", which unsettle the dominant from within' (1997: 85).

The second (and related) implication of the instability and 'doubleness' of discourse is that it enables the retrieval and recognition of difference. The object of postcolonial concern here is orientalist binary categorization (e.g. master–slave, colonizer–colonized, civilized–uncivilized, White–Black), into which the 'Other' is invariably incorporated. Postcolonialism seeks to preserve heterogeneity and to critique its aspersion or transcendence by any master discourse. Said likens this task to 'counterpoint' in baroque music, where several musical lines hold together without one dominating (1993: 51). Bhabha, for his part, coins 'third space' (1994: 37) as an in-between, incommensurable location in which minority or

STOP #1

'supplementary' discourses intervene to preserve their peculiarity. He also speaks of 'time-lag' as a way of validating different temporalities and 'reconstructing other kinds of histories' (1995b: 87). Here, metropolitan time (or Western 'modernity') is not allowed to be used as a standard or measuring rod for non-Western time(s) or 'traditions'.

One of the principal ways in which difference is valorized is by focusing on the marginalized. This is evident in Bhabha's above-noted work on the agency of the colonized and the migrant. But it is Spivak who may be said to emphasize it most. As a member of the Subaltern Studies Group (1988b: 197ff.), whose aim is to write history 'from below', Spivak declares her interest in 'subsistence farmers, unorganized peasant labour, the tribals and communities of zero work-ers on the street or in the countryside' (1988a: 288). But among these, she pays particular attention to the 'disenfranchised woman' whom she argues is the figure 'most consistently exiled from episteme' (1990a: 102-3; cf. 1985a, 1988a, 1993: 177ff.).

Paradoxically, while trying to retrieve the voice of the 'gendered subaltern', Spivak admits her failure. In perhaps her most famous text, 'Can the subaltern speak?' (1988a), she concludes that the nineteenth-century *sati* (the widowed woman who immolates herself/is immolated) *cannot speak* because she is never empowered *to* speak. Her voice, as Chapter 3 will further illustrate, is always mediated and appropriated by others (the colonial administrator, patriarchical institutions, the academic intellectual, etc.). Spivak concludes that, nonetheless, the role of the postcolonial critic is to record this silence/disappearance so as to valorize the 'difference' revealed by the disenfranchised woman and to critique the domination of imperial and patriarchical discourses.

A postcolonial critique of dependency

Before I stage the mutual critique — the postcolonial critique of dependency and the *dependentista* critique of postcolonial theory — the common territory between the two must be briefly noted. For, in many ways, this common territory forms a basis for comparison, but it is also *divided* territory that will enable the mutual critique.

Perhaps, more than anything, what brings dependency and postcolonial theory together is their shared commitment precisely to critique. In their own fashion, both are counter-modernist and critical of Western liberalism. And this critique yields a correspondingly shared critical politics, aimed principally at arresting the status quo of liberal modernity. In response to the liberal/modernization tendency to explain the rest of the world in Euro-North American terms, each attempts to shift the focus to the 'periphery'. As a reaction to the West's tendency to neglect examining its past, each accentuates the study of colonial/imperial history for understanding modernity in the Third World *and in the West*. In this sense, analyz-ing history amounts to analyzing the trajectory of hegemonic world systems, endowing both dependency and postcolonial theory with a global outlook.

Yet, their critique is shared only up to a point, as it rests primarily on the identification of a common foe — liberal modernity. Past this initial meeting of minds, both diverge significantly. Dependency singles out the inequality wrought by global capitalist development as crucial, while postcolonial theory zeroes in on the discursive power wielded by Orientalism. This tension — between focusing on 'capitalism' or 'representation', and over how best to fashion a matching politics that is *sufficiently* critical — is what lies at the heart of the debate.

argument

Dependency's Orientalism

From the postcolonial standpoint, dependency ignores (for the most part) culture and the politics of representation. Frank gives them no place in his analysis, and Cardoso and Faletto, while including ideology (e.g. nationalism, populism) and sociocultural groups in their dialectical approach, tend to treat these as superstructural or epiphenomenal. That is, culture *is* a factor, but it is viewed only in relation to the political economy. It matters only to the extent that it helps or hinders dependent development. Thus, they look at it as one element among many, and more precisely as a subordinate element, in their politics.[7] They do not examine the politics *of* (and within) culture, and are unaware of the way in which culture frames their very own analysis. Indeed, their (and Frank's) neglect of the politics of representation results in ethnocentrism.

culture missed in dependency

From the point of view of the *dependentistas*, this neglect is unfortunate, given their intention precisely to look at imperialism from the perspective of the periphery (Blomström & Hettne 1984: 37); but from the point of view of postcolonial theorists, it is not unexpected, given *their* argument (noted above) that counter-discourses often reverse or perpetuate orientalist representations. Such is the case with dependency's construction of binary opposites — 'developed–underdeveloped', 'centre–periphery', 'metropole–satellite' — which, although attempting to shift analytical focus to the second term, leave unexamined and untouched the power relationship between the two. The 'centre' continues to be just that — central and dominant — so that the West ends up being consolidated 'as sovereign subject' (Spivak 1985a: 247). Not surprisingly, many have argued that, despite intentions to the contrary, such a discursive hierarchy contributes to a psychology of perpetual dependence in the 'periphery', habituating colonized and ex-colonized subjects to being peripheralized (Fanon 1967; cf. James 1997: 207).

Dependency's ethnocentrism pervades its historical analysis as well. As Said states, historicism of the type put forth by dependency 'has meant that one human history uniting humanity either culminated in or was observed from the vantage point of Europe, or the West' (1985: 22). In equating its analysis of history with the analysis of the unequal development of global capitalism, dependency forgets that it is using (as did Marx and Lenin before it) Europe as a universal model. In this sense, it is not just capitalism, but the way capitalism develops in Europe that is 'made to stand for History' (Prakash 1992a: 15). Third World countries thereby become specimens of failed or 'dependent' capitalism, with capitalist economic

a fault(?)

10

growth as the 'unquestioned norm' and goal to emulate (Spivak 1985a: 260; Manzo 1991: 6; Werbner & Ranger 1996: 3; Nederveen Pieterse & Parekh 1995: 2). Even Cardoso and Faletto's dialectical approach does not escape this tendency: for all its complexity, their dialectics nonetheless strive towards an autonomous capitalist development (a prerequisite for transcendence to socialism).

The crucial problem from where postcolonial critics stand is that master historical narratives — dialectical or not — ignore, domesticate, or transcend difference: 'theories of accumulation on a world scale . . . depend . . . on a homogenizing and incorporating world historical scheme that [assimilates] non-synchronous developments, histories, cultures, and peoples to it' (Said 1985: 22; cf. Prakash 1990; 1992a: 8, 13; Werbner & Ranger 1996: 4). While not averse to using Marxist/class analysis herself (more on this point later), Spivak is particularly concerned with the way in which totalizing and economistic narratives tend to be blind to non-economic questions such as gender and race (1985a: 263ff., 265ff.). Part of the reason why she and Bhabha devote attention to the subaltern is to valorize their difference, or what Bhabha calls their 'struggle for the historical and ethical *right to signify*' (1995b: 51, italics in original). In this sense, postcolonial theorists attempt a 'catachrestic' strategy of 'displacing, and seizing the apparatus of value-coding' (Spivak 1990c: 228) so that difference is not allowed to be sublated and the West is relativized, de-ethnocentrized, and provincialized (Chakrabarty 1992). Bhabha's deployment of 'time-lags' and incommensurable temporal dimensions, as pointed out earlier, is precisely a way of denying modernity's linear and teleological time and showing how it is 'staged': '*belatedness* functions to critique certain priorities and myths about culture and modernization' (1995b: 58, 87). Stuart Hall summarizes it well when he writes:

> It is the retrospective re-phrasing of Modernity within the framework of 'globalization' in all its various ruptural forms and moments . . . which is the really distinctive element in a 'post-colonial' periodization. In this way, the 'post-colonial' marks a critical interruption into that whole grand historiographical narrative which, in liberal historiography and Weberian historical sociology, as much as in the dominant traditions of Western Marxism, gave this global dimension a subordinate presence in a story which could essentially be told from within its European parameters.
>
> (Hall 1996: 250)

Interestingly, while not identifying postcolonial/postmodern critiques of ethnocentrism as a cause, Frank modifies his stance on this issue. In his later work, which shifted notably to 'world system' analysis, he argues that the global (economic) system has been around for five thousand years, with Europe being its driving force for only a portion of that time. In fact, he contends that 'from a global perspective Asia not Europe held center stage for most of early modern history' (Frank 1998: xv; cf. xxv, 1ff.; Frank & Gills 1993: 3ff.; Frank 1977).

From a postcolonial perspective though, his economistic bias, and his partiality to 'totalizing narratives', remain.

Subjection and agency

As noted above, Spivak and Bhabha see politics as emergent from within the master discourse. Agency and subjection, in this sense, are intimately related: the type and degree of agency is tied to the type and degree of power. This argument provides a way of critically assessing dependency's views on power and politics.

Dependency and postcolonial theory concentrate on different configurations of power: the former on the power of imperialism/capitalism, the latter on the power within colonial discourse/Orientalism. Yet, both agree on the pervasiveness of this power. Frank and Said accentuate the overarching grasp of capitalism/Orientalism. And despite their reservations about Said's analysis of Orientalism, Spivak and Bhabha concur. In fact, their examination of everyday colonizer–colonized encounters, of what Bhabha (echoing Foucault) calls the 'microtechnics of [colonial] power' (1994: 116), demonstrates the extent of penetration of colonial discourse. In this regard, Spivak, while insistent on examining subaltern subjection, also reminds us that on the other side lie colonial agents, who 'are not only great names . . . but also small unimportant folk . . . as well as policymakers' (1985a: 254).

But unlike the postcolonial theorists, who see power as pervasive yet fractured, Frank constructs power as homogeneous and totalizing. He argues, as mentioned earlier, that Latin America is incorporated into the international division of labour as soon as it is colonized. Moreover, for him, capitalism 'fully penetrat[es]' and 'fully integrate[s]' the satellite (1967: xi-xii).[8] It is not surprising, then, that he advances no possibility of resistance to imperialism (at least under colonial rule), and in fact speaks of the periphery being 'condemned to underdevelopment'. For him, the only way to oppose power conceived as all-pervasive-and-without-remainder is to obliterate it by means of an equally totalizing and monolithic power — violent revolution. From the postcolonial standpoint, these arguments are deeply problematic. For, once again, they overlook that the replacement of one totalizing power by another strongly risks the continuation of domination and violence. Moreover, from the perspective of the periphery that Frank is purport-edly concerned about, the arguments are disempowering: the Third World is portrayed as a passive bystander in the imperial/capitalist game, with no will or ken to resist it.

It should be noted here that Frank's winner-takes-all view of power resembles Said's (at least the Said of *Orientalism*). However, Said strays considerably from Frank in never espousing violence or 'revolution'; and, as suggested earlier, in his later writings, he rejoins Spivak and Bhabha's arguments on the pervasiveness yet hybridity of imperial/orientalist power.

In contrast to Frank's, Cardoso and Faletto's structural, yet dialectical and differentiated, notion of power shares much with the postcolonial understanding of it as discursive yet split. Just as agency, for Bhabha/Spivak, springs from *want overthrow Colonialism*

within (and despite) discursive subjection, politics for Cardoso/Faletto is emergent and possible within the capitalist frame: development can happen in spite of dependence. But, once again, there is a crucial difference: whereas for the former, agency is always possible (it derives from the ever-hybrid character of discourse), for the latter (including Frank), it is possible only in the wake of political independence from colonialism.

hybridization of culture

From the postcolonial perspective, dependency's thinking on this question contains several problematic assumptions. Dependency's agent/subject of change appears only after the colonizer has relinquished political power. The postcolonial critics beg to differ. Not only are Spivak/Bhabha critical of the orientalizing and incapacitating tendencies of this position, but they also show how colonial discourse's production of subjects is witnessed by numerous acts of subversive resistance on the part of these colonized subjects. Moreover, contra Frank, the subversive acts are testimony to why the colonies were never able to be 'fully' colonized, or why colonization was never completely 'effective'; and contra Cardoso/Faletto, these acts show that Third World politics does not have to wait to happen until the end of 'formal' colonialism (cf. James 1997: 219).

A further assumption is that agency is only possible from within the confines of the nation-state. For Kate Manzo this is indicative of dependency's entrapment 'within a modernist discourse which relies on the principles of nineteenth-century liberal philosophy, [and] which treats the individual nation-state in the Third World as the sovereign subject of development' (1991: 6). In this connection, Bhabha, in the only direct critique he makes of dependency, avers that:

> The postcolonial perspective departs from the traditions of the sociology of underdevelopment or the 'dependency' theory. As a mode of analysis, it attempts to revise those nationalist or 'nativist' pedagogies that set up the relation of the Third and First Worlds in a binary structure of opposition. The postcolonial perspective resists attempts to provide a holistic social explanation, forcing a recognition of the more complex cultural and political boundaries that exist on the cusp of these often opposed political spheres. . . . It is from this hybrid location of cultural value — the transnational *as* the translational — that the postcolonial intellectual attempts to elaborate a historical and literary project.
>
> (Bhabha 1995b: 49)

On the one hand, Bhabha is critical of the equation of the political subject with the nation-state. As already noted, he, like Spivak, shifts focus away from the 'grand' politics of state and class to the everyday and 'marginal' acts of the subaltern. On the other hand, he is also suspicious of the very idea of the 'nation', at least to the extent that it refers to a unitary and undivided subject. He argues instead for the replacement of the presumed homogeneous and 'pure'/'authentic' national identity with a liminal, split, and ambivalent identity, and of the 'horizontal, homogenous empty time of the nation's narrative' with the 'double' and 'disjunctive

13

temporality' of the people (1994: 145-9). Of particular interest to him are how national cultures are 'being produced from the perspective of disenfranchised minorities' (1994: 6), not only in the Third World but also in the West (i.e. by migrants, refugees, or diasporas hailing from the ex-colonies). For, once again, this production shows up for him the artificial and differentiated character of the nation-state, while also complicating the 'cultural and political boundaries' between periphery and metropole.

To conclude this section is a brief summary of the postcolonial critique of dependency just staged. While not denying that both camps have notable common concerns, and while even suggesting some partial convergences between Frank and Said, as well as between Cardoso/Faletto and Spivak/Bhabha, I have attempted to bring out the main vulnerabilities of dependency from the vantage point of postcolonialism. Postcolonial theory argues that dependency's counter-modernist and critical inclinations are not, ironically, counter-modernist and critical enough, principally because it does not shed its modernist past. As Manzo suggests, 'even the most radically critical discourse easily slips into the form, the logic, and the implicit postulations of precisely what it seeks to contest, for it can never step completely outside of a heritage from which it must borrow its tools — its history, its language — in its attempt to destroy that heritage itself' (1991: 8). Thus, dependency is unaware of its Orientalism: despite itself, it ends up incorporating the non-Western world into a Eurocentric and teleological historiography, ignoring or flattening difference, and denying agency to the Third World. When it does bestow agency, the agent is identified with the nation-state. But here again dependency overlooks how its nationalist/statist proclivities can dismiss or suppress heterogeneity and subalternity.

A *dependentista* critique of postcolonial theory

To turn now to the blind spots and weaknesses of postcolonial theory, as teased out by dependency. This critique will be carried out on the basis of two considerations: the status of capitalism in postcolonial theory; and the breadth of postcolonial historiography and politics.

The status of capitalism

From the perspective of dependency, postcolonial theory does not adequately appreciate the role of capitalism, resulting in significant political problems. This critique applies somewhat differently to Said/Bhabha than to Spivak. Said and Bhabha assign capitalism no significant place in their respective analyses. The very titles of some of their works (e.g. *Culture and Imperialism*, *The Location of Culture*) reveal their bias towards cultural, as opposed to economic, arguments. Said's writing, as indicated earlier, repeatedly underlines his interest in the politics of representation. Bhabha makes occasional references to 'multinational capital' and the 'multinational division of labour' (1994: 241, 6), but nonetheless

14

errs on the side of semiotics.[9] This is evident in such formulations as: 'popular rebellion and mobilization are often *most* subversive and transgressive when they are created through oppositional *cultural* practices' (1994: 20, italics added; cf. Parry 1996: 8-9; 1987).

The problem is that questions of economic inequality, so central to dependency, tend to be given short shrift by this semiotic approach to politics. It is as though interactions or 'negotiations' among and between colonizer and colonized are barely affected by their differential socioeconomic status. As Moore-Gilbert points out, Bhabha 'assumes that the affective economies of mimicry and ambivalence operate equivalently for all colonial subjects irrespective of their positioning in the social hierarchy' (1997: 168; cf. 110; Ahmad 1997: 370; O'Hanlon & Washbrook 1992). Does the colonized subject's status in the capitalist economy not impinge on her/his ability to represent or negotiate, or on how forcefully s/he can represent or negotiate in relation to another subject? Bhabha appears to provide no answers. As above, he asserts that oppositional cultural practices are 'often most subversive and transgressive' (presumably, relative to 'material' ones), but offers no comparative political economy analysis to support this claim.

In this regard, it is significant that Bhabha, or for that matter Said, does not focus on capitalistic transactions or economically-oriented subversive agency by the subaltern or migrant (e.g. non-payment of colonial taxes, revolts against landlords, action against inhuman working conditions, etc.). In keeping with his poststructuralist politics of representation, he prioritizes agency in the 'post-materialist', symbolic sphere — resistance to colonial education or the subversion of Western Orientalism and stereotypes. As a consequence, several critics accuse postcolonial theorists like him of ignoring such key 'material' issues as distribution or poverty in their politics (Sylvester 1999: 703; Nederveen Pieterse & Parekh 1995: 13; Sunder Rajan 1997: 615). They point out as well that, contrary to the implication that social struggles are primarily over 'symbolization', many of today's social movements are struggles 'for' development (i.e. for better access to health, environment, jobs, etc.) (Storey 2000: 42). The postcolonial culturalist bias, then, is out of kilter with the significant and continuing 'materialist'-oriented forms of subaltern agency in the Third World.

While Spivak may be said, at least in part, also to display some of the above-mentioned weaknesses, it must be noted that she does pay significant attention to the role of capital. She draws on class analysis, and often quotes the work of Marx, Gramsci, and Althusser. But the problem for the *dependentistas*, as for Marxist analysts generally, is not that capitalism is merely acknowledged as playing a role; it is, rather, the relative importance given to this role. For them, capital is foundational or ontological. This is attested to by Frank's argument (underlined earlier) about a single world capitalist system, a position supported by Cardoso/Faletto: 'without the concept of capital . . . it is not possible to explain the movement of capitalist society . . . history becomes understandable when interpretations propose categories strong enough to render clear the fundamental relations that sustain and those that oppose a given structural situation in its globality'

(1971: xiii). In contrast, postcolonial theory approaches capitalism epistemologically. Aijaz Ahmad characterizes this as the 'literary-critical habit of seeing all history as a contest between different kinds of narrative, so that imperialism itself gets described not in relation to the universalization of the capitalist mode as such but in terms of the *narrative* of this mode' (1997: 376, italics in original). As a consequence, as Ahmad goes on to explain, postcolonial critics treat Marxism 'as a method primarily of *reading* . . . [thus reducing it] to an element among other elements in the analytics of textual reading'. It is not Marxism per se, then, but '*reading* [that becomes] the appropriate form of politics' (Ahmad 1992: 4-5, 3, italics in original; cf. 70; Dirlik 1994: 335; O'Hanlon & Washbrook 1992). The trap, as Hall submits, is assuming that, because a narrative has been read and deconstructed epistemologically and theoretically, 'therefore it has been displaced *politically*' (1996: 249, italics in original).

Spivak appears to confirm Ahmad's above-mentioned characterization, although it must be noted that she does equivocate. Her writings contain references to the 'real' as independent of representations or sign-systems, so that the international division of labour is portrayed as responsible for subject-constitution (Moore-Gilbert 1997: 100-3). An example of this tendency is the following statement: 'Woman's body is thus the last instance in a system whose general regulator is still the loan: usurer's capital, imbricated, level by level, in national industrial and transnational global capital' (1993: 82; cf. 1999: 315). But more often than not, she speaks of 'facts' as 'constructed' and of the mode of production as a 'narrative' (e.g. 1985a: 258; 1990a: 101, 162).

This epistemological approach to capitalism should come as no surprise, given postcolonial theory's anti-essentialist leanings. As the postcolonial historiographer Gyan Prakash reminds us, the idea is not to make capitalism a 'disposable fiction' but rather to warn that 'making capitalism the foundational theme amounts to homogenizing the histories that remain heterogeneous within it' (1992b: 176). Yet, this position has several questionable consequences. That there are no ultimate foundations may be an important and valid stand, but it evades the important point that some explanations/narratives are better or more convincing than others. In her attempt to valorize incommensurability and heterogeneity, Spivak provides no way of sifting through different epistemologies, or to use Cardoso/Faletto's above-quoted words, no 'strong enough' categories to decide which representations are more important. For example, given the current intensification of capitalist globalization and spread of multinational corporations, Spivak supplies few clues[10] about how to either recognize the magnitude of the problem or prioritize effective political responses. And she has no way of adjudicating between, say, the claims/narratives of anti-immigrant neofascists and new immigrants or refugees.[11] Whose claims are more compelling, and how are we to assess or rank them? Her (and her postcolonial colleagues') refusal to erase, check, or adjudicate difference runs into notable political conundrums in these not uncommon types of situations.

The breadth of history and politics

Postcolonial theory, as argued earlier by Bhabha, resists 'holistic social explanations' and focuses instead on heterogeneity and ambivalence. In the place of chronological or dialectical history, for example, it offers discontinuous historical narratives. In particular, Bhabha and Spivak (but not Said) zero in on isolated historical incidents and agents, refraining from providing any 'meta-'historiography. This is a problem from where dependency sits, for history then becomes merely a collection of fragmentary narratives. In this connection, Ahmad writes that the 'work of Bhabha is particularly telling of the way this kind of hermeneutic tends to appropriate the whole world as its raw material and yet effaces the issue of historically sedimented differences. Indeed the very structure of historical time is effaced in the empty play of infinite heterogeneities' (1997: 370; cf. Parry 1996: 11). The advantage of dependency's structural-historical perspective is that it enables the recognition of broad patterns and trends, which in turn allows one to relate the present to the past, or learn from past mistakes to change the future. Postcolonial theory's 'sedimented' historiography makes many of these tasks difficult, if not impossible.

A similar problem arises with postcolonial agency/politics. The emphasis on local discourses and action tends to result in the neglect of broader influences and impacts (Joss 1996: 245; cf. Dirlik 1994: 345; Hall 1997). Global concerns may be central to the postcolonial analysis of cultural hegemony and Orientalism, but it remains unclear how postcolonial political interventions impinge, in turn, on global power. In fact, it is difficult to imagine how the micro-political scale of postcolonial agency, as well as the micro-size of its agents, *can* meaningfully affect macro-politics. The postcolonial suspicion and deconstruction of the nation-state does not help here either. Although not without its limitations, the state may sometimes have to take on an increasingly important role. As the *dependentistas* insist, the proliferation of multinational capital makes the establishment of a semi-autonomous state a must if dependency/imperialistic ties are to be minimized. In contrast, the sub-national and decentred character of postcolonial agency risks allowing corporate power to overshadow it, and may even end up aiding, not regulating or altering, corporate propagation.

To conclude this section, I would like to draw attention to the way in which the *dependentista* critique brings out the limitations of the types of questions being asked by postcolonial theory. Postcolonialism's emphasis on cultural and representational issues leads it to inadequately reflect upon important material concerns (e.g. poverty, health, etc.). To the extent that it does consider materialist questions, it often approaches them epistemologically, shying away from the important political task of prioritizing or adjudicating among differing narratives (be they economic, cultural, social, environmental). Finally, although it examines global–local questions, these tend to be one-sided: they illuminate well how global power is reproduced in the local, but when it comes to politics, they reveal only local agency, not global consequences.

Conclusion

While both sides in the above-staged debate are critical of Western/liberal modernity, their critiques are different, with the result that each one accuses the other of being *insufficiently* critical. Dependency points to postcolonial theory's narrow politics and inadequate consideration of the socioeconomic inequality engendered by capitalist modernity. Postcolonial theory reproaches dependency for its lack of self-reflexivity, and hence for adopting a modernist framework that is totalizing, ethnocentric, and prone to erasing sociocultural and political difference(s). This mutual critique helps reveal the strengths and limits of both sides. Often, what one party sees as significant, the other construes as problematic. The debate, as a consequence, teases out important tensions between several of the ingredients of Third World politics: materialism and culture, state and subaltern, centralized and decentralized agency, local/national/global interventions, totality and specificity/heterogeneity, teleological historiography and discontinuous historical narratives, structuration and hybridity, transcendence and incommensurability, dualism and ambiguity.

The staged debate also helps shed new light on dependency. While many may consider dependency old-fashioned today, put into conversation with postcolonial theory, it regains relevance and contemporaneity. Although much more work and thought are required, its insights into the historical/global workings and impacts of capitalism in the Third World appear highly pertinent to current research on globalization. It can also be seen as acting as a materialist counterbalance to postcolonial-inspired discursive/representational analysis currently popular in the study of global issues. Finally, its statist and 'holistic' perspective, while not without reproach, is a cautionary note to postcolonial theory's decentred and, so to speak, 'globalization from below' approach.

2

THE CULTURE OF DEVELOPMENT POLICY

Basic needs, structural adjustment, good governance, and human rights

In mainstream development circles, one seldom hears 'culture' and 'policy' uttered in the same breath: the domain of culture is often seen as marginal to development policy, and any suggestion — evident for instance in the expression 'the culture of development policy' — that the policy formulation process might itself have cultural dimensions, is likely to be met with incredulity. Policy-making is typically viewed as a technical and institution-laden process, and while culture may become an *object* of policy, it is thought to have little to do with the *process* of policy-making. Yet, the construction and institutionalization of policy involve noteworthy representational practices: to make policy is necessarily to *imagine* it, to *speak* and *write* about it, to *discuss* and *debate* it, and to *see* it implemented (or *be seen* to be implementing it) in this or that way. Development policy is thus semiotically mediated, that is, it is culturally embedded and transacted, involving the production and systematization of particular languages, images, rhetorics.

This chapter will examine this postcolonial 'semiotic' view of culture and its implications for development policy. But before doing so, it is important to explicate the more conventional wisdom about culture that has so dominated the field of development. Indeed, culture is treated in either of two ways. On the one hand, it tends to be ignored. In neoclassical economics, as we shall see, it is constructed as a domain that cannot and should not be afforded by 'poor' countries. Instead, it is a 'luxury' to be indulged only by wealthy, post-materialist societies. The implication most often is that development policy needs to prioritize economic growth and, based on the West's industrialization experiences, recommend strategies that help fulfil people's material needs first. Culture, then, is to be put aside until such time as developing countries can pay for it. There is no consideration here about the culture *of* growth-focused policy; the latter is portrayed as objective and culturally neutral, so that it can be transposed anywhere around the world.

But on the other hand, culture *has* been taken more seriously by some quarters in development. Modernization theory, over four decades old now but still influential, makes culture a central area of concern. Development is deemed to require modern (i.e. 'Western') values, attitudes, personalities, and institutions (cf. Lerner 1962; McClelland 1967). Emphasis is placed on the cultivation of self-motivation, entrepreneurialism, scientific beliefs, thrift, investment, and a

19

free and thriving media. The implication is that the cultural infrastructure of non-Western societies is at least in part to blame for their socioeconomic backwardness. 'Traditional' practices (superstition, ethnicity, religion, caste) are seen as hindering modernization; they need to be surmounted if growth is to take root.

What is remarkable here is that, while culture is posited as central to the modernization project, it ends up playing second fiddle to economics. Culture is valued not for its own sake, but only insofar as it can be strategically deployed *for* capitalist growth. (All said and done, this ends up remarkably close to the position taken by those who ignore culture.) Both Western and non-Western cultures are, ironically, simplified and instrumentalized, forever fixed as either 'modern' or 'traditional'.

A recent variant of the modernization view is the liberal-multicultural view, with Samuel Huntington's *Clash of Civilizations* (1996) as one possible representative.[1] Like the modernization theorists, Huntington defines culture as 'ancestry, religion, language, history, values, customs and institutions' (1996: 21). He is more careful than his predecessors, however, in his characterization of non-Western cultures, refraining (at least outwardly) from privileging the West. For him, the world consists of a plurality of 'civilizations' (eight to be exact), each distinct and unique. He emphasizes the inherent cultural differences between each, believing they will inexorably result in conflict, notably one involving the West against 'Islam'. His recommendation is that the West, led by the US, should refrain from interfering in the affairs of other civilizations (1996: 208, 312).

Huntington's view of culture, typical of multicultural politics, is essentialist. His central question appears to be 'what is the nature of culture?', and his resulting methodology is about finding 'real' and 'authentic' cultural traits and fault lines. Each world cultural system is unique and discrete, bounded by what he sees as clearly identifiable national/geographic or religious boundaries. And similar to the modernization perspective, each cultural system emerges as fixed — closed, stable, homogeneous, never changing. He pays little consideration to the diversity and historical interactions within and between cultures, nor to each one's ongoing transformation. Moreover, there is an unmistakable 'culturalization of politics'[2] at work here, so often the mark of multiculturalism and identity politics: others will be tolerated, but only insofar as they are kept at a distance — contained, isolated, anesthetized; we will interact with them, but only to the extent that their differences (i.e. precisely what makes them unique) are diluted or cleansed; other cultures are equal to ours, but we must nonetheless protect ourselves from them. For all intents and purposes, Huntington's politics is modernization's by the back door; it may well be more polite and tolerant, but it is equally orientalist.

But there is another perspective on culture — the semiotic one mentioned earlier. I am calling it 'postcolonial', although this may be a sleight of hand, given that it has multiple variants and relies on several sources (cultural anthropology, cultural marxism, discursive analysis, deconstruction). I would like to draw out two notable dimensions for the purposes of this chapter. First, rather than asking

Huntington's 'what is culture?', which gives way to the reification of culture, the postcolonial perspective asks 'how is culture made?', emphasizing the more active and transformative role of culture. Culture is seen as a semiotic practice (Geertz 1973), grounded in everyday life and through which shared signs and symbols are deployed to represent our world. Raymond Williams refers to it as 'the *signifying system* through which necessarily . . . a social order is communicated, reproduced, experienced, and explored' (1982: 13, italics in original; cf. Hall 1977: 328). Rather than focusing on cultural identity, which fixes and unifies culture, the idea here is to see culture as signifying *process*: this means that culture is dynamic rather than static, slippery and unfixed rather than stable, plural and hybrid rather than whole, and 'negotiated and constructed rather than a "given"' (Clammer 2005: 103; cf. Williams 1979: 154; Bhabha 1994; Appadurai 1996: 12; Nederveen Pieterse 2001: 70).

The second dimension is what gives the postcolonial perspective its critical bent — its discursivity. The semiotic construction of culture involves a 'will to power', wherein knowledge is systematized and disseminated (Said 1978: 12; 1983: 216). This process includes the deployment of discursive strategies, for example the use of rhetoric or the construction, repetition, and reification of powerful images and stereotypes (Bhabha 1994: 66ff.; Derrida 1982: 307ff.). It also includes the enactment of discourse in institutional practices, for instance by funding and widely disseminating a favoured body of knowledge. A power politics is thus at play, entailing domination and/or contestation, and as a result of which some representational practices triumph over others.

What this postcolonial perspective enables us to do is to view culture, not as something separate and 'out there', whose outlines can be precisely and objectively determined from afar (*à la* Huntington or modernization theory), but rather as an immediate and inescapable lens or horizon. Its contours may well be shifting and imprecise, but we cannot view, interpret, or make our world without it. Culture tints, filters, gives perspective; yet, privileging one colour means excluding others; filtering in also means filtering out. The implication for development policy, as underlined at the start, is that, far from being neutral or objective tools, policies are always cultural artifacts. They emerge from a time and place, and are framed according to institutionally generated narratives and constrictions.

What follows, then, is a postcolonial semiotic critique of some of the major development policies of the last four decades — basic needs, structural adjustment, good governance, and human rights — in rough historical order.[3] My intent is to try and analyze their key cultural underpinnings. This will often entail recognizing the implicit or explicit cultural imprints of neoclassical economics, modernization theory, and multiculturalism, as outlined above. But more importantly, it will involve exposing each policy regime's discursive strategies: its ideological suppositions and rhetorical constructions; its gaps, disavowals, and discontinuities; its production and naturalization of hierarchies; and its institutional tendency towards reproducing or extending power.[4]

21

Basic needs

The basic needs approach emerged out of a crisis in modernization strategy: the latter's promise of 'trickle-down growth' bore little fruit during the 1960s and 1970s, and this across most of the developing world. Not only was there evidence of lacklustre growth, but there was also little to show regarding wealth distribution. As a result, by the mid-to-late 1970s, the ILO and UNESCO began advocating for a 'basic needs' (BN) development strategy. BN was seen as a 'minimum standard of living which a society should set for the poorest of its people', comprising food, shelter, clothing, sanitation, education, and health (ILO 1976: 7, 32; cf. Streeten & Burki 1978).

Soon, this thinking was taken up with interest by the World Bank. In 1981, it published what became the most famous BN reference text, *First Things First: Meeting Basic Human Needs in Developing Countries*. The book was authored by Paul Streeten, with contributions from, among others, Mahbub ul Haq, the Bank's then director of policy planning and programme review.[5] Haq, it should be noted, subsequently became one of the main proponents of the UNDP's human development approach (now named 'sustainable human development'), which draws heavily on BN. In this sense, BN can be said to have continuing influence on development policy, stretching up to today.

In contrast to modernization's emphasis on growth, BN advocates for a poverty alleviation agenda. It is a consumption-oriented approach, calling attention to a minimum threshold required for people to become productive members of society, and below which no one should fall. Absolute poverty is defined in terms of the provision of a fundamental set of socioeconomic goods and services, as opposed to a guarantee of basic levels of income. There is thus a strong welfarist bent to BN, with the attendant requirement for a strong state to ensure minimum levels of consumption (cf. Streeten 1981: 56). The Sri Lankan, Tanzanian, and Cuban state-led development strategies of the late 1960s and early 1970s are often cited as models for the BN approach.

BN's priority to human and social development, as opposed to only economic growth, and its concern with education and health, as opposed to more strictly defined 'material' needs, are usually seen as improvements upon modernization. But I would like to point out that its cultural underpinnings are at least equally as problematic. In support, I offer the following three arguments: BN is a dubious cultural fiction, it betrays strong paternalistic tendencies, and it is an ideological attempt at justifying inequality.

To start, it is important to probe both of BN's key terms — 'basic' and 'needs'. The first is meant to conjure up something obvious, universal, primary, natural. It is as though humans everywhere can be stripped bare of all social bonds, so that all we are left with are the most 'basic' needs. As long as humans have food, shelter, clothing, etc., they can survive, or so the story goes. This is classic Robinson Crusoe or 'state of nature' fiction.

And fiction it is. For, it is unlikely that there would be anything recognizably 'human' left if someone were indeed stripped of her/his sociocultural relationships.

Like it or not, it is precisely our access to language, our socialization, that human-izes us, that induces us *to* need (details on this below). What is more, this bare needs, desert island fiction is contradicted by the now ample anthropological evidence that 'poor' societies (in fact, *all* societies) have often given precedence to the sacred over the profane, for example by building extravagant holy or religious sites, in spite of relative poverty. The idea, as Gilbert Rist writes, is that 'Before one can eat, a share must be set aside for the gods; before one can have somewhere to live, the temple must be built' (1997: 168). Impoverished people, like anyone else, can and do choose to afford 'luxuries', even if this threatens their material livelihoods.

Not only is the term 'basic' a fictionalized construction, then, but it also creates an artificial distinction and hierarchy between 'primary' and 'secondary' needs: the former are viewed as absolute socioeconomic prerequisites, the latter — including such things as politics, culture, and spirituality (all notably absent from BN) — as 'luxurious' pursuits. The result is a simplistic and ahistorical narrative that occludes the multidimensionality of people's lives.

Moving on to 'needs', what stands out is BN's attempt to naturalize them. For example Streeten speaks of a 'pure basic needs approach' and about human beings as 'endowed with needs and a natural inclination to satisfy them' (1981: 55, 73). Yet, to naturalize needs and disavow the social in this way is to engage in what Jean Baudrillard calls 'magical thinking': you posit a 'real' and independent subject alongside 'real' objects and then proceed to establish a relationship between the two by means of a mythological invention you call 'pure need' (1981: 63, 71).

BN's argumentation must be turned on its head. As Baudrillard puts it, 'If he [man] [*sic*] eats, drinks, lives somewhere, reproduces himself, it is because the system requires his self-production in order to reproduce himself: it needs man' (1981: 86). Not only are needs socially generated, then, they are also generated for a specific reason — to ensure a 'productive' population. Streeten writes, for instance, that 'the emphasis on *making the poor more productive* has remained an important component of the basic needs approach' (1981: 3, italics mine). The logic is thus to create a productivist society, and people are constructed as naturally inclined towards precisely those basic needs (i.e. food, shelter, clothing, health, and education) that yield such a society: 'people discover a posteriori and almost miraculously that they need what is produced and offered on the market-place. . . . To become an end in itself, every system must dispel the question of its real teleology' (Baudrillard 1981: 71).

We can discern here more than a tinge of First World social engineering and paternalism. Indeed, BN's framing is premised on a series of paired hierarchies — rich–poor, culture–nature, luxurious–basic — that conveniently fit its North–South orientation. The narrative goes something like this: the poor of the South live in a state of nature and we, cultured policy advisors, must rescue them. Such a story supports the notion of BN as a fiction, but in addition it raises questions about whose needs are really being satisfied and to what extent 'needs' are being confused with 'wants': given BN's top-down and social engineering dimensions, might it not be conjectured that BN is constructed first and foremost to satisfy the policy framers' own needs/wants? In other words, might this not be a case of 'we' (policy experts embedded in the development machine) wanting 'you' (the Third World poor) to need? In the end, is it not our desires that dictate what you need to need?

Such conjecture is buttressed by two notable details: BN's emphasis on a strong state to provide for basic services, and its insistence that the selection of basic needs, as well as the indicators to measure them, are 'best left to technical experts' (Streeten 1981: 93). This first perpetuates the dependency of the poor, while the latter justifies the expert's role in BN.[6] BN thus appears to bolster well the policy-maker's needs/wants — controlling and managing the Third World poor by judging, defining, and measuring their 'needs', while at the same time rationalizing the requirement for both policy intervention (by the state or donor) and the expert's 'expertise'.

Where does all of this leave the 'poor', the purported beneficiaries? It essentializes them by positioning them as passive and lacking. Streeten refers to them as 'target groups' that are politically 'weak and inarticulate' (1981: 52); while the ILO goes so far as to encapsulate them by means of a 'reference man' — aged between 25 and 39 years, weighing 65 kg, healthy, and, tellingly, physically fit for an active eight-hour work day (quoted in Rist 1997: 166). The production of this BN subject means ignoring the rich tapestry of pluralistic Third World societies, while also excluding options for marginalized communities to define and address their own priorities. BN postures about increasing poor people's access to essential services, but it also constructs them as 'weak', incapable of helping themselves. Hence the need to save them. The one construction (a lack) opportunely leads to the other (a rescue mission).

There is, finally, the issue of BN's justification of inequality. Outwardly, this is evident in the way in which the policy approach localizes and individualizes development, addressing poverty on a micro-scale, without regard for broader structural, national, or global inequalities. Streeten admits as much when he writes that 'equality as such is probably not an objective of great importance to most people other than utilitarian philosophers and ideologues . . . meeting basic needs is morally a more important objective than reducing inequality' (1981: 17). And he goes on to say that 'It is very doubtful whether closing the income gap [between 'rich' and 'poor' countries] in the near future is either desirable or possible' (1981: 160-1).[7]

Not only can such arguments be taken as an acceptance of inequality, but *pace* Streeten, they are precisely an ideological rationalization. For, as intimated by my analysis up to this point, 'basic needs', like the supposed 'scarcity' that engenders the survival of the 'poor', are both artificially created, not 'natural'. They are both 'determined residually', as Baudrillard reminds us, 'by the fundamental urgency of an excess: the divine or sacrificial share, sumptuous discharge, economic profit' (1981: 80; cf. Rist 1997: 169). As a consequence, 'a certain surplus coexists with a certain poverty. But the crucial point is that it is always the production of surplus that regulates the whole. The survival threshold is never determined from below, but from above' (Baudrillard 1981: 81). By insisting on the local, by focusing on micro interventions, BN is thus obfuscating, if not disavowing, the intimate links between luxury and survival, wealth and scarcity, inequality and poverty. So much for Streeten's above-cited moral mission (or his basic need?) to protect 'most people' from 'ideologues'.[8]

Structural adjustment

If BN is a turn away from trickle-down growth, structural adjustment is a return back to it; and if BN is suspicious of narrow economic development in favour of greater social development, structural adjustment is a valorization of the economic realm to the exclusion of others. Indeed, structural adjustment emerged in the early-to-mid-1980s, inspired by neoclassical economics. In 1989, its ideological grounding was consolidated by what came to be known as the 'Washington consensus', as a result of which the IMF, World Bank, and US Treasury agreed to a set of economic orientations that were to greatly influence development policy-making for at least the next 15 years. This consensus centred mainly on a critique of Keynesian state welfarism and the prescription of government cutbacks, privatization, and free market policies.

Specifically, structural adjustment has come to involve IMF and World Bank short and long-term loan packages, typically extended to developing countries on the following conditions: the establishment of short-term stabilization policies to address balance of payments and trade deficits, currency devaluation, and price controls; and the institution of long-term structural policies that include downsizing the civil service, cuts to social spending (e.g. health and education), privatization of 'inefficient' public sector firms, and pro-market tax and investment measures (World Bank 1994b). Structural adjustment programmes have been secured across the Third World, particularly in Africa: for example between 1980 and 2000, the World Bank implemented 537 adjustment operations in 109 countries (World Bank 2001: viii, 2), with African countries subjected to by far the most (Koeberle & Malesa 2005: 4).

What I wish to highlight are the ways in which structural adjustment, as well as the development economics that underpins it, are cultural and discursive. This is evidenced by their affirmation of a particular set of values and categories, their dogmatic exclusions, and their disciplinary practices, particularly in relation to Africa.

For a start, it must be noted that economics, itself dominated by its neoclassical variant, has long been a hegemonic discipline within the field of development. The two code words — 'poverty' and 'development' — that dominate the field have without doubt derived their meaning from the discourse of economics more than any other, organizing what it means to be poor or wealthy, industrialized or rural, developed or underdeveloped (Zein-Elabdin & Charusheela 2004: 1).

Moreover, there is an unmistakable allure and authority of economics, which stem from its self-presentation as a rational science, supported by empirically tested methods and professional management techniques. This means that implementing structural adjustment in the Third World brings with it not only the institutional and financial power of its proponents (the IMF and World Bank), but also the cultural weight and discursive authority of the discipline of economics.

It is worth dwelling a little on the cultural underpinnings of economics, and by association, structural adjustment. The historical narrative that both espouse is a teleological one, placing the Third World in the pre-modern past and the West in the modern present. Such a historical ordering renders the Third World knowable and controllable: as Antonio Callari suggests, 'only on the grounds of such knowability could the other be placeable in a historical ordering . . . the West came to know about and of the other only what it wanted to know, and then only in terms of its own conceptual grid, in order to fit into the structural historicist order (the narrative of its own history) it was producing' (2004: 120-1; cf. Zein-Elabdin 2004: 31; Brohman 1995: 124). It is this 'we know, we've been there' sleight of hand that has authorized such policy prescriptions as structural adjustment, sold to Third World governments as a catch-all and catch-up solution.

The principal driver of this teleological historical tale is the quest for material accumulation. Growth is key, with people seen mainly as workers, consumers, and taxpayers. The implication here is that structural adjustment policies are historically neutral and that economics itself is 'disembodied from culture' (Zein-Elabdin 2004: 28). The Euro-North American capitalist growth process is assumed as universal model for development, transposable in present-day Uganda as much as Indonesia.

Added to the universalization of its teleology is the generalizability of economics' organizing categories. It is these categories, after all, that help maintain the hegemony of the discipline, establishing it as universal 'rather than part of a larger historical cultural episteme' (Zein-Elabdin 2004: 32). First, there is the question of selecting those categories that count, which in the case of neoclassical economics are 'national accounts', 'market equilibrium', 'maximizing behaviour', 'private property', and 'individual preferences', to name only a few. Referring to the applicability of such categories, Deepak Lal, for instance, states that even 'uneducated' peasants, migrants, and workers in developing countries 'respond to changes in relative prices much as neoclassical theory would predict' (quoted in Zein-Elabdin 2004: 29). Any non-selfish, non-profit maximizing behaviour is thus deemed 'irrational', if not pathological. Non-market forms of sociality or solidarity (e.g. community solidarity, communal property) or non-institutionalized activities (e.g. informal sector markets) are similarly looked down upon as 'archaic' (Callari 2004: 119; Brohman 1995: 127). And in the present context of globalization, even non-national categories such as transnational family networks and remittances are given short shrift (Danby 2004). There is a noteworthy process of double-erasure going on here, as Eiman Zein-Elabdin argues: 'erasure of certain cultures by theorizing them as inferior (less developed), and erasure of . . . the work of cultural hegemony' (2004: 28), as evidenced by the universaliza-tion of neoclassical economic categories.

Not to be forgotten is the methodology used to collect information according to these categories. In economics, and neoclassical economics especially, the methodology of choice is usually a positivist one, focusing only on the measurable and empirically quantifiable. As a result, monetized and market-related categories dominate, and either sociocultural and political factors are ignored, or they are treated very narrowly (e.g. education is measured only with quantifiable literacy indicators). Social complexity and heterogeneity are thus occluded (Zein-Elabdin & Charusheela 2004: 8). These problems are compounded in economic model-ling, *de rigueur* in any structural adjustment country analysis: it breaks down economies or societies into discrete and quantifiable variables (cf. Brohman 1995: 126-9), but thereby misses such key multidimensional and dynamic phenomena as institutional politics, cultural adaptation, or changing eco-systems.

Given this cultural backdrop, given the imposition of simple and quick techno-logical fixes and the rationalization of accumulation, market expansion, and resource exploitation, it should come as no surprise that economics is seen to be closely associated with colonialism. Zein-Elabdin and Charusheela maintain in this regard that 'Economics is epistemologically comfortable with the notion of colonialism and imperial domination. . . . [It] can thus be soundly characterized as a colonial discourse grounded in exclusion and erasure of the unfamiliar' (Zein-Elabdin & Charusheela 2004: 2-3).

What gives structural adjustment its particularly novel or neocolonial bent is its added biopolitical dimension (cf. Foucault 1979: 143, 137): here, classical domi-nation over vast territory and masses of people is replaced by more indirect and micro forms of control. By indirect control I mean manipulation from afar, what one might today call 'transnational e-control', when, for instance, the World Bank does not need to be physically present in Tanzania in order for its prescriptions to be followed. It can monitor and shape economic policies at one remove (e.g. electronically or through the financial markets) so as not to be seen as interfering in the country's internal affairs. Achille Mbembe labels this 'tutelary government' (2001: 74), whereby the IMF and World Bank have influence, not directly over the post-colonial African state, but more subtly (and yet efficiently) over its finances, economic policies, privatization and rural transformation programmes. Mbembe argues that such arrangements have led to new forms of power and violence, taking special note of '*the direct link that now exists between, on the one hand, deregulation and the primacy of the market, and, on the other, the rise of violence and the creation of private military, paramilitary, or jurisdictional organizations*' (2001: 79, italics in original; cf. 102).

By micro control, I mean power over people's minds and bodies, over their routine chores and daily activities. This brings to the fore the supervisory and disciplinary dimensions of adjustment conditionalities. I am referring here, in particular, to the strict spending limits imposed on public service managers, to their need to continually monitor their own activities and those of their partners (suppliers, NGOs) through such devices as performance measures and benchmarks. In this regard, a recent DFID White Paper revealingly declares, 'we need improved surveillance — better monitoring of the performance of developed and developing country economies . . . financial supervision will only work if there is an effective surveillance mechanism to monitor . . . implementation' (2000b: 53). While the ostensible (neoliberal) purpose of performance measurement is to help improve the public sector's efficiency and financial accountability, its accompanying proclivity, as the DFID statement perhaps inadvertently conveys, is to help better police people (cf. Winstanley & Stuart-Smith 1996), thus expanding the reach of donors into the routine tasks of civil servants. Some studies even show that managers end up spending too much time on the rituals of performance management (e.g. collecting performance data, monitoring results) and not enough time managing (Adcroft & Willis 2005: 398).

But I am also speaking here of the more corporeal disciplining that results from structural adjustment free trade and investment measures. The need to quickly expand exports means, for example, that free trade zones (FTZs) are opened up, wages are kept relatively low, and unionization is banned. Several studies show, for example, that the number of such FTZs have increased under adjustment.[9] Workers must work long hours in small, enclosed spaces, that facilitate their close supervision. Also implied is a certain engineering of bodies, especially female workers' bodies. Remarking that free trade zones in the Third World are primarily dependent on female labour, Medley and Carroll submit: 'Disciplining female workers to exhibit "female" traits, such as passivity, dependency, and malleability, factory owners seek to construct a generalizable worker, one suited to labor in Free Trade Zones' (2004: 146; cf. Kamel & Hoffman 1999). Aiwa Ong similarly remarks on the infantilization of women, on their need to fit a certain mould — they must be half-witted, docile, dexterous, patient (1987: 152). What all these connections reveal, once again, are not just the non-material cultural hierarchies and linguistic exclusions of the discourse of neoclassical economics, but equally its adumbrated institutional surveillance techniques and corporeal control mechanisms.

A final note on 'Africa': it has become the most structurally adjusted region on earth, and has consequently been subjected to much more than its share of discursive power and biopolitics.[10] In this sense, adjustment perpetuates colonialism's invention of a 'savage' or 'chaotic' Africa, which as Valentin Mudimbe argues (1988; 1994: xiv) is produced by the West to rationalize Euro-North American superiority and the need for quick technocratic fixes such as adjustment. The IMF and World Bank have tended to view Africa (in the singular) as a black mark to economic modernity, and the African state as anti-reform, thus eliding once again the sociopolitical plurality of the region. As a consequence, Mbembe writes, 'African politics and economics have been condemned to appear . . . only as a sign of lack' (2001: 8; cf. Ahluwalia 2001: 13). It is as though Western discourse on Africa has become authoritative, not because of overwhelming evidence, but because of overwhelming repetition, circulation, and intertextual references, stretching back to the nineteenth century (this is what Said calls 'strategic forma-tion'; cf. 1978: 20). The IMF and World Bank may thus be seen, willy-nilly, to be acting upon such stereotypical images of Africa as 'dark continent', 'famine stricken', 'basket case', and 'corrupt', not only in the context of structural adjust-ment but, as we shall presently find out, 'good governance' as well.

Good governance

The World Bank defines good governance as 'sound development management', referring in particular to the way in which 'power is exercised in the management of a country's economic and social resource[s]' (1992: 1; cf. 1994a). Good gover-nance usually includes four main components: sound public sector management; the accountability of public officials; the establishment of legal frameworks for development (e.g. the rule of law, an independent judiciary); and transparency (of information, of government procedures) (World Bank 1992).

In many ways, the governance agenda was constructed in the negative aftermath of structural adjustment, when it was discovered that free markets and price incentives were not enough to spur growth. This realization happened mainly during Joseph Stiglitz's tenure as the Bank's chief economist: inspired by institutional economics and insights from the East Asian development experience, his reasoning was that supporting markets and democracy required state capacity, often lacking in much of the developing world after the retrenchment years of structural adjustment (Hewitt 2006: 52; cf. World Bank 1997a). Complementing this claim was the recognition of the positive role that can be played by civil society in both democratization and policy-making. Good governance was thus a kind of awakening to the need for politics in development.

A dilemma faced by the Bank was that, in taking up the governance agenda, it was important not to be seen as interfering in the internal politics of recipients. In fact, the Bank's Articles of Agreement specifically state that 'The Bank and its officers shall not interfere in the political affairs of any member' (World Bank 2007: Article IV(10)). The solution was to make governance complementary to economic reform: governance was deemed a prerequisite to the success of adjust-ment policies, and was viewed as helping encourage local 'ownership' of reforms. Good governance thus became integral to loan extensions and a condition of aid.

During the 1990s, most donors jumped on the Bank-led governance bandwagon. Some added further activities to the Bank's list of essential gover-nance ingredients (e.g. public participation), while others emphasized particular elements of governance, for example the 'watchdog' role that civil society organizations can play in making governments more accountable (cf. UNDP 1997: 4-5; DAC 1993; Jenkins 2001).

Since the mid-to-late 1990s, anti-corruption activities have gained increasing prominence. Spearheaded by the Bank and developed in close cooperation with Transparency International (TI), an international NGO, the anti-corruption agenda is portrayed as critical to public sector transparency and better functioning markets (cf. World Bank 1997b). According to the Bank, so detrimental is corruption in some countries that, for example, starting in 1997, loans to Kenya had to be suspended because of the perceived lack of anti-corruption reforms there; and, more recently, sectoral loans have had to be withheld for Chad, Kenya, Congo, India, Bangladesh, Uzbekistan, Yemen, and Argentina over fears of corruption (Bretton Woods Project 2006). Corruption, we are told, damages incentive structures and negatively affects investment and growth (Transparency International 2000: 3). While the state is a focus for anti-corruption activities, it is not the only culprit; the private sector is also singled out as having to accept its share of the blame. Thus, TI publishes its now famous 'Corruption Perceptions Index' and 'Bribe Payers Index', intended to expose both governments and corporations involved in corruption (Transparency International 2007a-b).

To begin the task of examining the cultural/discursive construction of good governance: one is struck first by the qualifier 'good'. It conveys a moralistic tone, implying not simply that developing countries have 'bad' governance, but also that the West is the model for good governance and Western donors are the arbitrators of what is 'good' and 'bad'. Of late, many donors have woken up to these outward faux pas and dropped the term 'good', but the stigmata of the governance discourse still remain.

What is noteworthy about the discourse is that it is inspired by the 1960 to 1990 East Asian experience, yet one cannot help notice that many of the main elements of governance (e.g. accountability, transparency) are notably absent from the state-directed economic 'miracles' of Korea, Taiwan, Singapore, and Hong Kong during that period. In fact, several of these elements are conspicuously absent in the contemporary West itself, where neither political leaders nor civil service are immune from inefficiencies, less than rational decision-making, or indeed corruption. The criteria for good governance, in this sense, are an ahistorical and idealized fiction that even the West hardly achieves. I would argue, in fact, that not being able to achieve them turns out to be a useful maneuver: it means that aid recipients always fall short, which only strengthens the power the governance agenda has over them.

But good governance is a ruse in another important way, too: it is a self-fulfilling prophecy that serves to rationalize further external intervention and consolidate neoliberalism. Indeed, in 1989, the Bank published *Sub-Saharan Africa: from crisis to sustainable growth*, which was the first to broach questions of lack of government efficiency and effectiveness, direly predicting the 'collapse of public sector capacity' in Africa (1989: 8; cf. Idahosa & Shenton 2004). Yet, the implementation of structural adjustment had already begun to take its toll in the region by then, so that the Bank's predictions are more accurately characterized as advance warning. When the good governance agenda was initiated in 1992, the ingredients required to rationalize it were already in place. The civil service and social programmes had been gutted, the state's regulatory capacities had been considerably weakened, and the illegitimacy and violence of many African states had increased (cf. Mbembe 2001: 76). Good governance was therefore responding to a 'crisis' to which it had itself greatly contributed but disavowed.[11] It was able nonetheless to pose as another rescue mission. It was also able to use the opportunity to advance the cause of neoliberalism: given its positioning as complement to adjustment, many of its provisions could (and did) involve creating an 'enabling environment' for private sector-led growth (World Bank 1989: 2). Thus, for example, its law reforms have most often focused on updating business law, debt recovery, taxation, corporate governance, intellectual property, and landownership (Shihata 1997: 75-90).

A significant feature of governance is its commitment (outwardly, at least) to refrain from direct political interference, often going so far as to euphemistically categorize its programming as 'technical assistance'; yet, there appears to be nothing more political than reconfiguring a country's institutional decision-making processes. Nonetheless, this non-interference stance appears to tar much of the governance discourse, and notably its conception of 'state' and 'civil society'. Typically, the state is viewed through the lens of rational choice theory which, not surprisingly, is ideologically aligned with neoclassical economics. Accordingly, the state is seen as a neutral, autonomous, and homogeneous set of institutions that collect resources, respond to citizens' rational choices, and provide value for money (Harrison 2005: 245). This is a naive and mechanistic conception, giving little or no consideration to the state's social embeddedness or its internal fragmentation and power struggles. The implications are far-reaching, particularly for anti-corruption measures, as we shall see below.

The conceptualization of civil society is equally naive. In his study of USAID's governance programming, Rob Jenkins characterizes the agency's construction of civil society as a kind of 'political ombudsman, reflecting the values of fair play, and commitment to public welfare' (2001: 268). This is an idealized and normative construction, which according to Jenkins ignores 'the manifestly illiberal tendencies of many "actually existing democracies," including the United States' (e.g. labour strife, press censorship, trade union restrictions, etc.) (2001: 266). The problem, however, is that it is also a construction that leads the USAID to a sanitized form of governance, whereby funding goes mostly to those NGOs deemed neither threatening nor overtly political. In Sub-Saharan Africa particularly, many such NGOs are already linked to other donors or transnational organizations such as the Bank (cf. Ferguson 1998: 3-4). The end result, perhaps not unsurprisingly, is building a type of civil society that conforms to a neoliberal form of governance (Jenkins 2001: 263).

Finally, there is the issue of corruption. Usually defined as the misuse of public power for private gain, the overwhelming tendency is to blame it on bad values, greedy civil servants, and a general 'culture of political corruption' (LeVine 1993: 274). Most often, it is Africa that is singled out here, the implication invariably being that the African state is anti-democratic, authoritarian, and infiltrated by family and 'tribal' loyalties (cf. Mbembe 2001: 8-9). There is, once again, a noticeable moral tone to this discourse, allowing donors to sit in judgement. The typical maneuver is to blame the problem on the country's *culture*, insinuating that it take responsibility for its own plight. Yet, it is ironic that when there are cases of corruption in the West — the recent spate of corporate scandals (Enron, WorldCom, Hollinger, Savings and Loans) comes to mind — the problem is never blamed on 'Western culture' but rather 'rogue individuals' and 'poor business practices' (Visweswaran 2004). Moreover, rarely is there mention in the governance/corruption discourse of the broader socioeconomic and global causes of corruption (e.g. inequality, unbridled profit maximization, market domination). Narrow cultural explanations make it easier to ignore, or divert attention from, the bigger picture.

Not unexpectedly, the anti-corruption strategies implied by this discourse are inclined to be woefully shallow. They rely on the idealized notions of state and civil society mentioned earlier. Accordingly, the idea is that civil society will act as watchdog against state corruption, and the culture of corruption will be routed out in favour of a professionalized and transparent civil service (cf. Transparency International 2000). Not only is it unrealistic to expect NGOs to be good citizens and confront often powerful states, but the possibility that NGOs may themselves be participants in the business of corruption appears to elude the likes of the Bank and TI (cf. Jenkins 2001: 255, 257).

To believe that 'state culture' can be engineered, moreover, is ahistorical and unrealistic. The Weberian or rational choice claim to a professionalized bureaucracy (itself idealized) comes out of a particular Euro-North American history, which cannot be arbitrarily imposed on the diversity of Third World states (cf. Theobold 2002: 435; 1990). Many African governments, for example, do have clientelist practices; but these have complex sociopolitical origins, rooted in top-down colonial resource extraction and rent seeking. Attempts at eliminating such practices, at establishing 'clear' lines between the public and private — which, importantly, would not pass muster even in the West — in order to create a professional civil service, are therefore likely not to work. Cultures are not easily changed, and certainly not from the 'outside'. As Mlada Bukovansky suggests, anti-corruption strategies 'will lack legitimacy unless they are embraced and internalized by the culture on which they are imposed'; they demand not external brow-beating and quick fixes, but meaningful, slow, and often difficult public debate about the meaning of corruption, and its complex social causes and solutions (2006: 184).

In fact, there is little evidence that donors' anti-corruption strategies have worked, and growing recognition that they may be counterproductive. Graham Harrison contends that, in the context of several African states' clientelist practices, the Bank's policies of privatization and deregulation 'can have the unintended effect of consolidating new forms of clientelism . . . that epitomise "bad" governance' (2005: 253). Moreover, by opening up developing country markets, adjustment and governance may well have increased, not decreased, opportunities for transnational corporate graft. Taking a different tack, Mbembe and others suggest that, given the severity of adjustment in Sub-Saharan Africa, corruption has likely acted as a safety valve, preventing a 'slide into completely arbitrary rule and raw violence' (Mbembe 2001: 75; cf. Bukovansky 2006: 196; Hasty 2005). Similarly Manthia Diawara makes the case *for* market corruption and smuggling in helping people cope with the hardships of adjustment policies by providing more choice and lower prices (1998: 123; cf. Ahluwalia 2003).

But whether the corruption/governance agenda is successful or not is perhaps not really the point. One way or the other, its deployment has aided the Bretton Woods institutions to further secure their hegemony in the global economic system. It has given pride of place, as well, to such transnational NGOs as TI: Barry Hindess writes that the 'case of TI reminds us, at the international level, that the agenda of neoliberal reform should not be seen simply as the province of states and other international organisations. It also relies on agencies, such as TI, which have no coercive powers of their own and which operate rather through persuasion and example' (2005: 1397). Bukovansky hints at another (Žižekian?) angle: she compares the anti-corruption campaign to 'pornography' (2006: 186), which I take to mean authorizing a Western gaze on the Third World, allowing us to pleasurably and voyeuristically pore over the 'failings' of the other.

Human rights

Human rights-based development is now very much part of the development mainstream. Like basic needs, it sets minimum, universal standards; the difference though is that rights are framed as entitlements recognized in internationally agreed-upon legal treaties, while basic needs are constructed on an a priori consumption model. Most bilateral development agencies (e.g. AusAID 1997: 226) and multilateral organizations (e.g. UN organizations, World Bank) have taken on the rights agenda in some form or another. Some have even adopted a 'rights-based approach' to development (cf. DFID 2000a; SIDA 2007), which often implies making development programming conditional upon a country's human rights record. Many transnational NGOs (e.g. Oxfam, Amnesty International, CARE, Save the Children) have joined the human rights bandwagon, choosing to make rights issues a major focus of their programming (cf. Cornwall & Nyamu-Musembi 2004).

There is now a substantial corpus of international human rights instruments, which development agencies rely upon as a guide for programming. These comprise three main areas: civil and political rights (e.g. the Universal Declaration of Human Rights); social and economic rights (e.g. the International Covenant on Economic, Social and Cultural Rights, and the CEDAW or Convention on the Elimination of All Forms of Discrimination Against Women); and cultural and collective rights (e.g. the Indigenous and Tribal Peoples Convention). While there is overlap between these instruments, most often they are incompatible: there are disagreements, in particular, over whether precedence should be given to individual over collective rights, and civil/political over socioeconomic rights. Most often, it is those treaties emphasizing a Western and individualist conception of rights (i.e. the civil/political rights treaties) that are hegemonic (cf. Robbins & Stamatopoulou 2004: 427).

To draw out the cultural underpinnings of the human rights discourse in development, it is important to critically examine the universalism-cultural relativism debate that has so preoccupied the field. Universalists argue for the general applicability of (Western) laws on the basis of a universal essence or human nature. Their claims are usually made in terms of 'natural law', which they see as transhistorical and axiomatic. This is by and large the position taken (implicitly or explicitly) by most mainstream development organizations in both First and Third World. In contrast, cultural relativists are critical of what they see as the individualist focus of the Western legal system, arguing instead for the communitarian values of non-Western legal traditions (Confucian, Islamic, Hindu, etc.). This is often labelled the 'Asian values' position, notably championed by such Asian leaders as Lee Kuan Yew, Mahathir Mohamed, and Benazir Bhutto.

But both positions are problematic, in my view. The latter position appears as merely a reaction to Western hegemony: it is caught up in the same modernity-tradition dualism as its opponent, thus reproducing an essentialist view of rights (namely all non-Western legal traditions are communitarian, individual rights are uniquely Western and therefore bad, traditional law is necessarily good). Moreover, it is a view that tends to prop up nationalist elites, justifying their often non-democratic state practices under the pretence of 'collective rights' protection. Thus, during the 1990s, Hindu nationalists quite successfully propagated a view of the 'traditional Indian woman' to buttress their politics, causing those women's groups that resisted to be accused of betrayal for being too 'westernized' (Narayan 1997). This narrow, ghettoized take on culture, it must be pointed out, shares much with Huntington's earlier-mentioned multicultural politics.

The universalist position is equally essentialist. I would like to dwell on it a little, given its relative global dominance. Universalists tend to overlook that their project is a deeply cultural, and hence partial, one. As Sally Engle Merry maintains, they delude themselves that 'there is no culture in the conference halls of New York and Geneva [where they draft rights treaties] .... The transnational elites who populate these halls think they are doing law but they are actually making culture' (2003: 70). They call human rights transhistorical and 'natural', yet they are drawing on a particular tradition (i.e. the Western liberal rights tradition of Euro-North America), and on a political history that originates in granting rights to the few (male property owners) and denying them to the many (women, non-propertied classes, non-white people). The end result is that the promulgation of human rights amounts not to the promotion of universal rights, but to the universalization of the *Western* legal tradition.

Now it is true that, over the years, many human rights have been fought for and extended. But even today, it is arguable whether they universally apply. As Hannah Arendt has persuasively pointed out, the rights discourse purports to include all humans, irrespective of creed, race, social position, and so on; yet at the international level, rights pertain only to 'citizens', whose claims are dependent on exclusionary national citizenship criteria (1958b: Ch. 9). Human rights, in other words, derive from a system of state sovereignty, under which non-citizens (refugees, 'illegal' migrants) have no rights and hence are no longer even 'recognized or treated as humans' (Arendt 1958b: 297; cf. Balfour & Cadava 2004: 280-1).

A significant criticism of the universalist position is that, by positing the West as the site of progress (Narayan 1997), it is inclined to dismiss 'local culture'. This is modernization theory reincarnated: human rights are considered modern, and non-Western cultures are hastily equated with inequality, patriarchy, and religious 'fundamentalism'. Even 'critical universalists' such as Martha Nussbaum fall into this trap. Her stance is non-foundationalist, arguing for a culturally and socially constructed view of law. She is critical of both Western universalism and 'tradition', readily admitting they can both be oppressive to women and minorities (1995a, 1995b: 4-5). Yet, she nonetheless champions a cosmopolitan humanitarianism, which happens to be Western and coincidentally the 'best' (because of its commitment to equality). All said and done, there does not appear to be much she can learn from 'tradition'. Spivak thus reproaches her for appropriating and judging Third World women's narratives in order to 'find a philosophical justification for universalism'; rather than being open to the other, Nussbaum brings 'the other into the self' (Spivak 2004: 567-8).

As intimated in the Nussbaum–Spivak exchange, the problem of the universalization of human rights is particularly visible in the domain of gender rights. The main issue here is that women's rights discourse essentializes and besmirches 'local culture'. CEDAW, for example, takes Western rights as modern, and equates 'culture' with 'prejudices and customary' practices (CEDAW 1979: Articles 2, 5). Merry shows that the CEDAW committee's legal commentaries locate the source of women's oppression mainly in the domain of beliefs and values, reinforcing 'the idea that it is culture that is subordinating women and modernity that frees them. That modernity is also a cultural system seems lost in this formulation. Culture is relegated to the domain of the past, to religious extremism, and to irrational "taboos"'(2003: 62; cf. CEDAW 1979: Article 16; Gideon 2006: 1272; Razack 1998: 88ff.). And the problem is not just confined to legal treaties. Media and transnational organizations alike are prone to focusing on violence against women. Issues such as female genital mutilation, dowry deaths, and rape are fetishized, reinforcing notions of uniformly barbaric and patriarchic African, Hindu, or Islamic traditions. A 1999 Human Rights Watch report, 'Crime or Custom? Violence Against Women', even states that Pakistani women are 'second class citizens as a result of . . . social and cultural norms and attitudes' (quoted in Visweswaran 2004: 496).

Uma Narayan calls such representations 'death by culture' (1997: x, 84). They provide fodder for battling over women's bodies and genitalia (Merry 2003: 58), but they miss that violence against women is not simply culturally constructed. It has many causes. Most often it is the result of sociopolitical conflict: gang rape in Pakistan, for example, is more frequently the result of local politics than 'culture' (narrowly defined) (Merry 2003: 55; Visweswaran 2004: 487); and women's subordination is not necessarily the product of 'traditional patriarchy', but time and again stems from unequal state property/inheritance laws or male domination in the advancing cash economy (cf. Gayle Binion, quoted in Visweswaran 2004: 510; Merry 2003: 69). The culturalization and individualization of women's rights divert attention, once again, from broader questions of inequality, elite politics, and deficient state policy.

It is easy to forget, too, that even while human/gender rights are being promoted by Western development organizations, many Western governments have their own human rights abuse records — e.g. the promulgation of the death penalty, civil rights denials to minorities, the marginalization of indigenous peoples, the production of 'welfare mothers'. The same governments also have a history of supporting brutal, authoritarian regimes in the South — e.g. US backing for the past military regimes of Latin America, French aid to Zaire's Mobutu, and the West's arming of Saddam's Iraq. Moreover, it is important to note that many human/gender rights violations are the direct result of structural adjustment policies, promoted by some of the same donors that now dispense human rights. As alluded to earlier, states' flaunting of rights by banning unionization, disciplining women workers, supporting child labour, allowing lower-than-minimum wages, turning a blind eye on toxic working conditions, and cutting food and educational subsidies — all are the legacies of neoliberal adjustment policies (cf. Cornwall & Nyamu-Musembi 2004). If such is the case, then it must be said that even those development agencies critical of structural adjustment (namely UN organizations, human rights NGOs) are de facto condoning it when they promote liberal-universalist human rights: each side serves to further the mandate of the other, the one abetting rights violations, the other fighting them.

In many ways, the rights agenda serves to promote institutional power and state sovereignty. It helps absolve the West from responsibility, yet it can be used as an alibi for strategic or military intervention, often under the pretence of 'liberation', 'humanitarianism', or 'manifest destiny' (e.g. Iraq, Afghanistan): as Slavoj Žižek avers, 'war is okay insofar as it really serves to bring about peace, democracy, or to create conditions for distributing humanitarian help' (2004: 508).

So where does all this leave us? My purpose in critically studying the cultural dimensions of human rights discourse has not been to dismiss it, but to interrogate its construction, to recognize its limits, dangers, and violations. Many rights are important and have been hard-won; which is to say, as Spivak suggests, that their 'enablement must be used even as the violation is renegotiated' (2004: 524). And Jacques Derrida adds: 'We are in need of [human rights] and they are in need, for there is always a lack, a shortfall, a falling short, an insufficiency; human rights are never sufficient. Which alone suffices to remind us that they are not natural. They have a history — one that is recent, complex, and unfinished' (2003: 132-3).

One of the key problems with both the universalist and relativist positions in development is that each appears so focused on culture that neither adequately grapples with the political character of rights. That is, if rights are indeed culturally embedded and hence partial, then they can only apply universally, as Fred

Dallmayr argues, if they emerge from 'interaction, collaboration, and appropriate institutional [and equitable resource] arrangements' (2002: 177). This means that universalism can neither be imposed nor taken for granted; it must be generated through ongoing and difficult cross-cultural learning and global dialogue: 'Such a rethinking or reconfiguration treats universality not as a *fait accompli*, but rather as a hope or yearning; above all, it deprives any given culture — especially Western culture — of pretensions to monopolize universal "truth," placing its trust instead in the difficult process of interactive dialogue potentially enlisting participants around the globe' (Dallmayr 2002: 185).[12]

Conclusion

By foregrounding the *culture* of development policy, I have been able to scrutinize the representational practices and strategies of development organizations. I have contended that a move to ignore or deny a given policy's cultural make-up so often speaks to attempts at naturalizing a position, imposing and universalizing it under the guise of neutrality or technical/scientific authority. Nothing is more political than this, as the cases of basic needs, governance, and adjustment have shown, resulting in significant social engineering and economic and political restructuring. The move to embrace culture is similarly suspicious: it so often surrenders to essentializing and homogenizing cultures, privileging and praising some, and judging and paternalizing others. Nothing is more politically distracting than this, as anti-corruption and human/gender rights strategies have indicated, diverting attention away from such broader issues as inequality, imperialism, and state violence. Yet, the development machine moves on, constantly evolving differentiated policies and strategies. This leaves the postcolonial critic in the difficult position of being vigilant to these ever-morphing representational maneuvers, while trying to ensure against generalizing or essentializing one's own critique.

Part II

POSTCOLONIAL COMPLICITY
AND SELF-REFLEXIVITY?

3

HYPER-SELF-REFLEXIVE
DEVELOPMENT?

Spivak on representing the Third World 'Other'

'Can the subaltern speak?' (1988a), Spivak's influential, albeit controversial,[1] article, underscores what has become her untiring concern — the proclivity of dominant discourses and institutions to marginalize and disempower the Third World 'subaltern'.[2] Her article examines the ethics and politics involved in this othering process, seizing on the question of representation of the Third World.

Spivak begins the piece by pointing out how 'progressive' Western intellectuals such as Foucault and Deleuze tend to engage in gross universalizations when they speak on behalf of the Third World 'masses', or refer to '*the* workers' struggle' in a way that ignores the international division of labour (1988a: 272-4). She goes on to show how colonial and 'native' representations are similarly problematic. Focusing on widow-sacrifice (*sati*) in colonial India, she examines the British move to abolish the practice, which was justified on the basis of the British 'civilizing mission' in India (a move which Spivak captures in the now famous phrase: 'White men saving brown women from brown men') (1988a: 297). She contrasts this position with the then dominant Hindu one, which excused the practice by arguing that the widows *wanted* to die. Spivak indicates how each representation legitimizes the other: one purports to be a social mission, saving Hindu women from their own men, the other a reward, allowing the women to commit a 'pure' and 'courageous' act. But all the while, the widow's *own* voice is ignored. 'Between patriarchy and imperialism, subject-constitution and object-formation, the figure of the woman disappears. . . . There is no space from which the sexed subaltern can speak' (1988a: 306-7). Spivak ends the article by pointing out that, even when the female subaltern does speak, she cannot be heard (1988a: 308). In this regard, she mentions the case of Bhuvaneswari Bhaduri, whose suicide in 1926 is interpreted as *sati* resulting from illicit love, in spite of her deliberately leaving signs that she committed it for other (i.e. political) reasons.

The crux of Spivak's argument is that the above representations of the Third World conflate two related but discontinuous meanings of 'representation' (1988a: 275-6): (1) 'speaking for', in the sense of political representation; and (2) 'speaking about' or 're-presenting', in the sense of making a portrait. Thus, the British abolition of *sati* rests on a claim to politically represent the Hindu widow *and* portray her 'as she really is or desires'. But not only does this claim end up silencing her, it also erases the role the British play when staging her representation. In conflating the two meanings, in speaking for her *even as they re-present her*, the British neglect their own complicity in the representational process. And Spivak holds not just imperial and dominant nativist discourses to account here; even Foucault and Deleuze, whom she calls 'two great practitioners' of the critique of the subject, and the 'best prophets of heterogeneity and the Other', are guilty: 'The banality of leftist intellectuals' lists of self-knowing, politically canny subalterns stands revealed; representing them, the intellectuals represent themselves as transparent' (1988a: 275).

Spivak writes, of course, from the point of view of a literary/postcolonial critic; but I would like, in this chapter, to argue for the pertinence and significance of her concerns for the field of development. Many of us who work in this field as researchers and/or development workers[3] struggle with the dilemmas that her writing raises. What are the ethico-political implications of our representations for the Third World, and especially for the subaltern groups that preoccupy a good part of our work? To what extent do our depictions and actions marginalize or silence these groups and mask our own complicities? What social and institutional power relationships do these representations, even those aimed at 'empowerment', set up or neglect? And to what extent can we attenuate these pitfalls? Spivak encourages us to ask such questions. She underlines how our discursive constructions are intimately linked to our positioning (socioeconomic, gendered, cultural, geographic, historical, institutional), and therefore demands a heightened self-reflexivity that mainstream development analysts (e.g. Robert Chambers), and sometimes even those 'critical' development analysts among us (e.g. Escobar, Shiva), can fail to live up to. I shall attempt to examine Spivak's numerous writings to illustrate the reasons, advantages, and limits of this hyper-self-reflexivity.[4]

Who represents?

Spivak underlines how we cannot encounter the Third World today without carrying a lot of baggage. She joins Said in maintaining that her own discipline of literary criticism is unavoidably invested in Orientalism, so that literary writing (especially on the Third World) always already means reproducing various forms of Western hegemonic power over the Third World.[5] The same may be said of the field of development. As the 'postdevelopment' theorists (e.g. Escobar 1984, 1995; Sachs 1992) have reminded us, working in development inevitably positions us within a 'development discourse', where the North's superiority over the South is taken for granted, and Western-style development is the norm. Our encounters with, and representations of, our 'subjects' are therefore coded or framed in terms of an us/them dichotomy in which 'we' aid/develop/civilize/empower 'them'. Changing this relationship is not a question of mere good intentions or semantics: for instance, development organizations or researchers may now call their subjects 'beneficiaries', 'target groups', 'partners', or 'clients', instead of 'poor', 'underdeveloped', or 'disadvantaged', but this does not by itself change the discourse or dismantle the us/them power relationship. So caught up are we in this coding that it becomes important in our encounters with the Third World to ask who represents, and what baggage positions us in this us/them manner.

An inheritance that Spivak frequently emphasizes is the history of imperialism. Showing her Marxist leanings,[6] she reminds us of the materialist dimensions of this history, especially the way in which colonialism incorporated the colonies into the international division of labour and thus initiated a process of global inequality and socioeconomic impoverishment, particularly in the Third World. For Spivak, this is a process that continues today under the rubric of 'globalization', with women bearing the brunt of the costs: 'Marx's prescience is fulfilled in postfordism and the explosion of global homeworking. The subaltern woman is now to a rather large extent the support of production' (1999: 67). But Spivak supplements this political-economy argument with an important semiotic one: like Said, she recalls imperialism's cultural production and domination of colonial societies, a process she refers to, as pointed out in Chapter 1, as the 'worlding' of what we call the Third World (1985a: 247). 'Worlding' for her is akin to Marx's 'commodity fetishism', where commodities are so fetishized under capitalism that the (alienated) labour process involved in their production is obscured. For Spivak, the epistemic violence of imperialism has meant the transformation of the 'Third World' into a sign whose production has been obfuscated to the point that Western superiority and dominance are naturalized (1999: 114ff.).

One does not have to look too far a field in international development to see this obfuscatory process at work. As several analysts have pointed out (e.g. Frank 1967; Sylvester 1999: 717; Escobar 1991: 675-6), modernization thinking (e.g. Rostow 1960), which has so dominated the field, barely even mentions colonialism. For it, Third World history begins post-World War II, with First World growth patterns serving as history's guide and goal. The pervasiveness of such thinking is visible, for example, in the structural adjustment and free-trade policies of the Bretton Woods institutions. The policies proceed by a disavowal of the history of imperialism and the unequal footing on which such a history has often placed Third World countries in the global capitalist system. They also proceed by buying 'a self-contained version of the West', which for Spivak amounts to ignoring both its complicity in, and production by, 'the imperialist project' (1988a: 291).

Thus, according to Spivak, the disavowal of the 'worlding' of the Third World allows the Westerner to overlook the interrelationships between the West and imperialism or globalization and the conditions of homeworkers. It places the Third World at bay from the West, and either ignores colonialism, or situates it securely enough in the past as to make one think it is now over and done with. Moreover, it reinforces Western ethnocentrism and triumphalism. Spivak writes, for example, that 'the student [where Spivak teaches, at Columbia University,

New York] is encouraged to think that he or she lives in the capital of the world. The student is encouraged to think that he or she is there to help the rest of the world. And he or she is also encouraged to think that to be from other parts of the world is not to be fully global' (2003a: 622).

But Spivak is careful not to conclude that such thinking happens only along a geographic, West/Third World axis. Increasingly, her work refers to a 'class apartheid', in which the cultures of class are often more important than national or spatial positioning:

> There is an internal line of *cultural* difference within the 'same culture,' apart from the usual mechanisms of class formation. It is related to the formation of the new global culture of management and finance and the families attached to it. It marks access to the Internet. It also marks the new culture of international nongovernmental organizations, involved in development and human rights, as they work on the lowest strata in the developing world.
>
> (Spivak 2003a: 618, italics in original; cf. 2002: 7)

For Spivak, this elite global professional class, made up of both First- and Third-Worlders, is so embedded in managerialist culture that it is easily blind to the Third World subaltern or is prone to projecting developmentalist/ethnocentric mythologies onto the subaltern.

Spivak never shies from implicating herself in her critique of the above-mentioned historical, geographic, cultural, and class positionings, often confessing, for instance, to being a privileged Third World academic working in the West (e.g. 1990a: 57, 60, 75-94). It is perhaps for this reason that she also devotes quite a bit of space in her writings to what she calls the 'native inform-ant', not hesitating once again to implicate herself. She borrows the admittedly problematic[7] term from ethnography to denote a person positioned to speak on behalf of his/her ethnic group or country, typically *for* the benefit of the Western investigator or audience (1999: 6, ix; cf. Khan 2001). The term refers specifically to informants from the Third World or Third World diasporas living in the West[8] (like Spivak, I fit the latter category). Spivak is skeptical of the now fashionable celebration of 'marginality' and multiculturalism, and the increasingly important role that native informants play in/for the West. She is weary of these individuals' uncritical embrace of the West's validation of multiculturalism. The problem is that the native informant can too readily don ethnicity as a badge. S/he may indeed be a well-informed and prepared investigator, but 'clinging to marginality' (1993: 9) also runs the risk of essentializing one's ethnic identity and romanticiz-ing national origins. It can lead, for example, to ahistorical or fundamentalist claims (e.g. 'feminism is un-Islamic') which, in turn, may be used by those in power to justify the repression of women or subalterns (e.g. censorship of progressive Muslim women's groups). It can also lead to shaky claims about the native informant as keeper of esoteric 'ethnic' or subaltern knowledge.

Being postcolonial or 'ethnic', according to Spivak, does not necessarily or naturally qualify one as Third World expert or indeed subaltern (1999: 310); in fact, valorizing the 'ethnic' may end up rewarding those who are already privileged and upwardly mobile, at the expense of the subaltern.

While defending identity-based movements' attempts at recognition and protection of minority group rights, Spivak is critical of privileged diasporics capitalizing on postcoloniality by claiming comparative advantage or disadvantage. She states that, in the academic or political sphere, the 'diasporic' or 'subaltern' has become a 'kind of buzzword for any group that wants something that it does not have' (1996: 290). Similarly, in the economic/business sphere, 'difference' is increasingly becoming commodified, with ethnic culture now being packaged and 'niche'-marketed. She sees upwardly mobile Third-Worlders and Western diasporics, spurred by the desire to assist their 'home' culture, playing a greater role in this commodification process: as 'well-placed Southern diasporic[s]' or natives, they help advance corporate multinational globalization through the patenting of indigenous knowledge and agricultural inputs, microcredit programmes for women, or population control (1999: 310; 2003a: 611). She therefore concludes that this new-found 'nativism' yields a reverse ethnocentrism: 'It is as if, in a certain way, we are becoming complicitous in the perpetration of a "new orientalism"' (1993: 56; cf. 277).

But Spivak is quick to examine the other side of the equation. She reproaches Western researchers/academicians for sometimes too easily distancing themselves from postcoloniality by uncritically situating the native informant as authentic and exotic 'insider': they say '"O.K., sorry, we are just very good white people, therefore we do not speak for the blacks." That's the kind of breast-beating that is left behind at the threshold and then business goes on as usual' (1990a: 121). By placing themselves as 'outsiders', they duck their own complicity in North–South politics, often hiding behind *naïveté* or lack of expertise, all the while congratulating themselves as the 'saviors of marginality' (1993: 61). This inside/outside separation either helps contain and depoliticize ethnicity, or puts the onus for change and engagement exclusively on the Third World subaltern (or on the native informant as its representative).

Thus, for Spivak, it is dangerous to assume that one can encounter the Third World, and especially the Third World subaltern, on a level playing field. Our interaction with, and representations of, the subaltern are inevitably loaded. They are determined by our favourable historical and geographic position, our material and cultural advantages resulting from imperialism and capitalism, and our identity as privileged Westerner or native informant. When the investigating subject, naively or knowingly, disavows its complicity or pretends it has no 'geo-political determinations', it does the opposite of concealing itself: it privileges itself (1988a: 272, 292). It is liable (as discussed above and detailed further below) to speak *for* the subaltern, justifying power and domination, naturalizing Western superiority, essentializing ethnicity, or asserting ethnocultural and class identity, all in the name of the subaltern. In so doing, it is liable to do harm to the subaltern.

As Linda Alcoff writes, 'Though the speaker may be trying to materially improve the situation of some lesser-privileged group, the effects of her discourse is to reinforce racist, imperialist conceptions and perhaps also to further silence the lesser-privileged group's own ability to speak and be heard' (1991: 26).

Why represent?

Perhaps the most common answer in the field of development to the question about why we represent the Third World is that we want to better get to know it so as to be of help (to the 'less fortunate'?). Yet, Spivak stands with Foucault (and Said and Escobar) in arguing that such noble and altruistic claims are never just that: knowledge is always imbricated with power, so that getting to know (or discursively framing) the Third World is also about getting to discipline and monitor it, to have a more manageable Other; and helping the subaltern is often a reaffirmation of the social Darwinism implicit in 'development', in which 'help' is framed as 'the burden of the fittest' (2002: 22). We have already examined how our framing is influenced by our geopolitical positioning; but Spivak adds and underlines that the 'why' of our representations cannot be divorced from our institutional positioning.[9] She insists, in fact, that there is no such thing as a 'non-institutional environment' (1990a: 5), and hence that our representations are constructed, at least in part, based on such an environment. I propose, in this section, to examine her argument in relation to some of the key organizations in which we researchers/professionals work — academic institutions and governmental and non-governmental development organizations.

Universities have tended to pride themselves as institutions where knowledge can be pursued for its own sake, and where education is delivered in a neutral and objective manner. But of late, these claims have fallen into disrepute. Far from being pure and unmotivated, knowledge and learning are shown to be subject to myriad institutional demands (Bérubé & Nelson 1995; Kuhn 1970; Miyoshi 2000): pressures to 'publish or perish' (for faculty tenure and/or promotion); the imperative for prestige and 'originality'; competition (among students and faculty) for research funding and grants; jockeying between students for high grades; or 'turf wars' among researchers. These institutional demands are shaped, in turn, by external factors, such as government funding or cutbacks to education, corporatization of the university, the relative availability of research funds for humanities/social sciences versus natural sciences, or state policies on immigration or multiculturalism (that may affect pedagogical content and style, for example). Spivak encapsulates this intersection of academic learning and will to power, this knowledge framing according to institutional demands and pressures, under the rubric of 'teaching machine' (1993; cf. 1990a: 5). But she casts a particularly critical eye on how this knowledge framing intersects, in turn, with Third World.

She is concerned primarily with the politics of knowledge production, specifically the way in which Western university researchers, armed with personal/institutional interests, go to the South to do fieldwork and collect data. She calls this a process of 'information retrieval' (1990a: 59), wherein the Third World becomes a 'repository of an ethnographic "cultural difference"' (1999: 388).[10] It is, for her, another form of imperialism, the Third World once again providing 'resources' for the First World; but unlike classical imperialism, it is 'extraction of surplus-value without extra-economic coercion' (Spivak 1988a: 290; cf. Best 1999: 486, 492). Seen in this light, Western intellectual production mirrors, and is many ways complicit with, Western imperialism. Cultural imperialism supplements classical (socioeconomic) imperialism, with the Third World producing both 'the wealth and the possibility of the cultural self-representation of the "First World"' (1990a: 96; cf. 1988a: 271).

Spivak picks up two specific dimensions of this cultural imperialism. The first is what she refers to as the 'benevolent first-world appropriation and reinscription of the Third World as an Other' (1988a: 289). She means by it the retrieval of information from the South, not to encounter the Third World on its own terms, but for other, usually First World, purposes. To illustrate, she takes Julia Kristeva, the noted French feminist scholar, to task over her book, *About Chinese Women* (1977). Ostensibly a feminist book about ancient Chinese matriarchal institutions, Spivak reproaches it for being ahistorical (for too easily extrapolating the category of 'woman' to ancient Chinese social institutions), romantic (for implying that contemporary China has 'declined' relative to the former idyllic age), and colonialist (for benevolently using the Chinese example, but to argue for the ultimate Western feminist political agenda — a non-patriarchic feminist utopia). For Spivak, Kristeva is not interested in Chinese women per se, but in appropriating them for her own purposes. This amounts to exoticizing and orientalizing the women, treating the 'margin' as tourist (1988b: 134-53).

A second dimension of academic cultural imperialism is the privileging of theory (1988a: 275). Spivak has in mind here researchers who see themselves as transforming 'raw facts' or 'information' gathered from the South into 'knowledge'. Thus, the 'field' becomes the repository of data, the academy the 'centre' for value-added theory; subalterns/women tell stories, (male) researchers theorize for them; workers have concrete experience and practice, intellectuals distil and systemize them; social movements do local politics, academicians formulate 'new social movement theory'. The Third World is 'worlded' on the basis of this theory/practice binary, which perpetuates the pattern of placing the Western academy and intellectual at the centre. That the researcher does not see subaltern stories as sophisticated theory probably says more about her/him, and what she constructs and values as 'theory' and 'story', than the subaltern. Moreover, what s/he disavows, according to Spivak, is that 'the production of theory is also a practice' (1988a: 275), and conversely, that practice and narrative are never free from theory or theoretical bias. But in this mêlée, once again, the subaltern is not heard.

Perhaps because she is herself an academician, Spivak has more to say on academic institutions than development organizations; however, she does seize on the issue of gender and development. She describes gender programmes as the 'matronizing and sororizing of women in development' (1999: 386). The programmes often represent Third World women as oppressed by 'second-class cultures' (1999: 407) (as also underlined in the last chapter), thus rationalizing feminist intervention and reinventing, under guise of enlightened benevolence, the colonialist 'civilizing mission'. For Spivak, gender specialists in development agencies 'must learn to stop feeling privileged *as a woman*' and refrain from assuming 'women's solidarity *because* they are women' (1988b: 136; 1990a: 137; cf. Marchand and Parpart 1995; Mohanty 1991; Sylvester 1995: 956). By generalizing themselves, by speaking for all women's desires and interests, they disavow the many obstacles to gender liberation and equality *in the West*. They also neglect the historical, cultural, and socioeconomic differences among and between First and Third World women's groups.

Although she does not specifically consider other institutional dimensions of development, several of Spivak's arguments are pertinent. Just as universities can lay claim to 'pure' knowledge (as mentioned above), development organizations can promote the image of benevolence and disinterestedness. I will broach this issue more fully in chapters 4 and 5; for the moment though, let me point out that the construction of development as 'aid' and 'assistance' to the Third World is belied by what can be called the 'business' and 'conditionality' of development. Thus, in a fashion not untypical of all aid organizations, the Canadian International Development Agency (CIDA) justifies its aid budget to Canadian 'taxpayers' by boasting that 70 cents on every Canadian aid dollar returns to Canada through the creation of jobs and the purchase of goods and services (i.e. a large portion of Canadian aid is tied),[11] and that such aid sustains 30,000 Canadian jobs and provides contracts to 2,000 Canadian businesses, 50 universities, and 60 colleges (CIDA 2003). The aid programme may (or may not) help or reach its Third World audiences, but in the meantime, it is a state subsidy to First World businesses and a job creation programme for NGOs. It is also laced with power by dint of its conditionality: in this case, it means tying the recipient to procurement of Canadian goods and services; but in other cases (e.g. an IMF/World Bank structural adjustment programme), it could mean the recipient must buy into an ideological programme (neoliberalism) and carry out serious socioeconomic structural reform. Finally, an aid programme can be used as a pretext to open up developing-country markets for Western businesses. Here, Spivak cites the World Bank's recent promotion of itself as a 'knowledge organization' and consequent encouragement of developing-country and subaltern group access to new telecommunications technologies (computers, Internet, cell phones): the by-product of 'selling access to telecommunications-as-empowerment' is capitalist penetration by global computing and telecommunications industries (1997: 3; 1999: 419; 2003a: 613).

Like university programming, development programming is also subject to numerous procedural demands. Technical requirements, deadlines, budgetary time frames, funding priorities — all of these intervene in programme delivery, having little to do with on-the-ground needs. In a Foucauldian vein, many (postdevelopment analysts) in fact maintain that these bureaucratic procedures and interests are integral to the disciplinary and regulatory character of development institutions. James Ferguson's study (1990) of World Bank poverty reduction schemes in Lesotho, for example, shows how the representation of communities as 'underdeveloped' and 'poor' helps justify and reproduce bureaucratic red tape and power. He argues that, ultimately, it does not matter whether the schemes are a success or failure; the main outcome is the depoliticization of poverty issues and the advancement of state authority (1990: 256). Thus, rather than working themselves out of a job by reducing poverty, development administrations (local and external) can often ensure, through the construction and/or strengthening of a bureaucratic and technical apparatus, their own survival, if not expansion.

Not just the state or the large international or multilateral development organization such as the World Bank is complicit here; NGOs are, too. Spivak is skeptical of them because they tend to be 'too involved in the New World Order — in terms of the big players like the World Bank, the International Monetary Fund and the World Trade Organization as the economic arm and, unfortunately, more and more, the United Nations as the political arm' (1997: 4). Yet, even those NGOs that stand at the margins of the New World Order are not necessarily immune. Sangeeta Kamat's recent analysis (2002) of grassroots organizations in India demonstrates how small, ostensibly 'progressive', organizations can succumb to a development straitjacket. Comparing the work of a more mainstream organization (Seva Sansad, devoted to the health and literacy of bonded labourers) and a more radical one (Shramik Hakk Sanghatana, a workers' trade union), Kamat concludes that each in its own way ends up casting off its political militancy: each may well oppose the state through court cases or denunciation of corruption, but neither meaningfully questions 'development', by challenging, say, property laws or socioeconomic inequality (2002: 161). In spite of being financially autonomous and relatively independent of state/international development institutions, each is reluctant to contravene state authority. Both end up choosing band-aid, technical solutions over political ones, thus legitimizing state hegemony and reproducing development discourse.

Of course, the above critique is not meant to pose as a comprehensive examination or indictment of academic and development institutions, or to argue that all such institutions are imperialistic all of the time.[12] Rather, Spivak's point is to underline that our representations of the Third World/subaltern cannot escape our institutional positioning and are always mediated by a confluence of diverse institutional interests and pressures, such as those described above. If professional motives dictate, at least to a degree, what and how we do (in development), we cannot pretend to have pure, innocent, or benevolent encounters with the subaltern. To do so, as argued earlier, is to perpetuate, directly or indirectly, forms of imperialism, ethnocentrism, appropriation.

At least two implications follow. The first is that, to the extent that our lenses are institutionally (or geopolitically) tinted, our representations of the Third World are likewise institutionally constricted (as some of the examples above illustrate).

The construction of development institutions and discourses is simultaneously the circumscription of what and how we can and cannot do (i.e. development discourse defines our type and mode of encounter). Invoking Foucault, Spivak writes, 'if the lines of making sense of something are laid down in a certain way, then you are able to do only those things with that something which are possible within and by the arrangement of those lines. *Pouvoir-savoir* — being able to do something — only as you are able to make sense of it' (1993: 34). The second implication is that we *produce* the Third World or subaltern (Said 1978: 3; Beverly 1999: 2), and to a rather large extent we produce them to suit our own image and desire. When we act in accordance with personal, professional, organizational interests, our representations of the Other say much more about us than the Other, or at a minimum, they construct the Other *only in as far as* we want to know it and control it.

Represent whom?

I would like, in this section, to examine the above Spivakian argument that our discourses circumscribe what/how we can and cannot represent, although more from the perspective of the subject of our representations — the subaltern. Specifically, I want to assess three attempts at 'allowing' the subaltern to speak. I shall argue, from a Spivakian viewpoint, that all three are problematic.

One such attempt is Participatory Rural Appraisal (PRA), an approach that has become enormously fashionable in both governmental and non-governmental development circles. Popularized and developed by Robert Chambers, PRA is 'a family of approaches and methods to enable local (rural and urban) people to express, enhance, share and analyze their knowledge of life and conditions, to plan and to act' (1994b: 1253). It is critical of top-down approaches dominated by outsiders and 'experts', and instead aims at valorizing local knowledge and 'empowering' the subaltern so that s/he can 'determine much of the [development] agenda' (1994b: 1255). Accordingly, outsiders become facilitators of a participatory process, in which the '*poor, weak, vulnerable and exploited. . . come first*' (1997: 11, italics in original). PRA evolves a number of techniques that ensure inclusion of marginalized groups, emphasize open and collective learning, and valorize oral, visual, and written inputs. These techniques are meant to secure subaltern participation in a number of development programmes, ranging from environmental management to gender and social programming (1994a: 959-62; 1994b: 1254-7).

But while outwardly benevolent in wanting to enable the subaltern to speak, PRA is naive in believing that it actually can. Chambers's bottom-up approach rests crucially on the idea that PRA helps make the subaltern voice transparent so that development organizations can hear and represent subaltern desires and interests. The reason is that, for him, PRA minimizes, if not eliminates, power from the PRA space, thereby freeing the subaltern to participate. To him, power is negative and repressive: 'For learning, power is a disability', and moreover,

'All power deceives, and exceptional power deceives exceptionally' (1997: 76). But he appears to neglect the knowledge/power problem, wherein every knowledge framing (that of PRA included) produces power relationships (Kapoor 2002b). For example, women, whom PRA purportedly takes great care to include in the public space, can feel intimidated (and *be* intimidated) when speaking in public, especially on such sensitive issues as sex, rape, and violence. Often, if they do participate, they soften their words or ask men to speak for them (Cooke & Kothari 2001; Mosse 1994; Parpart 2000). The participatory space is thus a panoptic one: even *if* subalterns speak, they (like anyone) may perform the roles they think are expected of them (by their own communities, the facilitator, the funding agency). They may modify their speech when under pressure, or exaggerate their praise to please the funder. So much, then, for Chambers wanting to banish power to enable the subaltern 'to speak'.

The problem is magnified when we consider the role played by socioeconomic inequality. Chambers appears confident that people can reach agreement through PRA, but he does so because his narrow and localized view of power ignores the macro social impacts of imperialism or such difficult issues as unequal land tenure (Mohan & Stokke 2000; Kapoor 2002b). The consensus-reaching process, for him, is a relatively tame and harmonious affair. It is as if people can leave important power imbalances outside the door of the PRA space. Thus, he achieves harmony and consensus through disavowal. But as Medevoi *et al.* point out, denying subalterns' subordination, in effect, reinforces their subalternity: it 'reproduce[s] the subalternity of the people at the very moment that it seem[s] to let them speak' (1990: 134). And Spivak adds, '"being made to unspeak" is also a species of silencing' (1999: 408-9; cf. 1990b).

Even when the subaltern does speak, Chambers takes no account of the numerous intervening institutional structures. As we have seen, far from being neutral relays, they filter, reinterpret, appropriate, hijack the subaltern's voice. PRA tries to get around the problem by advocating use of direct testimonials or multiple narratives (1994a: 959). However, here too, there is no avoiding the question of who edits the stories, how they are presented, for whom and what purposes they are framed, and so on. So much, then, for PRA's belief in development organizations hearing and representing the pure, unmediated subaltern voice. As Spivak observes, despite appearances, it is another case of the First World analyst or development organization 'masquerading as the absent nonrepresenter who lets the oppressed speak for themselves' (1988a: 292).

But it is not just this mainstream (liberal?) approach that is questionable in this context; I want to argue that even 'progressive' critics like Vandana Shiva and Arturo Escobar can be guilty (in the manner that Spivak thinks Foucault, Deleuze, and Kristeva can be).

Shiva's *Staying Alive* (1989) is considered one of the first analyses to focus our attention on Southern ecofeminist issues and problems. In many ways, the book inaugurates a feminist critique of development and mainstream science, as well as the validation of Third World grass-roots environmental movements. But the book also makes problematic claims. Shiva essentializes subaltern women by feminizing 'nature' through the retrieval of what she calls a 'feminine principle' (1989: xviii, 38ff.) *and* identifying subaltern women as the embodiment of the principle: she writes about 'Women's ecology movements, as the preservation and recovery of the feminine principle' and nature as 'the experiment and women, as sylviculturalists, agriculturalists and water resource managers, the traditional natural scientists' (1989: xviii). By depicting subaltern women as 'naturally' close to nature and giving them an epistemologically privileged position on (feminized) nature, Shiva creates too neat a divide between subaltern men and women, thus reinforcing gender roles and stereotypes.[13] In addition, to counter her critique of mainstream development and science, she champions Chipko, the now famous forestry movement in the North Indian Himalayas, as an ecological and feminist alternative (1989: 55ff.). She praises the movement's successes and women's active involvement in them. But she has been taken to task for painting too rosy a picture (Jackson 1995; Rangan 2000: 13ff.; *Seminar* 1987): critics reproach her for neglecting to appreciate Chipko's patriarchic political structures (significant male leadership, despite women's overwhelming participation) and ignoring the tensions between three main factions within the movement (an agro-ecological wing, advocating intermediate technological solutions; a Gandhian wing; and a radical student-led wing). Her strong political support for Chipko thus yields to a romanticization of the movement.

Escobar's work has been found wanting for many of the same reasons. As alluded to earlier, in many ways, his critique of development (1984, 1995) echoes Spivak's on the disciplinary character of hegemonic and institutionalized discourse. But like Shiva, his anti-development stance issues in a blanket endorsement of social movements as political alternative. Critics accuse him of romanticizing the 'local' and assuming social movements are necessarily benign, in spite of substantial evidence to the contrary (Kiely 1999; Mohan & Stokke 2000; Nederveen Pieterse 1998, 2000; Kapoor 2002a: 472). They argue that, far from being 'progressive', many movements are internally and externally sexist, racist, homophobic, xenophobic, and undemocratic (e.g. right-wing Hindu movements in India, left- and right-wing guerilla movements in Colombia, etc.). Moreover, the critics point out Escobar's overemphasis on grass-roots 'anti-development' struggles, showing that he misses the diversity of Third World movements and the fact that many are struggles in favour of development (i.e. demanding access to education, irrigation, technological inputs) (Nederveen Pieterse 1998: 363-4).[14]

Thus, both Escobar and Shiva fail to recognize the heterogeneity of the subaltern, ascribing to it a single and ahistorical consciousness. The popular movements they champion tend to be represented as monolithic, overlooking the many differences (regional, ethnic, linguistic, class, gender, caste, age, sexual, historical, institutional) within and between such movements. Partly, this may be due to their use of what Spivak calls 'catachreses' (1993: 139),[15] which are 'master' or 'code' words that are without literal referents (e.g. 'subaltern', 'people', 'social movements', 'women', 'workers', 'Third World', 'West').

Although we are all liable to use such abstractions, Spivak warns of the accompanying dangers of generalization and simplification. Nonetheless, partly, Escobar and Shiva do more than speak catachrestically: they essentialize. They tend to fix the political orientation of social movements or the 'nature' of Nature and women.

They also romanticize, tending to eulogize subaltern women, indigenous knowledge, and/or local politics. This gives the impression that subalterns are transparent to themselves, immune to struggle or failure; as Linda Alcoff puts it, it 'essentializes the oppressed as nonideologically constructed subjects' (1991: 22). Escobar and Shiva are not merely 'speaking for' the subaltern, they are attempting to produce an 'authentic' and 'heroic' subaltern. Yet such gestures, as Spivak indicates, are the founding act for the consolidation of an inside, of the self (1988a: 293). Escobar and Shiva's stinging critique of development requires, and is made possible by, a hyperbolic construction of the subaltern. This desire for the Other as heroine or hero, this species of 'reverse-ethnic sentimentality', is a desire of the intellectual to be benevolent or progressive; it 'gives an illusion of undermining subjective sovereignty while often providing a cover for this subject of knowledge' (Spivak 1988a: 289, 271). It is, ultimately, another form of silencing of the subaltern.

My (Spivakian) critique of the three analysts above is not meant as complete or definitive; rather, my point is to show that attempts at speaking for the subaltern, enabling the subaltern to speak, or indeed listening to the subaltern, can all too easily do the opposite — silence the subaltern. Chambers, Shiva, and Escobar are, in different ways, analysts that are taken seriously in our field, because they each have a systematic critique and a political vision. Yet, like Foucault, their critique of development can hide 'an essentialist agenda' and their 'much publicized critique of the sovereign subject [i.e. the West, modernity, patriarchy]. . . actually inaugurates a Subject' (Spivak 1988a: 272). What Spivak helps drive home to those of us working in development is how decolonization in both the North and the South has been a failure (she argues, in fact, that 'postcoloniality is a failure of decolonization'; 1995: 178). Or, to put it the other way around, what she reveals is decolonization as an unfinished project, and the extent and depth of anti-oppression thinking/acting that we all have yet to learn. So what specifically must we do, according to her?

How to represent

Spivak's work is largely an attempt to valorize the subaltern, although as we have seen, she proceeds by a *via negativa*, showing how the discursive space from which the subaltern can be heard is disabling. But this negative and deconstructive approach has often been the subject of criticism. As mentioned at the start,[16] she has been interpreted as saying that the subaltern cannot speak and has no agency (Parry 1987: 35, 39; Moore-Gilbert 1997: 104). She has countered that, on the contrary, her argument is that elite or hegemonic discourses are deaf to the subaltern, even when it does speak or resist (1996: 289; 1999: 308). 'Speaking', for her, is to be understood as a speech-act, wherein 'speaking and hearing complete the speech act' (1996: 292). As John Beverly writes, 'if the subaltern could speak in a way that really *mattered* to us, that we would feel compelled to listen to, it would not be subaltern' (1999: 66). There is no question, then, of denying the subaltern insurgency or action.

But there have also been other criticisms. Spivak is accused of paralyzing the intellectual and the pursuit of knowledge through her 'unremitting exposure of complicity' (Varadharajan 1995: 89). She has also been taken to task for not specifying how one is to validate and support the subaltern: Moore-Gilbert opines that 'While Spivak is excellent on "the itinerary of silencing" endured by the subaltern, particularly historically, there is little attention to the process by which the subaltern's "coming to voice" might be achieved' (1997: 106). Finally, she is charged, ironically, with reinforcing the West's self-obsession by focusing too much on questions of self-reflexivity. Here is Moore-Gilbert once again: 'Though one appreciates the irony of her reversal of the West's anthropological gaze, this focus nonetheless reinscribes the West as subject, leaving Spivak open to the kind of accusation she makes against Foucault and Deleuze' (1997: 105).

Spivak defends herself against these allegations, stating that she 'question[s] the authority of the investigating subject without paralysing him' and that deconstruction can lead 'to much better practice' (1988b: 201; 1990a: 122). She does not systematically lay out what such a practice may be (her musing, deconstructive style tends to be averse to so doing), but I think her work is strewn with arguments that respond to the above criticisms, while also revealing an approach to the question of representation of the subaltern, a way of looking at the world. In what follows, I have culled from her writings what emerges as a step-wise approach: a deconstructivist position, followed by a process of self-implication, which yields the possibility of an ethical encounter with the subaltern.

'Intimately inhabiting' and 'negotiating' discourse

Taking Derrida's lead, Spivak insists that deconstruction and critique are only made possible by what is already there, by what inevitably surrounds and inhabits you. 'The only things one really deconstructs are things in which one is intimately mired. It speaks you. You speak it' (1990a: 135). You can never represent or act from an 'outside', since you are always already situated inside discourse, culture, institutions, geopolitics. Spivak thus describes her deconstructive approach as the persistent critique of 'a structure that one cannot not (wish to) inhabit' (1993: 60). Not surprisingly, she warns against the total repudiation of one's 'home', arguing, as we have already noted, that it amounts to a disavowal of one's complicities and results in claims of purity, transparency, or triumphalism. Instead, she advocates negotiation from *within*. The point is to take seriously that with which one is familiar, to acknowledge that one is seduced by it, even as one engages in a persistent critique of it.

In a sense, Spivak is cautioning the likes of postdevelopment critics such as Escobar against throwing the baby out with the bathwater by being uncompromisingly 'anti-development' and arguing for 'alternatives *to* development' (Escobar 1995: 215). If development were that dominant and oppressive, then how could the critic claim to be outside it (this is unacknowledged complicity) or represent the subaltern and social movement as pure and untangled (which amounts to essentialization and romanticization) or indeed posit a utopic alternative (i.e. from where would such an alternative arise if not from the bowels of development itself? and how could it miraculously escape from creating its own disciplining/power structures?)? Hence Spivak motions: 'let us become vigilant about our own practice and use it as much as we can rather than make the totally counter-productive gesture of repudiating it' (1990a: 11). It is possible to work within the belly of the beast and still engage in persistent critique of hegemonic representations. Development may indeed be a shady business, but this does not mean one cannot retrieve from within it an ethico-political orientation to the Third World and the subaltern. Thus, for instance, the World Bank and IMF may well be 'imperialistic' organizations, but they are too important and powerful to turn our backs on; instead, we can engage them unrelentingly from all sides to try to make them accountable to the subaltern.

'Acknowledging complicity'

Acknowledging complicity is the most obvious implication from the above analysis of Spivak's work. Because we are all 'subject-effects' (1988b: 204), that is, inescapably positioned in a variety of discourses, our personal and institutional desires and interests are unavoidably written into our representations. We need, then, to be unscrupulously vigilant (i.e. hyper-self-reflexive) about our complicities. Acknowledging one's contamination, for Spivak, helps temper and contextualize one's claims, reduces the risk of personal arrogance or geoinstitutional imperialism, and moves one toward a non-hierarchical encounter with the Third World/ subaltern.

'Unlearning one's privilege as loss'

A concomitant step is the 'careful project of un-learning our privilege as our loss' (Spivak 1990a: 9; cf. 1988a: 287). In a sense, for Spivak, one cannot do 'fieldwork' without first doing one's 'homework'. The itinerary toward representing the Other 'over there', requires scrutiny of the 'here' (Visweswaran 1994: 112). Or it necessitates reversing the gaze, re-imagining what we mean by the 'field' or the 'there'. Thus, Spivak characterizes her teaching in the West (at Columbia University) as fieldwork, in a deliberate attempt to anthropologize the West (1993: 278; 1997: 5; 2003a: 620). What this means, in effect, is casting a keen eye on the familiar and the taken-for-granted. It is not enough to try and efface oneself, to benevolently try and step down from one's position of authority; in fact, as Spivak has reminded us, this gesture is often a reinforcement of privilege, not a disavowal of it (cf. Alcoff 1991: 25). Rather, the idea is to retrace the history and itinerary of one's prejudices and learned habits (from racism, sexism, and classism to academic elitism and ethnocentrism), stop thinking of oneself as better or fitter, and unlearn dominant systems of knowledge and representation. This is what Spivak calls a 'transformation of consciousness — a changing mind set' (1990a: 20), and what others have variously penned as 'decolonization' (Fanon), 'conscientization' (Freire), and 'accountable positioning' (Haraway).

'Learning to learn from below'

'Learning from below' is a tried and tired formula, particularly in development. For Spivak, despite its politically correct message, it results mostly in more of the same. Serious and meaningful learning from the subaltern requires an anterior step: *learning to learn*. I have to clear the way for both me and the subaltern before I can learn from her/him. In effect, this is the on-the-ground application of the above-mentioned unlearning process. It is suspending my belief that I am indispensable, better, or culturally superior; it is refraining from always thinking that the Third World is 'in trouble' and that I have the solutions; it is resisting the temptation of projecting myself or my world onto the Other (Spivak 2002: 6). Spivak cautions, for instance, against assuming that such concepts as 'nation', 'democracy', or 'participation' are natural, good, or uncontestable. To impose them unproblematically in the field is to forget that they were 'written elsewhere, in the social formations of Western Europe' (1993: 60). Unlearning means stopping oneself from always wanting to correct, teach, theorize, develop, colonize, appropriate, use, record, inscribe, enlighten: 'the impetus to *always* be the speaker and speak in all situations must be seen for what it is: a desire for mastery and domination' (Alcoff 1991: 24; cf. Spivak 1990a: 19).

It is this itinerary of decoding which, for Spivak, can yield to an openness to the Other, enabling the subaltern to become not the object, but the subject of development. It of course requires patient and painstaking work, but as Spivak underlines, 'our engagement with the world's disenfranchised women has to be as thick as the engagement with our students' (2003a: 615). Being open to the subaltern ensues in meaningfully coming to terms with her/his difference and agency, ready to accept an 'unexpected response' (2002: 6). It implies, specifically, a reversal of information and knowledge production so that they flow from South to North, and not always in the other direction. One of Spivak's suggestions, to this end, is that we 'learn well one of the languages of the rural poor of the South' (2002: 18). By so doing, we begin the process of not defining them, but listening to them name and define themselves. We lay the groundwork for a two-way conversation and non-exploitative learning. Spivak sometimes likens this process to reading a novel: when we read, we put ourselves in the protagonist's shoes, suspend belief, and let ourselves be surprised by the twists and turns of the plot. In fact, while maintaining that empirical/fieldwork is important, Spivak recommends literature as a way of remembering again how to imagine, because the imagination, for her, 'is the possibility of being somewhere that is not the Self' (1997: 2).

What emerges about Spivak's project of 'unlearning' and 'learning to learn from below' is that it turns crucially on establishing an *ethical* relationship with the subaltern. Spivak's goal of enabling the subaltern is about issuing a 'call' to the 'quite other', or what Derrida refers to as 'rendering *delirious* that interior voice that is the voice of the other in us' (quoted in Spivak 1988a: 294; cf. 1999: 427; Morton 2003: 140; Landry & MacLean 1996: 3, 10). If we are able to have a conversation across wide differences, suspend our beliefs to experience the impossible, then we are beginning to respond to the appeal of the Other. It is 'not so much a sense of being responsible for, but of being responsible to, before will' (Spivak 2002: 9):

> the dominant redefines himself in order to learn to learn from 'below,' learns to *mean* to say . . . I need to learn from you what you practice, I need it even if you didn't want to share a bit of my pie; but there is something I want to give you, which will make our shared practice flourish. You don't know, and I don't know, and I didn't know, that civility requires your practice of responsibility as pre-originary right.
>
> (Spivak 2000: 16)

This, then, is Spivak's response to the earlier-mentioned criticisms. Far from paralyzing the intellectual or researcher, her project is an appeal to acknowledge our complicities and unlearn our prejudices as a way of clearing the space for the subaltern speech act. This may not be an easy task, but it is not an incapacitating one; indeed, it may well be a challenging and motivating one. Far from refraining from specifying how the subaltern voice might come to the fore, moreover, Spivak traces a clear enough itinerary for the investigating subject. That this itinerary insists on a prior unlearning phase is not an evasive or delaying gesture; it is a crucial step in being able to encounter the Third World, without which representing the subaltern or 'learning from below' will continue to be a benevolent and self-consolidating act. And a similar response is due the other charge: Spivak's hyper-self-reflexivity can hardly be accused of being a navel-gazing exercise that reinforces Western ethnocentrism when it is expressly carried out *in order to* clear the way *for* an ethical relationship with the Other.

But while I disagree with the criticisms of Spivak on these points, I believe there are other points on which her thinking appears incomplete, if not unclear. Her hyper-self-reflexivity may not be paralyzing; however, it tends to be inadequately layered, in my view. That is, it does not distinguish between varying *degrees* of complicity. Now Spivak may respond that this type of objection is really an exculpatory attempt, aimed once again at self-validation ('I am not as guilty as X, so therefore I am better than X'). It can be. But it can also be important, as Chapter 1 emphasized, for the purposes of strategizing and prioritizing. For example, an advocacy group may need to distinguish between complicities to

57

assess if these NGO activities are more benign than those World Bank ones, and hence decide where efforts and resources are better spent for organizing against them. Unfortunately, Spivak provides no way of making such assessments. Her deconstructivist approach may have an unmistakable ethico-political horizon, but it lacks any adjudicative mechanism for sorting among and between greater goods and lesser evils.

Moreover, Spivak is adamant about taking account of institutional positioning in representation; yet, she appears to neglect the institutional implications of the ethical encounter with the subaltern. She points, ultimately, to the necessity of a one-to-one relationship for it to be intimate, caring, and non-exploitative. Reflecting on her own recent work training primary school teachers and spending quality time with 'tribal' (*adivasi*) children in Bangladesh and India, she refers to such a relationship as striving towards '"answer"ability' and 'ethical singularity' (1999: 384; cf. 1996: 276; 1997: 5; 2003a: 622-3). Her reasons for prescribing a face-to-face encounter are important, but the institutional consequences are unclear and perhaps untenable. How does a personalized and micrological approach translate into institutional or macrological politics? Given the scale and depth of global and local inequalities, how practicable is a one-to-one approach on a large scale? Is an intimate relationship with the subaltern even compatible with institutional processes, let alone on a large scale? Unfortunately, Spivak leaves these types of questions unanswered. Yet, not attending to issues of do-ability gives her work a romantic, utopic dimension. It endows her discussion of the ethical encounter with the subaltern with a quasi-mystical, ecstatic character that is at odds with her otherwise Marxist-deconstructivist leanings.

Working 'without guarantees'

A final and important Spivakian test is being able to work 'with no guarantees' (2001: 15). This is because we need to recognize that, ultimately, not only is the subaltern heterogeneous, it is 'irretrievably heterogeneous' (1988a: 284) and hence 'non-narrativisable' (1988a: 284; 1990a: 144). Coming to terms with the Other's difference is precisely reckoning with the impossibility of knowing it, accepting that it exceeds our understanding or expectations. This includes being open to the 'non-speakingness' of the subaltern, its refusal to answer or submit to the gaze and questioning of the ethnographer. Thus, the subaltern's various silences (as distinguished from its silenc*ing*) need to be recognized as forms of resistance and agency: reticences, equivocations, lies, secrets, refusal to be named or labelled, etc. (Visweswaran 1994: 60; cf. Morton 2003: 122-3).

Working without guarantees is thus becoming aware of the vulnerabilities and blind spots of one's power and representational systems. It is accepting failure or, put positively, seeing failure as success. The implication for development is that we need to learn to be open, not just, in the short-term, to the limits of our knowledge systems, but also to the long-term logic of our profession: enabling the subaltern while working ourselves out of our jobs.

Conclusion

Spivak's call to action, as I have tried to argue, is compelling and highly pertinent to development studies/work. It demands vigilant self-implication and painstaking, ethical engagement. While it recognizes that our representations cannot escape othering, it argues for us to be scrupulous in so doing, especially in the case of unequal power relationships, i.e. when representing the West's Other (the Third World) and the Third World's Other (the subaltern). This is a much-needed wake-up call to those of us who unquestioningly and unaccountably narrativize the Third World. It is also a reminder that our narration does not take place in a vacuum: we function in geopolitical institutions that circumscribe what and how we narrate. Spivak shows us, in fact, that such entanglements can both produce and disable the subaltern. In the end, she steers us toward a face-to-face ethical encounter with, as opposed to an institutionally prescribed narrativization of, the subaltern. Her proposed mode of encounter may be impractical, but her challenge to us to engage in an intimate and dialogical manner remains.

4

PARTICIPATORY DEVELOPMENT, COMPLICITY, AND DESIRE

At a time when imperialism looks naked and pervasive, when 'freedom' and 'democracy' are all but forced on people (e.g. in Iraq), any North-to-South exchange appears particularly suspicious. Thus, due at least in part to the growing influence of the Western-dominated Bretton Woods institutions, the field of international development struggles harder and harder to escape its reputation as Trojan horse. And now, so does one of its newest offspring — participatory development (PD), and this in spite of the latter's 'noble' goals.

PD ostensibly implies discarding mainstream development's neocolonial tendencies, Western-centric values, and centralized decision-making processes. It stands instead for a more inclusive and 'bottom-up' politics, which takes two dominant institutional forms: (i) Participatory Rural Appraisal (PRA), which, as the last chapter noted, aims at promoting local community 'empowerment'; and (ii) country 'ownership' of development programmes, where the state and/or international development agency seeks civil society involvement for policy development and agenda-setting.[1] In one form or the other, PD has become development's new orthodoxy, so much so that you would be hard-pressed to find any NGO, donor agency, or development institution that has not integrated it into programming.

But of late, PD has faced notable scrutiny and criticism. Critics point out that, far from being inclusive and bottom-up, it reconfigures power and value systems which may end up being exclusionary, if not tyrannical (Mosse 1994; Cooke & Kothari 2001; Kapoor 2002a). It is shown to be gender-biased, frequently ignoring and reinforcing patriarchic structures (Parpart 2000). And it is seen as a 'liberal populist' approach to development that fails to address either class inequalities or the negative impacts of macro-socioeconomic structures (Mohan & Stokke 2000).

I would like, in this chapter, to include and extend the above criticisms by carrying out a postcolonial and psychoanalytic reading of PD. Postcolonialism helps point out that our discursive constructions of the Third World say more about us than the Third World; while psychoanalysis helps uncover the desires we invest in the Other. Thus, to the question, 'why do neoimperial and inegalitarian relationships pervade PD?', I want to answer, 'because even as it promotes the *Other's* empowerment, it hinges crucially on *our* complicity and desire'; and 'because disavowing such complicity and desire is a technology of power'. In other words, I want to argue that complicity and desire are written into PD, making it prone to an exclusionary, Western-centric, and inegalitarian politics.

I write 'our' in an effort at self-implication: it seems to me that whether we are critics or advocates of PD, we are implicated in it. As development workers and researchers, as intellectuals and academics, we may make (at least a part of) our careers off it. As Westerners, some of our sociocultural values and practices may inform PD (as we shall see below). As members of Western(ized) elites participating in the global capitalist economy, we may be direct or indirect contributors (as taxpayers, consumers, voters) to those national or transnational institutions that 'invest' in PD. True, there are different degrees of contamination here; but my point is that not owning up to the range of these complicities ensures the reproduction of inequality and empire.

Complicity and desire

To begin the task of excavating complicity and desire from the depths of PD, I take my cue from Said, Spivak, and Žižek. Said's significant contribution, of course, is showing the Orient to be a discursive construct. He points out how Orientalism is integral to imperialism, serving both to subordinate the Third World and rationalize Western imperial rule. The important point for us here though is his implication that Orientalism, while ostensibly staging the (Third World) Other, actually reveals the West: 'Indeed, my real argument is that Orientalism is — and does not simply represent — a considerable dimension of modern political-intellectual culture, and as such has less to do with the Orient than it does with "our" world' (1978: 12).

Much of Spivak's work is an extension of this insight. As the last chapter showed, she cautions that, in speaking about the Other, we often disavow our own role in the representational process, as though we are transparent and neutral relays. Like Said, she thus believes that it is important that we turn our anthropological gaze upon ourselves before we investigate the Other. Because we are part of organizations that have their own class, gendered, cultural, and/or organizational demands, we cannot pretend to purity or objectivity in our dealings with the Third World.

Žižek, in my view, provides a depth psychology to the contaminations and complicities that Said and Spivak alert us to. Relying on Lacanian psychoanalytic theory, his argument proceeds something like this: 'reality' goes hand in hand with, but is opposed to, the 'Real' (Žižek 1989: 69; 1999: 74). Reality is what we (mistakenly) take to be wholeness or harmony, while the Real denotes the impossibility of wholeness, a fundamental lack that troubles any attempt at closure and consistency. For Žižek, from the moment we enter into the world of language, reality is where we escape to avoid the Real (1989: 45, 47): we desire and enjoy fullness (e.g. the perfect car, pure love, an ideal democracy), and find it difficult to come to terms with incompleteness (that is written into the very structure of language), and so we construct a fantasy world. Desire thus involves the misrecognition of fullness, and fantasy is 'the support that gives consistency to what we call "reality"' (1989: 44).

While fantasy is an individualized or internalized psychic phenomenon, ideology interpellates us at the level of the social, from the outside. Like fantasy, it is a framework that forecloses the Real in order to make reality smooth and consistent. But Žižek is adamant that ideology is not a mask or veil covering the 'real' situation, a reality behind reality: it is 'not simply a "false consciousness", an illusory representation of reality, it is rather this reality itself which is already to be conceived as "ideological"' (1989: 21). In this sense, for Žižek, ideology is externalized and materialized: it is built into our sociopolitical practices and institutions.

But if it surrounds us and interpellates us, how do we go about distancing ourselves from it, critiquing it? *Not* through the development of some super-consciousness, since as just pointed out, there is no 'higher' ground from which to distinguish 'true' from 'false' reality. And *not* through some sort of postmodern ironic distance, in which we admit we know better than to do something (but nevertheless go ahead and do it): the TV viewer, for example, may mock and rail against TV advertisements, aware that they are commercial manipulations; but the point is that s/he still watches them, and does so with some delight. Irony or cynicism for Žižek, far from being critical, are built into ideology, underlining both how insidiously pervasive ideology is and how psychically enjoyable it can be (1989: 28, 33). No, ideology critique, according to him, can only be undertaken from within ideology itself, by being intimately alert to its machinations. And this means tracking and identifying ideology's Real — its slips, disavowals, contradictions, ambiguities.

What Žižek helps reveal, then, are the psychoanalytic dimensions of our complicities. He points up the psychical-ideological work that goes into desiring reality and disavowing the Real or, in our case, desiring to empower the Other and overlooking our complicity. And so, drawing on these insights, I want to show PD to be ideological. As we shall see, it is promoted as benevolent, but forecloses various complicities and desires. It is championed and propagated by development institutions, which nonetheless seek to obscure their own participation in participation. It supposedly puts local Third World communities at the centre of development, but actually centres on First World and/or elite institutional and geopolitical interests. The task ahead, then, is to track these complicities and desires, and to scrutinize their accompanying slips, disavowals, contradictions, ambiguities.

Tracking complicity and desire

This section examines complicity and desire as they manifest themselves in the assumptions, values, and goals of PD. We begin by dissecting PD's image of magnanimity, move on to investigating the unconscious desires it has written into it, and end with problematizing its objective of reaching consensus.

Narcissistic samaritanism

PD appears to be pulled in two directions at once: being promoted as benevolent, while professing neutrality in order to 'empower the Other'. As to the first of these, there is an unmistakable self-righteousness that pervades PD. Partly, this is the inheritance of the field of development, in which the mentality of the 'burden of the fittest' prevails: not only is pride taken in the philanthropic idea of 'us' helping 'them', but also in the assumption that we (elites and professionals) know better than they (impoverished Third World communities). Perhaps some of this self-congratulatory benevolence has faded lately, in the wake of harsh condemnation, notably of the socioenvironmental costs of IMF/World Bank-led structural adjustment programmes. But the emergence of PD appears to have neutralized some of these criticisms and saved the day. Armed with its message of enabling local community participation, PD has become a kind of development with a clear conscience. Its 'empowerment' dimension, in fact, gives it an almost sublime character, so that it has come to be associated with a series of seemingly incontestable maxims: PD is naturally progressive, community participation is inherently good, championing PD is blameless and honourable.

Added to this is a certain religious dimension, particularly noticeable in PRA. It is evident, first, in the figure of the PRA 'facilitator', who plays the crucial role of the change catalyst. Robert Chambers, charismatic enthusiast and promoter of PRA, stands as model here. Affable and earnest, he cuts a preacher-like personage (Henkel & Stirrat 2001: 175). His writings are strewn with moral exhortations, encouraging the PRA facilitator to shed hierarchical thinking and Westernized ways (1994b: 1256). Like the ascetic or monk who has overcome worldly attachments, the facilitator is expected to develop astringent powers (more on this below), and as Paul Francis puts it, enact 'an exorcism, of sorts, of phantoms of "conventional" development practice' (2001: 80). But PRA's religiosity is also evident in the way it envisions social change. PRA-led community discussions can become ecstatic experiences, causing socioeconomic elites (or 'uppers'), in particular, to rethink their privileges and undergo tremendous personal transformation: 'it means that those who are uppers and powerful step down, disempower themselves, and empower others. . . . It implies that uppers have to give up something and make themselves vulnerable' (Chambers 1997: 234). Seen in this light, then, the PRA exercise becomes a (Christian evangelical) religious ceremony, in which the facilitator-as-priest presides, privilege and power are purged, and the community is reborn.

Running counter (or so it appears) to the construction of a benevolent and quasi-religious aura around PD, however, is an attempt at self-effacement. The logic here is that outside interference and imposition must be minimized in order to facilitate civil society 'ownership' of programmes or enable community empowerment. The onus, once again, is on the convenor or facilitator to be neutral and objective so as to allow the community agenda to emerge authentically. Thus, PRA repeatedly underlines the need for 'handing over the stick',

urging in its facilitators the cultivation of such personal behaviour traits as transparency, honesty, humility, respect, and patience (Chambers 1994b: 1253, 1256).

But how is one to reconcile this self-effacement with the earlier self-regarding
benevolence? The answer, it seems to me, lies in the power relationships set up in
PD's community workshops or forums. The convenor or facilitator may well
portray him/herself as a neutral and fair arbiter, but the fact is that s/he manages
the proceedings almost every step of the way: deciding on the need for, and
purpose of, the meeting; selecting whom to include/exclude on the invitation list;
making up the agenda; choosing which participants speak, on what topic, and for
how long; and/or shaping the form and use of the meeting outputs. There are no
'objective', or indeed intersubjective, rules or procedures governing meeting
goals, logistics, or discussions. Power is tilted decidedly in favour of the
convenor, and while it may well be used accountably and democratically (as
Chambers hopes for), it can just as easily be abused.

Either way though, given the convenor's substantial discretionary powers, any
attempt at self-effacement, far from running counter to self-aggrandizement, is
likely another strategy *for* it. As underlined by Spivak in the last chapter, pretend-
ing to step down from power and privilege, even as one exercises them as master
of ceremony, is a reinforcement, not a diminishment, of such power and privilege.
Humility, patience, respect, etc., may be the public expression of PD's guilty
conscience ('I'm a bit ashamed of being in charge of your "empowerment" . . .
and isn't it nice of me to acknowledge it?'), but these may also be acts of self-
glorification and -gratification ('it doesn't really matter whether or not people are
"empowered", as long as I come off looking good!'). The result in both cases is
that PD centres not on the Other, but on the I.

PD fits well, then, the Žižekian definition of ideology as a 'lie which pretends to
be taken seriously' (1989: 30). It appears immaculate, founded as it is on enabling
unadulterated participation; upon such purity does its reputation as noble and
progressive rest. Yet, it hinges on a fundamental underside — the enabler's complicity.
Its ingeniousness rests on successfully negotiating this slipperiness. It creates a 'feel
good' community experience, but elides the behind-the-scenes stage management.
It promotes the sharing of power, but manages to centralize power by personalizing
and mythologizing the role of the facilitator. The latter feature is perhaps what
makes PD so desirable to the development establishment — its narcissistic pleasurability: not only does one get to stage the empowerment process, but one also gets
to be the centre of attention, deriving enjoyment and praise for it.

Transference

I would like to track another, related form of complicity by suggesting that PD is,
to a degree, the result of psychical transference. Transference is the displacement
of unresolved conflicts onto a substitute object, whereby for example, the lover,
analyst, or friend is a stand-in for the parent toward whom one feels aggression.
PD, I want to suggest accordingly, is the consequence of transference onto Third

World communities of the perceived inadequacies of our own liberal democratic political systems.

Several analysts (e.g. Habermas 1976; Kothari 1988; Mouffe 2000) have highlighted the rising 'democratic deficit' within mainstream political institutions in the First and Third World (see Chapter 6 for details). Public apathy and low voter turnout, they contend, are the product of increasingly distant and exclusionary party politics. The emergence of various fundamentalisms (religious, ethnic, nationalist), as well as grass-roots public protests and social movements, are responses to the unaccountability and corruptibility of the state and market. There is thus a wave of political dissatisfaction and a demand for a more participatory democracy that has entered our liberal democratic culture and, in turn, the consciousness of the development intelligentsia.

Of course, such frustrations and demands are channelled in various ways (e.g. through public protest), but some of them may be psychically transferred through our development work. PD then becomes a vehicle for us to try and resolve real or imagined liberal democratic deficiencies. (Such an argument, to my mind, does not appear to be a stretch: after all, a good deal of post-World War II aid and development was aimed at containing the Soviet 'threat' to meet Western foreign policy objectives, and at spreading 'free market' policies to help in the much-needed opening up of Third World markets for multinational capital. Moreover, a sizeable portion of development transfers today help resolve *economic bottlenecks*. Food aid, for example, is a way of disposing of Western farmers' food surpluses [e.g. in wheat or rice]; and the sizable US military aid budget helps prop up the country's military-industrial complex. The transference of which I speak is thus no different in its channelling of, as it were, surplus idealism and disgruntlement, so helping to address *political bottlenecks*.)

A sure sign of this transference is that, when it comes to PD, we ask more of marginalized Third World communities than we do of ourselves. All considered, how many of our own Western social institutions and programmes (e.g. employment, gender, or poverty-related programmes) are participatory? Very few, if any. The implication is that we hold the 'beneficiaries' of PD to a higher standard or ideal. As a consequence, Third World communities may well be a dumping ground or test site for idealized forms of participation.

Žižek helps tease out a further dimension of such transference via his discussion on 'canned laughter' (i.e. simulated audience laughter, usually on television comedy programmes). For him, the significance of canned laughter lies not in reminding us when to laugh, but in the fact that

> the Other — embodied in the television set — is relieving us even of our duty to laugh — is laughing instead of us. So even if, tired from a hard day's stupid work, all evening we did nothing but gaze drowsily into the television screen, we can say afterwards that objectively, through the medium of the other, we had a really good time.
>
> (Žižek 1989: 35)

Seen in this light, PD is a kind of canned laughter: it helps us work through our political idealism and discontent, relieving us from participating 'over here' and enabling us to partake vicariously through the other's participation 'over there'. *We* manage the process (and get the glory), *they* participate (as directed by us), and at the end of the programme we come away feeling satiated as spectator-participants.

Žižek interprets this phenomenon as symptomatic of 'commodity fetishism' under late capitalism: human relationships take on the form of relations between things, so that we increasingly interact with one another in abstract, vicarious, and alienated ways (1989: 34-5). The irony, in this case, is the prospect that commodity fetishism has colonized even participation, an activity meant precisely to overcome alienated human relations through intersubjective dialogue.

The fantasy of consensus

One of the main objectives of PD is arriving at a consensus. Once the key community 'stakeholders' are gathered, relevant information is collected, and people have had their say, a collective decision is reached. The development programming that ensues is thus taken to be not prescriptive but reflective of community interests and needs. But to the extent that consensus is an attempt at making development smooth and complete, it is a fantasy (in the Žižekian sense discussed earlier). To the extent that it is used to seek definitive decisions, thereby avoiding the risks and messiness (i.e. the Real) inherent in participation, it is the product of self-delusion. Žižek avers, as a result, that establishing '"real" democracy [or participation] necessarily brings about its opposite' (1989: 5), and Chantal Mouffe[2] speaks of consensus as the 'elimination of pluralism from the public sphere' (2000: 49).

Indeed, the quality of the consensus and the power relations involved in reaching it are crucial. One danger is that decisions are made on the basis of inadequate participation, for example when beneficiaries are consulted *after* the programming design and goals have already been set; or when agreement is justified through majority vote and frequent community meetings, rather than meaningful deliberation (i.e. open dissemination of information, airing of dissent and debate, inclusion of minority views). In the meeting space itself, moreover, there may be several micro-power processes at play. For instance, rhetorical devices — polemical or sensationalist arguments, technical or esoteric language, misrepresentation or over-representation of evidence, loud or aggressive speech, monopolization of airtime by a participant — can unduly influence opinion or silence and intimidate participants. While sometimes overt, these devices can be subtle, too, as when the meeting convenor invites technical or scientific 'experts' to speak to (i.e. persuade) community members.

The very condition of having to seek a consensus may also be a problem. When consensus-based decisions are single, as they most often are, they overlook or suppress community differences and tensions. Frequently, they ignore precisely those issues that are most difficult to address — class inequality, patriarchy, racism (cf. Chapter 6; Mohan & Stokke 2000; Mosse 2001: 22). Rather than confront these messy problems, they leave them unspoken or unresolved. The result is a simplified or distorted consensus. Thus, Kelsall & Mercer (2003) show how a World Vision participatory community development project in Northern Tanzania ends up concentrating power in the hands of established elites (church elders and employees, village council members, rich farmers) to the exclusion of poorer farmers and women. Not only does decision-making get monopolized by these elites, but so do project resources (access to funds and training, allocation of free cattle), thereby 'reproducing existing inequalities and perpetuating patterns of development which date from the colonial period if not earlier' (Kelsall & Mercer 2003: 302; cf. Mosse 1994: 508). The 'common good' becomes the expression of hegemonic privilege and subaltern loss.

My point is not to deny that decisions need to be made in PD. It is, rather, to warn against the fetishization of consensus, that is to say, the desire to reach a single (and perfect) agreement at any cost. The tendency of consensus-making is towards closure, and hence towards the privileging of some voices, and the simplification, suppression, and exclusion of others. In the absence of objective or intersubjective procedures governing participation (or perhaps even with them),[3] this proclivity is ever-present. Averting or abetting it is once again the responsibility of the convenor. It is his/her benevolence or self-interest that in large measure determines the quality of participation and the politics of consensus-making.

Complicity and desire institutionalized

Complicity and desire are present not just in PD's values and goals; they are also integral to PD's institutional arrangements. This section tracks them in PD's packaging and branding, its disciplining mechanisms, and its neoliberal conditionalities.

The packaging and branding of participatory development

When participation is incorporated into development programming, it is subjected to a plethora of organizational demands. It is made to conform, for example, to bureaucratic review and approval procedures, budgetary deadlines, and/or reporting requirements such as the collection of statistics (e.g. participation rates, frequency of meetings, gender breakdown of participants). It is thus gradually institutionalized, much as a hospital patient might be, after being admitted, tested, diagnosed, and classified. It is also moulded to suit project needs, becoming a management 'tool' to help increase project sustainability and results. 'Toolkits' and 'modules' are produced for this purpose (e.g. Srinivasan & Narayan 1994). As a consequence, PD is transformed into a package — discrete and manageable to suit the institutional culture, and modular to make it flexible and transferable to various project sizes, tasks, and contexts.

In addition to PD's packaging is its institutional marketability. It has become one of development's latest trends, following on the heels of 'women in development' (in the 1980s), 'sustainable development' (in the early 1990s), and 'human rights' and 'governance' (the 1990s and beyond), respectively. Such 'trendiness' is more than just incidental; it is surely deliberate. Just as product differentiation is a corporate strategy to ensure the reproduction of consumerism and capital, so each new trend safeguards development's renewal and marketability. The 'new' turns attention away from the 'old' (recurring problems, challenges), mobilizes new energy and resources, and inaugurates a 'fresh' start; and so the development machine keeps turning.

But participation is more than just a trend; it is also an institutional brand. Its marketability and fashionability mean that PD is now de rigueur in the development community. It has acquired a certain cachet or, as I discussed earlier, a subliminal aura. David Mosse (2001: 23-4) explains, for example, how the Kribhco Indo-British Rainfed Farming Project has donned participation as a mark of respectability, in spite of the fact that decision-making remains mostly top-down.

Participation's cachet acts in many ways like corporate 'lifestyle branding' (Klein 2000). PD is made into self-expressive lifestyle product: in the same way that to buy Starbucks is not just to buy coffee but to identify with 'community', or to wear Benetton is not simply to wear clothing, but to embrace 'multicultural diversity', so to institute PD is not simply to take on participation, but to enhance 'community empowerment', 'good government', or 'democracy' (presumably, a Western-style, wealthy democracy). Such branding brings instant recognition and respect, while enabling development institutions to build long-term trust and loyalty with their 'clients' (governments, communities, NGOs). And cultivating these long-term affective attachments is the best publicity development can't buy!

Packaging and branding are evidence of PD's institutional complicities. When it is managerialized and marketed, then what matters is not so much whether participation works or is well done, but how it can help protect and advance institutional authority (cf. Ferguson 1990). Consequently, far from being taken up for people's empowerment or democratic governance, PD is taken up, first and foremost, for institutional aggrandizement.

Panopticism

Panopticism, as briefly alluded to in Chapter 2, refers to the phenomenon of self-policing (Foucault 1984: 239). For instance, in contemporary societies surveillance has become increasingly pervasive (in the form of video surveillance, collection of social security or tax data, security assessments, etc.), so that people, even if they do not like it, end up internalizing it. This has important implications for PD, since participation is public, and a public participatory space can be a panoptic one. Under the watchful eyes of the community, participants perform roles by playing to an audience, living up to an expectation, or acting out a socially sanctioned duty. Thus, for example, the village leader personifies the authority figure, the facilitator acts as the benevolent arbiter, the woman performs her prescribed gender role, the minority group accentuates its status as 'dependent' or 'victim', and the community as a whole plays at pleasing the project funder. PD's public and panoptic character mean that power relationships are reconfigured, affecting the way people interact, information is expressed, and knowledge is exchanged.

The problem is that this reconfiguration of power does not happen in a vacuum; it happens in the context of already established community relations. As a result, unequal power relationships, far from disappearing, adjust to PD's new power/knowledge regime. David Mosse's work highlights this phenomenon with particular reference to PRA. He finds that what is taken to be 'local' knowledge or needs, for instance, can be a reflection of the preferences and biases not of the community, but of the authority to which it is beholden (e.g. the donor, the state). Hence, *adivasi* villagers in Western India are found to prefer using eucalyptus as timber for housing; they do so, however, not because they have had prior experience with it or as a result of some 'indigenous knowledge', but because the local Forest Department favours it (Mosse 2001: 20-1, 17).

The realignment of relations occasioned by PD happens, then, in favour of the powers that be. Dominant groups soon develop an 'interest' in the new truth regime, adjusting and rearticulating their interests in accordance with it. Government officials may discover it helps monitor community activities; husbands and fathers may see it as a way of keeping tabs on their wives/daughters; elites may take it as an opportunity to manage dissent; the PD convenor may find in it a way of manufacturing consent; and everyone may delight in its production of gossip and rumour about friends and neighbours. Eventually, following Foucault's logic, each community member will end up self-disciplining, that is, internalizing the socioeconomic, cultural, and patriarchic dos and don'ts. And before long, what were once select dos and don'ts — reflective of elite/institutional complicities — are taken for granted: they become naturalized, passing off as 'consensus', 'community will', or 'traditional knowledge'.

I cannot help but follow such panopticism to its ultimate conclusion: a *Nineteen Eighty-Four* scenario. The seeds of it lie in the institutionalization of PD. Indeed, most PD projects envisage their own periodic monitoring and evaluation (Makuwira 2004: 8). The idea, as touched on in Chapter 2, is to ensure that project resources are being used efficiently, and that the project is sustainable and effective. Yet, under a panoptic lens, such monitoring and evaluation translate into the totalization of panopticism — the monitoring of monitoring and the disciplining of discipline! Here, it is not just about people watching people anymore, but about putting in place institutional mechanisms that *ensure* that everyone is watching everyone. Now this may well be a far-fetched, nightmarish scenario, but as Žižek is quick to remind us, excess seems unreal and unthinkable to us, outwardly because we cannot integrate it with our own experience, yet psychoanalytically because we are in fact intimately familiar with it (2002: 19).

Calling it a 'nightmare' is our way of avoiding the Real, which in this case is about disavowing our socio-institutional complicities (i.e. our institutional panoptic and disciplinary tendencies, our voyeuristic desires) so that we/PD can appear pristine and pure. Thus, Žižek says about 9/11 that the US 'got what it fantasized about': a Hollywood disaster film — the ultimate American desire-fantasy — came true (2002: 15-16). And while characterizing 9/11 as 'unreal' was a way of coping, it was also a way of overlooking US state-abetted imperial activities around the world.

Conditionality

Two decades ago, participation was anathema to such transnational institutions as the World Bank and IMF. Now, in the aftermath of acerbic criticism about the top-down and exclusionary character of their structural adjustment programmes, not only do they embrace participation with panache — in itself a suspicious development — but they also make it a *condition* of assistance. Thus, for the Heavily Indebted Poor Countries (HIPC) especially, debt relief is contingent upon a poverty reduction strategy (PRS), which in turn requires local 'ownership' (World Bank 2003; 2000: 253). Recipient governments are expected to form 'partnerships' with civil society organizations when putting in place their PRS.

A case in point is present-day Tanzania. To access funds through the HIPC initiative, it has agreed to comply with various adjustment policies (i.e. privatization of 'inefficient' parastatals, public sector reforms, establishment of a pro-business investment climate) and form partnerships with NGOs for its PRS. But as Claire Mercer (2003) discovers, such partnerships are the result of a top-down government decision-making process that tends to privilege elite NGOs (i.e. professionally run, and usually donor-funded) at the expense of weaker, community organizations. Moreover, civil society participation amounts to little more than consultation, with government-initiated community forums as veiled attempts to convince participants of the wisdom of already agreed-upon strategies. As a consequence, Mercer writes, the 'increased profile of NGOs in policy-making engages them and other actors in a performance of partnership . . . which serves to legitimize continued (structural) adjustment . . . partnership has become a synonym for consensus on adjustment' (2003: 743, 751). Similar situations have played out in Rwanda and Bolivia (Renard & Molenaers 2003a-b), with participation serving, in the former case especially, as a cover for what is otherwise an undemocratic, if not authoritarian, state.

The erstwhile top-down structural adjustment regime is thus reconfigured to the specifications of the new PD regime. Championing PD and making it a condition of assistance accomplishes several tasks in one fell swoop: participation becomes a disciplinary mechanism for the World Bank/IMF to hold the poorest Third World states 'to account' (in both the financial and discursive senses of that expression) and, in turn, for these states to keep civil society organizations in check; and participation helps advance neoliberalism, promoting 'partnerships' to co-opt Third World states *and* (elite) NGOs into the structural adjustment programme.

Broader implications

My point in tracking the above complicities and desires in PD is not to argue that they show up all of the time and in every aspect of programming; it is to suggest instead that they are liable to (and do) show up somewhere and at least part of the time because they are integral to PD. The propagation of PD depends fundamentally on a propagator or convenor, who in the current geopolitical conjuncture tends to be *us* as members of elites and institutions in both the North and South. It is because of such inescapable complicity that personal and institutional benevolence in PD, while outwardly other-regarding, is deeply invested in self-interest (geopolitical, cultural, organizational, economic) and desire (narcissism, pleasurability, self-aggrandizement, purity, voyeurism, manageability, control).

But PD's propagation is premised on overlooking these contaminations (i.e. the Real), and to this extent it is an ideology, in the Žižekian meaning of the term discussed earlier. PD as ideology is attractive and pleasurably desirable (in indulging our self-centredness). It is marketed and branded as wholesome and unblemished. But even as it papers over its 'dirty secrets', what is notable about its ideological and misrecognizing force is the ability to appear open, inclusive, and transparent: 'The central paradox . . . is that the very process of production, the laying bare of its mechanism, functions as a fetish which conceals the crucial dimension of [its] form' (Žižek 1997: 102).[4]

Three implications follow. First, the disavowal of complicity and desire (i.e. the construction of PD as ideology) is a technology of power, as a result of which participation can easily turn into its opposite — coercion, exclusion, panopticism, disciplinarity. Here, 'participation as empowerment' morphs into 'participation as power'. PD may *appear* pure and unmediated, but for this very reason, as we have seen, it is likely deployed to wield authority, helping to maintain and further elite or institutional hegemony. Flashing PD as a badge, or romanticizing our involvement in it, will tend to be similarly dangerous: innocently or benevolently claiming that one is helping a Third World community become participatory is not just self-aggrandizing, but also risks perpetuating elite, panoptic, or institutional power, all at the expense of the Third Word community. (This of course conjures up the triumphalist Bush/Blair claim of bringing 'freedom and democracy' to Iraq.)

A second implication is that PD is a vehicle for various types of empire building — institutional, geopolitical, socioeconomic, cultural, personal.[5] One such instance, as underlined earlier, is the branding of PD to help widen institutional spheres of influence, while another is the World Bank/IMF construction of PD as conditionality, through which participation becomes a 'euphemism for [global] neo-liberal capitalism' (Roy 2004b: 56).[6] In either case, it is no wonder that PD is a vehicle for empire: in this era of mediatization, when image and spin matter so much, the construction of PD (or indeed of 'freedom' and 'democracy') as 'benevolent' and 'good' is an ideal cover.

Note that to make such an argument is not to maintain that power is conspiratorial (PD = empire building = Western conspiracy); on the contrary, it is to agree with Foucault in suggesting that power circulates, so that institutional and social complicities and desires adjust, and are reconfigured, to PD's new power/knowledge regime. Thus, as mentioned earlier, consensus building can align with elite/institutional interests, and community gatherings can end up helping state monitoring of local communities. Now it is true that, in the current global context, many of these complicities and desires *are* Western/westernized, reflecting Western economic, geopolitical, and cultural hegemonies. But they are not exclusively so (as I have tried to underline), also reflecting local hegemonies (class, patriarchal, institutional).

Moreover, it is because power circulates that we, Western(ized) elites and intellectuals, are implicated in empire. For example, as the earlier discussion on 'transference' stressed, our development work is psychically and politically conditioned, so that we, too, develop, amend, and transfer our interests and desires in accordance with PD's knowledge/power regime. This is why it is too easy and convenient to blame contemporary empire building on transnational corporations or the Bush/Blair administrations alone; the latter may well be more powerfully complicitous, but this is no reason for us to claim innocence or neutrality. Empire building, in this sense, may well be a broadly cultural sign of the times, implicating the 'noble' as much as the 'ignoble', 'participation' as much as 'trade', 'citizens' as much as 'leaders'. And this is also why dismantling empire, if it is to happen, must take place at so many levels simultaneously (personal–structural, local–global, social–institutional, North–South, etc.), a point I shall take up further below.

A final implication is that PD perpetuates the treatment of the Third World as object and resource. If empowerment centres not on the Other but on our own desire to be seen as benevolent, then Third World communities are in effect regarded as pawns.[7] If participation is a conduit for transference of our politico-cultural ideals and frustrations, then the Third World becomes a disposal site, in the way that it already acts as a dumping ground for toxic waste or hazardous multinational corporate products (e.g. milk substitutes, contraceptive implants). And if PD enables the collection of information or 'field data' for our research and disciplinary/managerial needs, then the Third World is made into both resource and laboratory. To repeat Spivak's pithy phrase: the Third World produces 'the wealth and the possibility of the cultural self-representation of the "First World"' (1990b: 96).

Conclusion: what to do?

My point is not that everything is bad, but that everything is dangerous, which is not exactly the same as bad. If everything is dangerous, then we always have something to do. So my position leads not to apathy but to a hyper- and pessimistic activism.

(Foucault 1984: 343)

[W]e can save democracy only by *taking into account its own impossibility*.
(Žižek 1989: 6, italics in original)

My point is not that PD is bad, but that it is dangerous. The reason is that it is fundamentally adulterated, so that along with its medicine comes its poison (cf. Parfitt 2004: 554-5). Yet, this is not grounds to discard it (lest its poison return in even more potent forms), but rather to 'confront the Real' (Žižek 1989: 48, 63), which in our case is about recognizing and coming to terms with our complicities and desires. In the preceding analysis, I have attempted to identify this Real by tracking its various forms; in the four possible scenarios that follow, I will try to come to terms with it by arguing for the broadening, deepening, and radicalization of participation.

Publicizing complicity and desire

The most obvious implication from the above analysis is the need to admit to our complicities and desires, that is, to make them open to scrutiny and discussion. Unilaterally moralizing about the correct behaviour of the facilitator (*à la* Chambers) is, as we have seen, a recipe for self-promotion and benevolent paternalism. In contradistinction, politicizing and publicizing the prejudices and prerogatives of the facilitator will likely help decentre and democratize power relationships. It will entail, for the facilitator, tempering and contextualizing one's claims and commitments, and for the participants, lowering one's hopes and expectations. It will also entail subjecting the PD meeting's rules and procedures, not just its contents, to public deliberation.

Of course, the risk of airing our complicities and desires is that participants may not want to have anything to do with us (why would they, if we were to really admit to empire building?). But though a failure for us, such an outcome would in many ways be a success for them: saying 'no' would move them from object to subject of development; it would be a meaningful sign of their 'empowerment'.

Yet, many pitfalls remain even here. The onus for PD's politicization continues to lie with us as facilitators/convenors; it remains dependent on our continued 'generosity' or cunning desire. Moreover, the likelihood is small that development organizations will be open to PD's radical democratization or willing to recognize failure as success.

Extending participation to the economy and development decision-making

There are two glaring blind spots in the deployment of PD: its integration into the economy and its application to the decision-making processes of the very development institutions that deploy it.

To be sure, proponents of participation appear only too happy to initiate projects in such areas as education or urban planning, but reluctant to do so in more politically difficult areas such as, say, manufacturing. When the economy *is* broached, PD is used, as we have seen, to push neoliberal capitalism, ignoring questions of distribution or inequality. Politicizing the economy is thus a taboo. Žižek, in fact, sees it as today's global Real (2002: 65). And so transgressing this taboo, while politically challenging, is PD's new frontier. It would mean extending participation to the economy by enabling greater social regulation of both the market and the freedom of capital. And it would mean the establishment, for example, of worker management schemes, peasant cooperatives, or community-run enterprises.

In a similar vein, there is a great deal of hypocrisy in advocating participation by the Other without looking at one's own institutional backyard. Often, the bureaucratic structures and management processes that sanction PD schemes are themselves hierarchical (which only points up earlier arguments about PD as a vehicle for managerialism and disciplinarity). A participatory organization would ostensibly reverse the flows of authority and knowledge. It would make management more accountable to its putative beneficiaries; and the resulting South-to-North and subaltern-to-elite flows would wean it into better learning from, as opposed to patronizing, Third World and subaltern communities.

Linking up with democratic politics

A notable hindrance is PD's 'packageability': it is meant, as discussed earlier, to make participation adaptable to individualized projects rather than broader structural politics. It allows power to be managed by fetishizing the 'inside' meeting space (i.e. acclaiming community 'togetherness', eulogizing the facilitator), while ignoring the unmanageable 'outside' (the power of socioeconomic elites, the forces of globalization, etc.). This depoliticized approach to participation is what ensures that the latter centres not on empowering the Other, but on furthering our own complicities and desires.

One way to break the stranglehold of complicity and desire is to link PD with broader democratic movements (cf. Chapter 6; Mohan & Hickey 2004). This would involve building bridges between PD projects and wider local and transnational efforts for democratizing state and market and politicizing new spaces/issues (e.g. urban slums, sexual politics, biotechnology, water). But this would also mean having to give up on our desire for mastery and embrace long-term democratic struggles, with all the risks and setbacks that they entail (i.e. their success is never guaranteed).

Hijacking participatory development

That I have focused on the dangers of our complicities and desires does not mean that the 'beneficiaries' of PD are necessarily passive bystanders. As Glyn

Williams points out, PD may 'indeed be a form of "subjection", [but] its consequences are not predetermined and its subjects are never completely controlled. . . . [It may] open up new spaces for political action' (2004: 557). The reason is implicit in the above analysis: the disavowals, slips, and contradictions (i.e. the Real) in PD — empowering the Other while protecting our own interests, desiring to appear benevolent while stage-managing community meetings, seeking consensus while ensuring it is single and smooth, facilitating open deliberation while exploiting panoptic constraint — make it unstable and susceptible. PD's hybridized script, in other words, is grounds for agency (cf. Bhabha 1994); its slippages render it vulnerable to reinterpretation, diversion, hijacking. Chapter 1 has already broached this Bhabhaian type of politics, and chapters 7 and 8 will elaborate it further.

Much more research is required on these types of political tactics, but there is already evidence of their use in the realm of PD: Jenkins & Goetz (1999) document how participation inspires a right-to-information campaign challenging government corruption and accountability in Rajasthan; and Hildyard *et al.* (2001; cf. Williams 2004: 569-70) speak of a PD project in which women participants, rather than using loans to buy dairy cattle, divert the funds for their own purposes (e.g. to recover family heirlooms used as loan equity).

What this means is that the three opportunities just discussed (publicizing complicity and desire, extending participation to the economy and decision-making, linking up with democratic politics) do not depend only on us,[8] but may be exploited by PD's subjects as well. The latter could conceivably shame us into facing up to our complicities, demand more transparent rules for deliberation and project management, or manipulate our need to look benevolent by cajoling us into providing more funding or better minority political representation.

This is not to announce the end of empire building through PD; but it is to say that even imperial power can be (and is) resisted and redeployed. Power, no matter whether it is hegemonic or authoritarian, is always hybridized (or haunted by the Real), making its triumphalism shaky and its victories temporary. Thus, PD's gaze may well be constrictive, but as Bhabha would say, there is nothing to prevent its subjects from returning a menacing glare or a mocking glance (1994: 119), thereby inaugurating their agency.

5

FOREIGN AID AS G(R)IFT

In his work on the gift, *Given Time* (1992), Derrida quotes a short story by Baudelaire in which two friends encounter a beggar on the street. Both give the beggar money. One friend offers a large sum, thus demonstrating his generosity, but also eliciting in the other feelings of remorse for appearing selfish. Later, the 'generous' friend admits to having passed the beggar a counterfeit coin. Here is Baudelaire's narrator:

> My friend's offering was considerably larger than mine, and I said to him: 'You are right; next to the pleasure of feeling surprise, there is none greater than to cause a surprise'. 'It was a counterfeit coin', he calmly replied as though to justify himself for his prodigality.
>
> (quoted in Derrida 1992: 32)

Given Time proceeds by taking up some of the themes of this story — generosity, recognition, selfishness, one-upmanship, deception — the point being to investigate the *aporia* of the gift (i.e. its internal divisions, contradictions). On the one hand, for Derrida, the idea of the gift carries with it the promise of genuine, 'pure' generosity, without self-interest or expectation of reward: 'for there to be gift, there must be no reciprocity, return, exchange, countergift, or debt' (Derrida 1992: 12). In fact, in shunning symmetry or reciprocation, gifts are supposed to be '*aneconomic*'; they are meant precisely to interrupt market relations and suspend the circle of economic calculation and exchange (1992: 7, italics in original).

But, on the other hand, Derrida argues that the gift is also always associated with an injunction to respond. It involves a cycle of giving-receiving-taking back. On the side of economics, gift-giving must take account of reciprocal exchange: 'One cannot treat the gift . . . without treating this relation to economy' (1992: 7). Giving, accordingly, most often involves recompense (or the calculation of it), interest, debt, credit. And on the side of symbolism, gift-giving implies some form of recognition: a symbolic return, a thank you, the expectation of a thank you. Here, recognizing the donor is itself a kind of giving back, a 'symbolic equivalent' of the gift: 'the gratifying image of goodness or generosity, of the giving-being who, knowing itself to be such, recognizes itself in a circular, specular fashion, in a sort of auto-recognition, self-approval, and narcissistic grat-itude' (1992: 13, 23). The same is true of accepting a gift, refusing it, or being seen to accept or refuse it. Indeed, the 'simple identification of the passage of the gift' (1992: 14) from donor to recipient constitutes a symbolic return, thereby annulling any idea of non-reciprocation.

The paradox of the gift is thus its promise of unburdened generosity, yet its tendency towards economic and symbolic reward; its claim to purity alongside its unmistakeable contamination. And so Derrida concludes: 'It is perhaps in this sense that the gift is the impossible. Not impossible but *the* impossible. The very figure of the impossible' (1992: 7).

Two aspects of this discussion are worth pondering. The first is Derrida's impli-cation that, for there to be gift, a donor (and for that matter, a recipient) has to be determined and identified. He writes that a gift

> supposes a subject and a verb, a constituted subject, which can also be
> collective — for example, a group, a community, a nation, a clan, a tribe
> — in any case, a subject identical to itself and conscious of its
> identity, indeed seeking through the gesture of the gift to constitute its
> own unity, and precisely, to get its own identity recognized so that the
> identity comes back to it, so that it can reappropriate its identity: as its
> property.
>
> (Derrida 1992: 10-11)

Self-construction is therefore integral to the gift. In giving, the donor is fashion-ing her own identity and seeking recognition by others (i.e. the recipient, other donors, other recipients).

A second aspect is the relationship of Derrida's argument to that of Marcel Mauss, often considered pre-eminent on the question of the gift. Mauss sees gifts as 'total social phenomena' (1950: 3): they help establish complex, multidimen-sional social relations (e.g. reciprocity, exchange, debt, obligation, status). But he laments the movement away from a gift economy to a capitalist economy, contending that gifts could act as a corrective to such modern ills as individual-ism and war (1950: 81-2).

Derrida takes him to task on both these issues. Since, for Mauss, the gift always involves obligation and return, Derrida believes he 'speaks of everything but the gift' (1992: 24). That is, absent for Mauss is the very idea of non-reciprocation that makes the gift a 'gift'. Moreover, Derrida sees Mauss's beckoning for the gift-as-alternative-to-capitalist-exchange as romanticization and myth-making, likening it to a 'gesture which consists of winning "paradise economically"' (1992: 82). In fact, he wonders whether the very title of Mauss's book, *The Gift*, is indicative of such empty posturing — is it announcing Mauss's book as gift to the world? proclaiming a book, whose call for social solidarity can itself be taken as a calling out for 'credit' and recognition (1992: 43, 82)? Derrida is being crit-ical, in other words, of the lack of self-reflexivity in such gestures.

And that, it seems to me, is the nub of Derrida's overall argumentation here: gift-giving demands vigilance. The point of emphasizing the aporia of the gift is not to set up an ideal on one side (the unconditional gift) and a 'real world' practice on the other (giving with strings attached). It is, rather, to recognize the shifting limits within which any gift event takes place. Derrida is not saying that gifts are impossible, but that one has to always carefully negotiate between promise and practice, lest 'giving wholeheartedly' turns into taking back (materially or symbolically), and 'giving conditionally' fails to face up to the promise of the gift. Such constant negotiation and questioning, to be sure, is what makes gift-giving 'the' impossible.

What follows is an examination of the aporia of *foreign aid* as gift: on the one hand, the discourse of aid is constructed as non-reciprocated gift; but, on the other, the discursive practice of aid is also closely tied to conditionalities, be they economic (tied aid), ideological (neoliberalism), or political (foreign policy objectives). Picking up on Derrida's connection between gift-giving and self-constitution, my main argument is that foreign aid regimes have advanced the former (aid as gift) and covered up the latter (aid conditionalities) so as to shore up the donors' national self-image as benevolent and generous. In other words, my contention is that aid giving is strongly allied with the production of the nation, where the construction of a positive, single national identity is paramount, and hence where the nation's aid as 'gift' trumps its grift. This argument is made by linking the literatures on the gift (especially the work of Derrida) and foreign aid to the postcolonial literature on nationalism (especially the work of Bhabha). The chapter concludes with a consideration of political, ethical, and institutional possibilities — what some might call 'postnational' possibilities — for maximizing foreign aid as gift.

It should be noted that there is a vast literature on foreign aid, which can be roughly divided into two categories: one that focuses on the motives of aid (what are its political, economic, or foreign policy motivations?) (e.g. Mosley 1985; Raffer & Singer 1996; Stokke 1996; Pronk 2001); the other that treats the effectiveness of aid (what impacts does it have on recipients? how well is it used/targeted?) (e.g. Hellinger 1988; Arvin 2002; Pomerantz 2004). This chapter falls squarely into the former category,[1] but with some notable differences. I am wary, in particular, of any behaviouralist notion of a stable subject (in this case, nation or donor) with straightforward motivations: for, such a notion is deeply ideological, presupposing a homogeneous nation-state and fully rational and controlled policy-making. My purpose is to try to point up the conflictual, contradictory workings of foreign aid, in which some positions may win out, but neither donor nor motives are without ambiguity. My purpose is also to suggest that subject and motive are inseparable; that constructing national identity or donor image is at the same time constructing a discourse about the Other — the nation's positioning in relation to its internal or external adversaries, aid recipients, and/or competing donors.

Aid as gift/grift

In the post-World War II period, while an increasing portion of aid has been multi-lateral aid (more on this later), by far the largest portion has been bilateral aid, that is, state-to-state aid. Thus, in the mid-1960s, over 90 percent of Official Development Assistance (ODA) from Western or 'DAC'[2] countries was bilateral (Hattori 2001: 644). The current figure stands at just under 70 percent, with total DAC bilateral aid in 2004 reaching $54.4 billion (DAC 2005: Table 2). Just as Mauss analyzed it, this aid is given as a gift by states to develop and maintain relations with other states. But as will be argued in this section, its construction as gift is belied by its (equally constructed) practice as grift.

The construction of aid as gift

The discourse of aid is a highly invested one. A number of terms, whether in common parlance or 'official' jargon, act as code words for such a discourse: 'foreign aid' is perhaps the most widespread, but 'foreign assistance', 'develop-ment assistance', or 'Official Development Assistance' (the OECD/DAC term) are also prevalent. All such terms represent aid as a kind of gift — a unilateral offer of help, a pure act of generosity, an extension of resources for development (without obligation). But in addition to symbolizing aid as a gift, foreign aid discourse, like the broader 'development discourse' with which it is associated, also constructs and positions both donor and recipient.

The donor country — Western, of course — is rich and enlightened. Its privi-leged status makes it incumbent upon it to act with kindness and generosity, while its superior wealth and knowhow situate it as exclusive agent of development. There is more than a tinge of Christianized paternalism here, foreign aid some-times being associated with good conscience, charity, benefaction, salvation (as discussed in the previous chapter in relation to participatory development).

In contrast, the recipient country/community is stigmatized as poor and archaic. It is a victim of unfortunate circumstances (of its own making). And it is haplessly dependent on the benevolence and altruism of the Western donor (to which gratitude is owed). (My use of parentheses here is a way of noting some of the implied meanings of aid.)

The discourse of foreign aid thus fixes the nature of aid as gift, and simultane-ously, the nature and relationship of those who give or receive it. The binary oppo-sites (wealthy/underprivileged, expert/novice, kind/needy, self-sufficient/subordinate) that support the discourse may seem stereotypical, yet it is precisely such caricature that makes this discourse (like any other) powerful and pervasive: its meanings and values appear intuitive, natural. What this suggests is that not only is 'aid' code for the broader foreign aid discourse, but the mere mention of *one* of its associated terms (e.g. gift, wealth, help, generosity) evokes a *series* of related terms, values, and hierarchies (e.g. purity, superiority, inadequacy, victimhood), without any of them having to be made explicit. It is as if one can complete the foreign aid story with only a partial telling.

The following are examples — taken from current bilateral donor websites — of the representation of foreign aid, with some of the above allusions made implicit, if not explicit:

> Canadian International Development Agency: 'We want to help those in need . . . The Canadian aid program reflects values that all Canadians cherish: humanitarianism, social justice, generosity, and peace. Most Canadians believe that helping the less fortunate is the right thing to do' (CIDA 2006).

> United States Agency for International Development: 'The United States has a long history of extending a helping hand to those people overseas struggling to make a better life, recover from a disaster or striving to live in a free and democratic country. It is this caring that stands as a hall-mark of the United States around the world — and shows the world our true character as a nation' (USAID 2006).

> Netherlands Development Cooperation Programme: 'There is strong public support in the Netherlands for development cooperation. Many people contribute in some way, whether as volunteers or as donors. We take pride in this' (NDCP 2006).

> Australian Agency for International Development: 'Australia gives aid because giving aid reflects our desire to help those less fortunate than ourselves . . . Australians give aid because they believe it's the right thing to do' (AusAID 2006).

> Danish International Development Agency: 'The Government constantly works to ensure that Danish assistance fulfils its original goal of helping the poor by providing critical investments in education and health infrastructure plus support for the development of a private sector as an engine for growth' (DANIDA 2006).

It is noteworthy that, in constructing both aid-as-gift and the donor-recipient rela-tionship, these official donor statements resort to a collective 'we' to speak for the nation, to represent it as 'caring', and even to urge it to take 'pride'. This is consistent with the idea that the deployment of nationalist sentiment is closely connected to the perpetuation of the mystique of foreign aid, a point I will elabo-rate later.

It is also noteworthy that several national surveys recently conducted in Western countries report that, while the public generally supports foreign aid (Smillie 1999), it tends to be poorly informed about the subject (i.e. about how much aid is given, on what it is spent, and the extent of its returns to the donor, etc.) (CCFR 2002; Lagae 1990). Interestingly, the public tends to dramatically *over*estimate the size of aid expenditures: many Americans, for example, believe them to be 25 times higher than they actually are (CCFR 2002; Jepma 1996: 255; Lagae 1990; Mosley 1985). Such findings are perhaps a further indication[3] of 'the mystique of aid' and the image of national/Western generosity that aid discourse perpetuates. The details of aid appear less captivating than the bluster that surrounds it; or to return to my earlier theme, the details are inferred on the basis of that bluster.

The discursive practice of aid as grift

Yet, the discursive practice of aid also tells another story, one that is not dissimilar to Baudelaire's tale of fraudulent kindliness. This section will enumerate some of the main donor conditions and interests that impugn the straightforward construction of aid as 'gift'.

(i) Tied aid

> The biggest single misconception about the foreign aid programme is that we send money abroad. We don't. Foreign aid consists of American equipment, raw materials, expert services, and food.
> (1968 US State Department document, quoted in Jepma 1991: 47)

Tied aid has been a common practice since the 1950s. It can take several forms: product tying, whereby aid is tied to the purchase of products and services from the donor country; project tying, whereby specific project or programme aid is tied; and regional tying, whereby recipients must procure goods and services from a specified geographic region that most often includes the donor country. In effect, as pointed out in Chapter 3, tied aid is a state subsidy to domestic exporters and a job creation programme for NGOs. It contributes to employing the transnational professional class of policy advisors, technical experts, contractors, and trainers. Some donors have even been found to use it to help protect their weaker industries or strengthen their comparative advantage in exports (Jepma 1991: 33, 43).

While the DAC tied-aid average during the 1950s and early 1960s stood at almost 70 percent, this figure declined to about 30 percent in the early 1990s (Lumsdaine 1993: 48, 262; Hattori 2003b: 42; Jepma 1996: 240). In 2001, DAC members agreed to try to move towards untying aid. The current (2004) average is recorded as 10 percent; however, we cannot take this number at face value, since over 66 percent of the tying status of total DAC aid remains unreported (DAC 2005: Table 23). Some donors — notably Ireland, Norway, and the UK — have now untied all their aid. Others continue to tie theirs quite substantially (e.g. Austria at 48 precent, Canada at 43 percent). But the worst offenders over the past few years have been the US and Italy; they also happen to be donors that tend not to report their tying record to DAC. Nonetheless, Oxfam has estimated it at 70 percent and 92 percent, respectively (2002 figures) (Oxfam 2005: 51; cf. OECD 2001: 4; CRS 2004: 19). The inclusion of these figures would no doubt raise the DAC tied-aid average quite considerably, especially given the large size of US aid spending. Their exclusion helps make *all* donors look better.

But this unflattering data covers only formal or 'official' tied aid. What is left out is the substantial informal tying that goes on, when, for example, it is unofficially agreed or understood that the recipient will purchase a portion of programme aid from the donor. Several studies have shown this practice to be quite widespread. One study examined both formal and informal tying during the 1970-1980 period for 37 recipients and found the average to be 63 percent, standing out against the reported DAC average of 47 percent for the same period (Jepma 1991: 21).

And donors profit from the *untied* components of their aid, too. This is a direct outcome of the West's privileged position and comparative advantage in many of the economic and technological sectors of the world economy. Procurement studies done in the mid-1970s and early 1980s, for example, reveal that almost 70 percent of bilateral aid from Europe led to direct procurement (Jepma 1991: 25). Similarly, 81 percent of USAID's procurement during 2002-2003 came from US sources (CRS 2004: 19).

What does all of this mean for aid recipients? It means a reduction in the 'real value' of aid to them, by anywhere between 10 percent and 40 percent (Deen 2005; Petras & Veltmeyer 2002: 286; Jepma 1996: 251; Jepma 1991: 15): for tied aid results in the procurement of goods and services at often higher-than-competitive prices. Moreover, it means that the actual transfer of aid to the developing world is quite low. Oxfam puts it this way: 'by the time donors have paid their consultants, [and] covered their administration expenses . . . the remaining transfer of aid to developing countries is a mere 40 per cent of the total [2002 ODA] budget' (2005: 52; cf. Thérien 2002: 451).

(ii) Loans versus grants

Not only is some aid tied, but a proportion of it is also given as loans, as opposed to grants. Loans lead to debt; grants do not. Now it is true that DAC only reports loans as ODA if they are provided on 'soft' terms [i.e. if they have 'a grant element of at least 25 per cent', a low interest rate, and a long repayment period (DAC 2001b: 5)]. But this still means that a not insignificant portion of the loans passes off as gift, accumulating interest payments to the donor and debt to the recipient.

The proportion of DAC bilateral aid in loan form has been gradually decreasing, from an average of about 51 percent in 1965 to 13 percent in 2003-2004 (DAC 2005: Table 20; Hattori 2003b: 242-3; Lumsdaine 1993: 265). Currently, some donors (e.g. Australia, Ireland) provide all their aid in grant form, while others still extend quite large portions of their aid as loans (e.g. 59 percent of Japan's total ODA is given as loans) (DAC 2005: Table 20).

Despite a recent trend towards the conversion of aid from loans to grants, the problem of accumulated debt remains. Thus, we have tragic situations where heavily indebted countries such as Niger, Rwanda, and Ethiopia are receiving Western aid for debt relief, which is in the form of concessional loans but which nonetheless adds to, rather than reduces, their overall debt loads (Northover 2004: 2; cf. Boyce 2002: 243). Meanwhile, donors come off looking good: they have greatly publicized their recent $40 billion debt write-off for the 18 heavily indebted African countries. Yet, much of this write-off turns out to be part of already committed DAC bilateral and multilateral aid, often resulting in overall reductions in aid by the amounts being cancelled (Shah 2005; Eurodad 2005b: 4). In this regard, France has been found to have artificially inflated its recent aid figures showing increases in French ODA, with DAC reporting that 'a significant part of the current growth is due to debt cancellation processes in the framework of the HIPC Initiative. . . .The increase in ODA has barely translated into a flow of fresh money towards developing countries' (DAC quoted in Eurodad 2005a). The ensuing absurdity is that donors take 'credit', literally and metaphorically, for providing more and more aid that does not live up to that name, for forgiving debt to which that aid has itself contributed, and for providing aid that turns out to be a 'catalyst of reverse aid' (in the form of debt payments, among other things) (Petras & Veltmeyer 2002: 286).

(iii) Conditionalities

The conditionalities of aid are the direct result of its loan component. They refer not just to the 'technical' conditions of loans (e.g. interest payment terms), but also to the ideological conditions binding loan recipients. Previous chapters have referred to them as 'neoliberal conditionalities', alluding to the disciplinary requirements of structural adjustment programmes, so there is little need to provide much further detail here. Suffice it to say that, between 1975 and 1990, the period of intensified IMF/World Bank adjustment lending, 378 structural adjustment loans were made to 71 countries worth $118 billion (current dollars), with some 11 percent to 15 percent of these loans classified as ODA (Hattori 2001: 645). Since then, conditionalities have continued unabated and, in some cases, even increased: the average structural adjustment conditions per country in Sub-Saharan Africa rose from 32 in the early 1980s, to 56 in the late 1980s, to 114 in the late 1990s (Mutume 2001; cf. Devarajan et al. 2001: 32).[4] Currently, recipient countries face an estimated average of 67 conditions per World Bank loan (Eurodad 2006: 3, 89).

(iv) Military aid

Until the early 1970s, DAC used to count military assistance as aid; after that time, ODA has excluded expenditures on military equipment and services, although it includes the cost of military personnel used, say, to deliver humanitarian aid (DAC 2001b: 2). But the US, the world's largest provider of armaments, continues to categorize military assistance as foreign aid (under the 'foreign economic and military assistance' label) (CRS 2004: 7). Between 1945 and 1990, it transferred almost $400 billion to more than 120 countries (Hook 1995: 28). Currently, $4.8 billion of its overall $19 billion annual aid budget is devoted to military aid (2004 figures), taking an average of about 26 percent of the aid budget since 2000 (CRS 2004: 7). (The bulk of it goes to three countries — Israel, Egypt, and Colombia.)

The inclusion of such military spending, it should be noted, substantially inflates the US government's overall aid expenditures, making it look like the country devotes close to 1 percent of GNI (Gross National Income) to aid, as compared to the DAC figure of 0.17 percent, which, ironically, places the country as one of DAC's *lowest* aid donors by that measurement[5] (DAC 2005: Table 1; CRS 2004: 14-18, 21). It should also be noted that, while military assistance and ODA are ostensibly kept separate, there appears to be a correlation between the two: the UNDP estimates that, in 1992, high military spenders in developing countries got roughly 2.5 times more ODA per capita from bilateral donors (especially the main weapons manufacturers — the US, France, and Britain) than low military spenders (UNDP 1994: 75; Raffer & Singer 1996: 170-1). This finding can be explained by the fact that these donors use aid for their security and foreign policy objectives. More on that topic next.

(v) Foreign policy objectives

The use of aid as a political tool is nothing new. During the Cold War, aid was an integral part of superpower rivalry. Eastern European countries and Cuba received substantial aid from the Soviet Union, while such countries as South Korea, Taiwan, South Vietnam, Greece, and Turkey obtained large amounts of US aid as part of the latter's 'containment' policy (cf. Thérien 2002: 454; Tisch & Wallace 1994: 57-8; Tarnoff & Nowels 1994: 5). In the 1980s, the Reagan government showered El Salvador with (military) aid to back the Nicaraguan 'contras' and, more recently, the George W. Bush regime has devoted a high proportion of US aid to two countries (Iraq and Afghanistan) as part of its global 'war on terror'.

If US aid is often directed by strategic interests, those of France and Britain tend to be oriented by mainly colonial ties: most of the French aid programme is focused on Francophone Africa (Hook 1995: 59; Oxfam 2005: 49), and Britain's on the Commonwealth. Japan, for its part, tends to shape its aid policy on the basis of its regional interests. A large proportion of Japanese aid currently goes to Asian countries (especially Indonesia, South Korea, the Philippines, and China), much of it to further commercial goals (Hook 1995: 79).

Troublingly, there are several instances of withholding aid to suit foreign policy objectives. For example, the US cut aid to the Philippines in 1992 when the government there tried to bar foreign military bases on Filipino soil; and, in 1990, it discontinued economic and military assistance to Pakistan after indications the latter had developed nuclear weapons (cf. Tisch & Wallace 1994: 57-8). Similarly, there are instances of aid recipients being embroiled in the game of shifting political alliances. A case in point is Egypt, which received Soviet aid as a result of Nasser's non-alignment stance in the 1950s, Arab aid during the various Middle East crises of the 1970s, and US/Western aid after the signing of the Camp David Accords in the late 1970s (Raffer & Singer 1996: 126).

Even food aid, often seen as the most 'pure' form of aid because used for emergency or humanitarian purposes, can be politically motivated. During the North Korean famine in the late 1990s, for instance, the US and South Korea exploited their food aid to coax the impenetrable North Korean regime into peace talks. But they also used it as part of a public relations campaign to show the communist regime as incapable of meeting its people's most basic needs (Aaltola 1999: 376).

What these varied examples help determine is that not only do foreign policy objectives intersect with foreign aid, thereby further highlighting aid's contamination, but also that aid is highly donor-centred, thereby further revealing the 'gift' of aid to be first and foremost the donor's gift to itself. It should hardly come as a surprise, therefore, that more aid is received by politically and strategically important countries (e.g. Israel) than 'needy' ones (e.g. Bangladesh).

A 1968 Richard Nixon statement captures this situation well: 'Let us remember that the main purpose of American aid is not to help other nations but to help ourselves' (quoted in Collingwood 2003: 56). At one level, the statement is a candid representation of aid, showing it to be beholden to national interests. Aid can be used, as we have seen, to establish export subsidies, create debt, stipulate ideological conditionalities, and/or serve national military and security goals. But at another level, the statement also points up the aporia of aid that Derrida has alerted us to: Nixon's beckoning to us to 'remember' betrays his awareness of the importance of the idea of aid as 'help' and, despite his candidness, a certain anxiety about gift-giving as double-dealing (which is fitting, since deception is something for which Nixon is himself notorious). In fact, even as he made this statement, the US government (like other donor governments) continued to construct aid as gift and cover up its grift. Its manipulation of aid statistics, as we have repeatedly underscored, is indicative — inflating, hiding, withholding figures to make the nation look good, or as Derrida puts it, 'to pick up gratis the certificate of a charitable [nation]' (1992: 32).

Nationalism and the production of the 'generous nation'

My purpose in this chapter is not merely to examine the contradictory character of aid, but also to ask why aid as gift is hegemonic in relation to aid as grift. For an answer, I want to turn to postcolonial theories of nationalism. Their focus on national identity construction is helpful in understanding the urge by Western donors to produce a 'generous nation', thus echoing Derrida's linkage between gift-giving and self-constitution.

Nationalism

Homi Bhabha sees nationalism as an 'attempt by nationalist discourses persistently to produce the idea of the nation as a continuous narrative of national progress' (1990: 1). Nationalism is thus about constructing a single, master narrative that elides the cultural and social pluralism that makes up any nation. Faced with contradiction, the tendency of nationalist forces is to deny it, to suppress or repress anything that does not fit with the politico-cultural unity necessary for the nation. Ambivalence, for Bhabha, 'haunts the idea of the nation' (1990: 1; cf. 1994: 148, 152). Coherence, purity, authenticity, unanimity, fixity triumph over heterogeneity, hybridity, contamination, disagreement, fluidity.

Implied in Bhabha's argument is the Lacanian psychoanalytic view we discussed in Chapter 4: identification is based on a desire for fullness and an avoidance of the Real (i.e. lack, incompleteness, ambiguity). Such a desire is perhaps misplaced, but it is powerful nonetheless, often approaching a kind of religious zeal (Renan 1882). People are driven to imagine themselves as part of a community (Anderson 1983), to seek a sense of identity, belonging, and togetherness by affiliating with the nation. The nation may well be a fictive invention, but its myths are gripping, so much so that unpleasant memories associated with nation-building (colonialism, violence, racism, inequality) are set aside. Instead, people take pride and gain self-esteem from their national symbols — flags, rituals (remembrance days, holidays, parades), founding texts (the constitution, maps), figureheads ('founding fathers', heroes/heroines), and even sacrifice (the war dead) (Hayes 1966: 104ff.).

Self-identification, however, is always done at the behest of an Other. For the nation to be unified and exclusive, Others (internal or external enemies, strangers, critics, traitors, villains) must be identified, excluded, or even denigrated (Bhabha 1990: 4; Chatterjee 1986). The Other is perceived as a menace; it is s(he) who prevents 'us' from our desire and enjoyment, from achieving our potential and fullness as a nation (Žižek 1993: 206). And by denigrating him/her (e.g. through political ideology, jokes, or racist, sexist, and homophobic stereotypes), we look superior — more worthy, more manly, more advanced.

Producing the 'generous nation'

Just as patriots repress the ambivalences within the nation, so donors gloss over the aporia of foreign aid. Just as the joy of national unity triumphs over the embarrassment of colonialism and racism, so donor generosity overcomes the unpleasantness of self-interest. Aid as gift supersedes aid as grift. This image of donor kindness, in fact, is integral to the production of the nation. Being identified as big-hearted through the aid programme enables the nation to build its unity, to take pride, and so to become recognizable, if not unique. It also positions the Other — the recipient — as subordinate, less worthy, 'underdeveloped'.

In this sense, nationalist discourse (in the West) and aid/development discourse are bosom buddies. They both centre on and complement one another's insider/outsider distinctions. They also share what can be called an 'Occidentalism': while nationalism and aid each take on distinct national forms, both breed a broader cultural identification with the Occident that pits West against Third World.

I have already hinted at instances of the collusion between nationalism/ Occidentalism and aid: I have referred to the use by donors of the collective 'we' to represent their aid programmes, and to the manipulation of aid statistics to make the nation/West look good. I would like to elaborate this collusion further with the help of other examples.

(i) Flag-waving

While perhaps seemingly innocuous, the identification of aid by country of origin is revealing of the donors' need to be recognized. Flags on grain sacks, insignias on equipment, sponsor names on NGO literature — all aim at designating the nation's 'gift' and publicizing it to multiple audiences — recipients, other donors, home viewers, and the broader world public and media. Nationalist symbols permit donors to be identified, thanked, or envied; they also enable it to stake its territory, and perhaps to gloat, in relation to other donors. Let me quote Mika Aaltola at length in this regard:

> A donor country needs to attract attention to its donation to receive more benefits from it. An especially important benefit is the opportunity to show off its vitality and status. The ceremonies of this status demonstration include having as many witnesses as possible, which can be effected by international media coverage, a showy and often military operation of getting the food to the needy, having one's own people hand out the aid to the needy . . . Under the gift-giving rubric, things being exchanged are by no means simple neutral objects but objects that embody the qualities of their donor states. A concrete representation of this embodiment, national symbols such as flags, seals and emblems attached to international gifts convey a sense of presence of the donor state . . . The act of gift-giving extends the donor state's sovereignty beyond its territorial borders, making its presence felt at the international level, and thus increases its sovereignty and viability.
>
> (Aaltola 1999: 379)

(ii) Creating 'humanitarian heroes'

There are several examples of humanitarian heroes/heroines — Americans Jimmy Carter and Angelina Jolie, Canadian Craig Kielburger, or the French-identified transnational NGO, *Médecins Sans Frontières*; but perhaps the most obvious ones are Bono and Bob Geldof. Here are two celebrities, ostensibly trying to focus the West's attention on problems of Third World debt and 'poverty', but something else has also happened: they have been constructed as Western humanitarian idols, so much so that, in 2005, at the height of their respective global campaigns, Geldof was being considered for the Nobel Peace Prize (CBC News 2005), and Bono was *Time* magazine's 'Person of the Year'. It is as if we, British, Irish, Canadians, Westerners, so desire to be generous, and to be *seen* as generous, that we have produced them as heroes. They have emerged as contemporary incarnations of charity and salvation. The irony once again is that debt and poverty have become an afterthought, serving as excuse for nationalist/occidentalist idolatry.

This is not to deny the personal commitment and efforts of either of these men, or to suggest they are necessarily willing participants in such idolization. But, at the same time, it is difficult to ignore the sometimes expedient character of their gestures. Geldof's initiative, Live8, for example, watched by about three billion people, was intended to put pressure on the G8 leaders to reduce debt and increase foreign aid. But sadly, it also turned into a massive media event, advertised itself as the 'greatest show ever' (Live8 2005), sloganized and logo-ized debt and poverty ('make poverty history'), provided 'unpaid' performing artists with global exposure (and increased music sales), and served as advertising platform for several corporate sponsors (AOL Time Warner, the BBC, and Nokia, among others). One is left wondering, in the end, whether Live8 was the 'greatest show ever' for poverty or for self-promotion.

(iii) Guarding donor exclusivity

The OECD is a group of 30 'rich' countries, often characterized as the 'rich country club', with membership restricted to those committed to 'a market economy and a pluralistic democracy' (OECD 2006a). Within the OECD, DAC is an even more exclusive club, including only OECD donor members (currently 23, all Western)[6] and focusing on development policy and coordination.

DAC appears to place marked emphasis on its identity. To begin with, as Tomohisa Hattori argues, it acts as a kind of 'moral book-keeper', trying to ensure that aid giving is kept virtuous (2003a: 244, 237). For example, in ranking donors according to how much they spend and the aid conditions they impose, it urges donors to be more giving, often praising the Scandinavian donors for their generosity, while sometimes politely admonishing Japan and the US for not living up to their aid commitments.

DAC membership, moreover, is prized and guarded. Currently, many OECD members — Mexico, Czech Republic, Slovak Republic, Hungary, Poland, Turkey, and South Korea — are not DAC members (OECDb 2006; Hattori 2003b: 243), even though some of them have been aid donors. What is remarkable is that these all happen to be non-Western European and/or former Southern countries.

A similar pattern is discernible with regard to non-OECD donors. Over the years, several Southern countries — China, India, Egypt, Brazil — have emerged as substantial donors, but are, by definition and design, excluded from DAC membership.

To wit, China is currently the world's third largest food donor (*Globe & Mail* 2006). But perhaps the most significant exclusion has been that of OPEC donors. During the 1970s particularly, OPEC countries accounted for between 22 percent and 30 percent of all ODA; some OPEC members (Kuwait, Qatar, Saudi Arabia) even devoted a staggering 7 to 12 percent of GDP to aid at the time,[7] compared to the less than 1 percent devoted by Western donors (Raffer & Singer 1996: 123). To add insult to injury, OECD/DAC has recently been shown to have underestimated OPEC aid for that period, with some studies reporting, for instance, that OPEC aid in 1979 should have been $2 billion more than recorded (Raffer & Singer 1996: 130, 124-5). DAC's book-keeping, it seems, is 'moral' by omission, intended to protect the reputation of DAC members to the exclusion of others.

There is thus a hard-to-miss politics of inclusion and exclusion by DAC, whose aim is to maintain and protect its exclusive image and membership. Its clan-like behaviour is decidedly occidentalist, its members prizing their status as Western, rich, and self-sufficient. And its donor classification is selective and insular, effectively discriminating against non-Western European and Southern donors.

(iv) Taking pleasure

I have already hinted at the affective basis and power of nationalism, pointing to the kernel of *jouissance* or enjoyment in every identification (cf. Žižek 1993: 202). I would like to briefly pursue this point in relation to aid, by suggesting ways in which the gift is pleasurable to the nation.[8]

There is, of course, the sheer pleasure of giving. In the case of aid, such giving can be multiply pleasurable and, dare I say, auto-orgasmic. There is, first, the satisfaction derived from offering help and winning symbolic returns — world recognition and the acknowledgement and (presumed) gratitude of the recipient. Then, like illicit sex, there is the added excitement of stealthily enjoying the material returns of aid (tied aid, loan payments, etc.). In fact, this added excitement is three-layered: one enjoys the grift of aid, even as one constructs it as 'gift' *and* garners praise for it. This amounts to the nation applauding itself/being applauded for its narcissism, thereby further fuelling its narcissism.

But the pleasure does not stop there. Not to be forgotten is the gratification received from establishing superiority over the recipient. Bourdieu calls this the 'symbolic domination' of the gift, through which the recipient can be coerced into subordination, acquiescence, or admiration (1997: 205ff.); and through which, I would add, the donor can derive sadistic regalement. It is a domination that legitimizes global inequality and the privileged economic position of the West. In this regard, Hattori suggests that aid acts as a 'mechanism of consent to the capitalist order', in which there is 'no incentive to change [and indeed much satisfaction to take from] the underlying material hierarchy' (2003a: 153, 157; 2003b: 237; 2001).

Under such conditions, aid becomes an aphrodisiac for the nation. Hardly is it surprising to find donors constructing aid, not just as gift, but as gift 'beyond measure' (Derrida 1992: 38). For, the more immoderate the generosity, the greater the pleasure. Thus, when the G8 ministers announced their 2005 (alleged) relief package for highly indebted countries, the agreement was hailed as nothing less than 'historic', with Gordon Brown boasting that now was 'not a time for timidity but a time for boldness . . . .We are presenting the most comprehensive statement that finance ministers have ever made on the issues of debt, development, health and poverty . . . [which will] forge a new and better relationship, a new deal between the rich and poor countries of the world' (BBC News 2005).

Hardly is it surprising, too, to find commentators suggesting that donors have become hooked on aid (cf. Edgren 2002: 262, 264). For, the sado-narcissistic pleasures of the gift may be just too difficult to give up. In fact, they give new meaning to 'aid dependency': it is not just that some Third World countries may be habituated to the material benefits of aid, it is also that First World nations may be addicted to the psycho-symbolic indulgences of aid.

To conclude this section, let me make explicit what I have until now only implied: foreign aid as 'gift' is an ideological construction. The mystique of the gift covers over aid's political and economic dimensions. Let me also clarify, though, what I mean by 'cover'. I do *not* mean it in the classical Marxist sense, whereby ideology covers up 'reality' (cf. Bourdieu 1997: 206; cf. Osteen 2002: 24-5), or in our case, whereby the 'truth' is that aid is really grift, and aid as gift is only a cloak. Rather, as in the last chapter, I mean it in the sense of the former being hegemonic in relation to the latter. As Stuart Hall points out, national cultures are riven with internal differences and divisions, but are unified through cultural hegemony (Hall 1992: 297). Accordingly, foreign aid is internally contradictory and aporetic, with both its economic *and* symbolic pursuits integral to donor practice. Each is written into aid's institutional politics, and both are 'real'. So the ideology of aid is that which expulses any ambivalence between the two, unifying them by fixing and fetishizing the one at the expense of the other. And ideology critique is bringing attention back to this ambivalence, or rather, deconstructing what is always already unravelling, which is what I have attempted here.

Conclusion: towards aid as gift?

The foreign aid regime, it appears, is highly invested in its material and symbolic returns. As a consequence, what Derrida says of Mauss applies equally to aid: it involves 'everything but the gift'. The notion of non-reciprocation seems to have insufficient sociopolitical leverage to turn aid into 'gift'. So what might be done?

Of course, a first possible response is to altogether abandon the idea of foreign aid, in favour of alternative ways of doing development (e.g. development 'from below', social justice programming, etc.). Thankfully, much alternative development is already happening (although not without its own limits and dangers) (cf. Chapter 8). However, ending aid, apart from being unrealistic given the substantial interests invested in it, is probably also ill-advised: gift-giving, as Mauss suggests, is an age-old anthropological and cross-cultural phenomenon, and it would be a mistake to deny, ignore, or repress it, lest it return in equally (or more) nefarious and disguised forms than foreign aid (e.g. participatory development, as discussed in the previous chapter). It seems to me more salubrious to learn from the past mistakes and the ever-present perils of gift-giving in order to transform and better bring to account the global foreign aid regime.

Derrida offers a few hints here. He starts by suggesting that the genuine gift would require 'oblivion', that is, no memory, consciousness, or recognition of the gift (1992: 16-18). This would mean the anonymity of both donor and recipient — shedding one's identity as 'donor' or 'recipient', and putting distance between self and other in order that return, expectation, or debt not intervene. It would also mean that aid would cease to signify 'gift'. In this sense, the gift event would neither reveal itself nor be recorded. Derrida thus writes, '*At the limit, the gift as gift ought not appear as gift: either to the donnee or to the donor*' (1992: 14, italics in original). For this, he motions that giving would need to be accidental, spontaneous, unforeseeable, unexpected: the gift must 'let itself be structured by the aleatory; it must *appear* chancy or in any case lived as such, apprehended as the intentional correlate of a perception that is absolutely surprised by the encounter with what it perceives' (1992: 122, italics in original).

The challenge becomes trying to translate these inferences into a historically rooted and institutionally feasible politics (Derrida has been criticized for not doing just that; cf. O'Neill 1999: 142-3). In what follows, I outline some broad possibilities, with all the risks that that may entail.

Reconfiguring the nation?

As I have implied, the transformation of foreign aid needs to happen in the context of much wider change, which has to do with making the nation more self-reflexive. This is not to suggest doing away with nationalism; *that* is neither realistic nor feasible, and perhaps not even desirable.[9] Rather, the idea is to prevent nationalism from being the only game in town, to rethink the nation by reconfiguring identification, affiliation, and sovereignty.

The recent intensification of globalization has opened up avenues for such reconfiguration. The movement of peoples from the ex-colonies to the West, in particular, has occasioned a de facto globalization of the nation, and by extension a multiculturalization of the aid/development industry. Immigrant and diasporic communities are beginning to populate development agencies, bringing cross-cultural perspectives with them. Similarly, the information age and the growth of the civil society sector have enabled greater transnational communication, understanding, and politico-cultural exchange. All of this sets the stage for questioning the hegemony of single national identity and belonging. It helps disrupt the supposed cultural homogeneity of the nation. It troubles the inside–outside distinctions of nationalist and development discourses alike. And it authorizes non-national forms of association, cultivating *trans*national bonds and loyalties.[10]

But there are no guarantees. For globalization has also brought with it new forms of nationalism, occasionally in virulent and conservative guise, and notably from the ranks of both recently and permanently settled communities in the West (namely diasporic religious/nationalist fundamentalisms, anti-immigrant back-lashes). Moreover, globalization has helped accelerate transnational corporate affiliations, which can, for instance, reinforce aid's neoliberal orientations (namely conditionalities opening up developing-country markets to greater transnational corporate investment). The risk here, then, is that the nation can be reconfigured and transnationalized, but not necessarily in the desired direction.

A related, albeit equally risky, approach is rethinking national sovereignty in favour of a postnational politics. As long as aid is controlled exclusively by bilateral organizations as representatives of sovereign nation-states, there is no getting away from issues of national interest and pride. Instead, Derrida issues a call for a 'new International', 'another broader politics, another humanitarian politics, indeed a humanitarian commitment that *effectively* operates beyond the interests of Nation-States' (1999: 101; cf. 1994: 85). Two possible options in this direction include the multilateralization of aid and the channelling of gifts through NGOs.

Multilateral aid?

Multilateral organizations can act as a mediation between donor and recipient. This means that donors have much less of a say over aid decisions, while recipients identify the aid with the multilateral organization as representative of not a single country, but a community of nations. Hattori writes, in this regard, 'What originated and still predominates as a bilateral face-to-face practice has been progressively redefined and legitimised [by multilateral aid] as a collective endeavour of the former colonising states, expressing a civic virtue specific to the community of states' (2003b: 240; cf. 234).

The good news, if indeed it is, is that multilateral aid *has* been increasing over the years, at the expense of bilateral aid. Thus, in the mid-1960s, multilateral aid accounted for 5 percent of total ODA, as compared to 95 percent for bilateral aid. Today, the numbers stand at 32 and 68 percent, respectively (2004 figures) (Hattori 2001: 644; DAC 2005: Table 2).

But the bad news is that multilaterals are not necessarily benign. Indeed, they consist of relatively well-regarded agencies such as UNICEF and UNDP, but they also include such maligned organizations as the World Bank. [The UN development organizations comprise 19 percent of total current multilateral aid, while the Bank and regional development banks make up 34 percent (DAC 2005: Table 15.)] The Bank has come under criticism for its neoliberal policies (as already pointed out), but also for its lack of accountability: its decision-making processes are dominated by its major funders, mostly Western donor countries (World Bank 2006; Griffith-Jones 2002), without adequate representation from its borrowers — developing countries. In contrast, the UN agencies are generally better reputed, in great measure because they are seen as comparatively more accountable: the UNDP Executive Board, for example, has wide representation from developing countries (24 board members), double that of the major donor countries (12 board members) (UNDP 2006; cf. Hattori 2003b: 239).

Of course, this is not to say the UN aid network is without problems, a key one being that its decision-making processes are still largely dominated by the Westphalian system (i.e. only nation-states have legal standing and representation, to the exclusion of civil society groups). Nonetheless, a key ingredient for a more benign multilateral organization — and by extension, a more salubrious multilateral aid regime — is broad-based political accountability (ideally including non-national forms of representation). It helps ensure that aid decisions are not based solely on national interests or narrow affiliations, and can result in a greater anonymity of the gift.

Gifts through NGOs?

Channelling aid through NGOs may be another fruitful route. Like multilaterals, they are institutions that can act as a mediation between donors and recipients, with, in principle at least, the identity of both donor and recipient remaining relatively anonymous, and the donor's control over the gift reduced, if not eliminated. As civil society organizations fostering people-to-people exchanges, NGOs can be less bound by national loyalties, and more ethical. They can, as Godbout and Caillé suggest, be forums where strangers give spontaneous gifts to other strangers, as in the case of the donation of blood, human organs, or gifts to children (1998: 187, 93, 67-72). If so, we are seeing the playing out of Derrida's 'chancy' and unanticipated gift, with NGOs as a sort of ghostly association: 'Barely deserving the name community, the new International belongs only to anonymity' (Derrida 1994: 90).

But once again, one has to be wary. While several NGOs participate in grass-roots social justice movements, many are entrenched in the aid business (as underlined in chapters 2 and 3). Some lack accountability, seeking publicity and imposing their institutional identity on their 'clients' (cf. Godbout & Caillé 1998: 70-80; cf. Clifford 2006). Others are heavily dependent on funding from donor agencies, often advancing donor/national loyalties and interests. Not surprisingly, Arundhati Roy refers to them as the 'secular missionaries of the modern world' (2004a).

No guarantees, then. Even when we try, to the extent possible, to bypass the nation, we are confronted with the possibility of other interests contaminating the gift. Institutional intermediaries such as NGOs and multilaterals may solve one set of problems, but they also engender others, with the risk that their regime may be even worse than that of the bilaterals. This is in part because institutional gifts can never be pure or neutral: 'As soon as almsgiving is regulated by institutional rituals, it is no longer a pure gift. . . . It becomes prescribed, programmed, obligated, in other words bound' (Derrida 1992: 137). But the larger point is that it is such uncertainty that makes gifts 'the impossible', and in turn, such impossibility that enables freedom, responsibility, politics (cf. Derrida 1992: 31; 1997: 111, 219; 2002: 249). If pure gifts were possible, there would be no decision to make; it is the recognition of their contamination that can bring forth self-reflection and self-limitation. Which is why giving needs first to give pause . . .

Part III

POSTCOLONIAL POLITICS?

6

DELIBERATIVE DEMOCRACY OR AGONISTIC PLURALISM?

The relevance of the Habermas–Mouffe debate for Third World politics

In recent decades, one cannot have failed to notice the spread of Western liberal democracy throughout the world, whether in Eastern Europe or many parts of the Third World. Yet, the ascent of liberal democracy has been accompanied by 'ethnic' nationalisms, religious 'fundamentalisms', civil wars, and genocide. Furthermore, much like in the West, in those developing countries with already well-entrenched liberal democratic regimes, there has been growing public dissatisfaction with democratic institutions. This unease is evidenced by such phenomena as the rise of popular protest and social movements, lower voter turnout, and the inability of public institutions to adequately meet citizens' demands and needs.

Jürgen Habermas and Chantal Mouffe speak directly to this 'crisis of liberal democracy'. Both are democratic theorists who, while defending the gains of Western liberal democratic regimes, are critical of them, believing them to be far from sufficient or complete. It is not enough, Habermas and Mouffe contend, to have the outward trimmings and institutions of liberal democracy (i.e. elections, parliaments, rule of law, etc.); we also need to ensure the quality and inclusiveness of democratic processes in the multiple spheres of social life and within public institutions. Many of the sociocultural problems of nationalism, religious resurgence, and popular protest noted above, they argue, are precisely the product of political neglect and exclusion by regimes purporting to be democratic. Thus, both theorists make a compelling argument for the need to deepen or extend democracy.

However, Habermas and Mouffe differ on how to bring this about. Habermas's vision, which he labels 'deliberative democracy', relies on reasoned and inclusive public deliberation that is geared to reaching consensual decisions. His arguments foreground concerns about legitimacy and (universal) justice, concerns which he believes are ignored by poststructuralists to their peril. Mouffe's (poststructuralist) vision of democracy is critical of Habermas's defence of rationality and universalism, believing these to be inimical to pluralist societies. Her 'agonistic pluralism' accentuates ways for democratic politics to represent difference. Thus, the debate between the two theorists rests on how best to promote democratic participation and decision-making without impeding sociocultural difference; or, to put it another way, it hinges on democratically representing difference without thereby sanctioning injustice and intolerance.

I will attempt, in this chapter, to call attention to several significant dimensions of the debate. As just noted, while both theorists valorize, criticize, and wish to extend liberal democracy, each does so from a different ontological standpoint.[1] In this sense, each one's differences bring out the strengths and limits of the other's democratic theory. To appropriate Richard Bernstein's words (written in another context), in many ways, each is 'each other's other'; their debate can be seen as an '*allegory* of the "modern/postmodern" condition' and is a 'juxtaposed rather than an integrated cluster of changing elements that resist reduction to a common denominator, essential core, or generative first principle' (1993: 219, italics in original; cf. 201, 225).[2] This being the case, I will not attempt to reconcile the differences between the two theorists or integrate their democratic visions; rather, believing that (and showing) the tensions between them to be irresolvable but fruitful and educative, I will treat both theorists agonally to highlight some of the limits, strains, and possibilities of contemporary Third World democratic politics.

As compelling and relevant as Habermas's and Mouffe's democratic theories may be, surprisingly little work has been done to relate these theories to the political and postcolonial challenges of the Third World. A voluminous (and still growing) literature exists on Habermas's critique/vision of Western democracy, but very little exists on its application to the South.[3] Mouffe's work fares only slightly better here, primarily through the writings of the 'postdevelopment' theorists (especially those of Arturo Escobar),[4] who have used her work as it relates to new social movements. But nothing exists as yet on the *debate* between Habermas and Mouffe and its relevance to Third World politics, most likely because the debate is relatively recent. In what follows, I will attempt to fill this gap. However, I will do so with qualification and caution. There are limitations in applying First World theories to Third World actualities. In particular, Habermas's and Mouffe's democratic politics do not adequately address issues of particular significance to postcolonialism or Third World politics: the legacies of colonialism, the impact of socioeconomic inequality on democratic politics, the democratic participation of the subaltern, and the pivotal role of the (Third World) state.[5]

The structure of the chapter will reflect the sequence of arguments just laid out. After developing Habermas's views on 'deliberative democracy' and Mouffe's counter-proposals on 'agonistic pluralism', I will analyze the relevance of their debate to Third World politics in terms of both what they share and what sets them apart. I will then examine the limits, erasures, and gaps in their respective arguments from the perspective of Third World and postcolonial politics.

A final introductory note: the Habermas–Mouffe debate is one that has been constructed chiefly by Mouffe, specifically in two articles (1997, 1999) and a book (2000), in which she assesses Habermas's more recent work on deliberative democracy (Habermas 1996a-b, 1998). To date, Habermas has not replied to Mouffe, although his misgivings about her proposals can be teased out from his (and a number of Habermasian theorists') criticisms of poststructuralist politics.

Accordingly, this chapter will draw not only from the two theorists' recent work, but also from the larger body of their work and criticisms of it where appropriate to the debate.

Deliberative democracy vs. agonistic pluralism

Habermas's deliberative democracy

In his early writings, Habermas developed the notion of the 'public sphere' as a discursive space, distinct and separate from the economy and state, in which citizens participate and act through dialogue and debate (1989; cf. Calhoun 1992).[6] In more recent writings (1996a-b, 1998), he elaborates the specifically discursive aspects of this public sphere, arguing for a procedural model of democracy that he labels 'deliberative democracy'. For him, in order to encourage public participation and broaden/strengthen democracy, politics must be viewed as a public conversation governed by legitimating procedures and reason: 'democratic will-formation draws its legitimating force . . . from the communicative presuppositions that allow better arguments to come into play in various forms of deliberation and from procedures that secure fair bargaining processes' (1996a: 24). Habermas encapsulates these 'fair' procedures in what he calls an 'ideal speech situation', that is, a situation in which public dialogue is free and uncoerced. Democratic deliberation approaches an ideal speech situation if it satisfies the following formal conditions: (i) it is inclusive (i.e. no one is excluded from participating in the discussion on topics relevant to her/him, and no relevant information is omitted); it is coercion free (i.e. everyone engages in arguments freely, without being dominated or feeling intimidated by other participants); and (iii) it is open and symmetrical (each participant can initiate, continue, and question the discussion on any relevant topic, including the deliberative procedures) (1990: 88-9, 197; 1976: 107-9; Benhabib 1996b: 70).[7] It is worth noting that while the formal procedures entailed by the ideal speech situation enforce free and uncoerced dialogue, they impose no limits on the scope or agenda of public deliberations; topics are always open, determined only by those participating in the discussions and subject to revision if and when required.

Habermas recognizes that the ideal speech situation is not easy to bring about; he is aware that there are many obstacles standing in its way, not the least of which is trying to minimize power relationships among participants. For him, the ideal speech situation is not empirical; it is a regulative idea, a counterfactual stance from which to assess and criticize non-deliberative processes and power politics. In more recent writings, as a way of better guaranteeing, regulating, and expanding deliberative democracy, he argues for the institutionalization through legal and constitutional means of these legitimating rules (1996b). According to him, laws enacting 'fair' procedures can help organize democratic politics. For example, they can delineate, regulate, and check state powers to ensure better accountability of public institutions; in turn, this will help protect the public sphere from being overly influenced and colonized by state administrative and technocratic interests.

Habermas seeks not simply legitimating procedures, but just outcomes as well. For this purpose, he resorts to the use of reason. Yet for him, rationality cannot be autonomous, insulated from society and imposing its will without accountability; it must be a dialogical or 'communicative' rationality, through which participants advance arguments and counter-arguments. Consensual decisions are reached only by the (unforced) 'force of the better argument', so that, at the end of the deliberative process, all concerned are convinced by the decisions reached and accept them as reasonable (1990: 88ff., 160, 198). Like the discussion topics, these decisions can be revisited when information and participants change.

Several dimensions of this process are worth dwelling upon. First, communicative rationality not only helps coordinate information, plans, or actions, but performs an important critical and adjudicative function. By making speakers give (or test) reasons for the claims they advance, deliberative democracy enables participants to criticize unsubstantiated or unconvincing claims and distinguish between better and worse claims. Decisions reached are 'right' because they are supported by good reasons. Second, it is not the status of the speaker that counts, but the force of her/his arguments. Reason prevails over power. In this sense, Habermas complements his above-noted legitimating rules with communicative rationality to criticize and minimize power inequalities within the deliberative public space.

Finally, Habermas upholds the quality — the quasi-transcendental[8] quality — of public deliberation. For him, just outcomes are reached through '*higher-level intersubjectivity* of communication processes' (1996a: 28, italics in original). Decisions happen not by aggregating individual preferences, adding votes, or finding commonalities; rather, each participant begins with her/his interests, and through the course of deliberations, transcends these interests to seek the good of all. Thus, the outcomes represent a movement from 'mere agreement' to 'rational consensus' (1990: 67, 198).

It is such (quasi-) transcendence that gives consensual decisions their universal appeal, since all participants discover norms that are generalizable (or potentially generalizable) and accept them as universally binding. To this end, Habermas prioritizes morality (i.e. the domain of impartial procedures and universal right/justice) over ethics (i.e. the domain of differing conceptions of the personal and social good, or the 'good life'):[9] he argues for the need for communities to distance themselves from their taken-for-granted beliefs and traditions, so that they bring 'universal principles of justice into the horizon of the specific form of life of [the] particular community' (1990: 104; 1996a: 25). As a consequence, communicative rationality's transcendent qualities form the basis of his defence of justice and universalization.

Mouffe's agonistic pluralism

Mouffe enters the debate with Habermas equipped with a different set of priorities: hers is a postmodern world that valorizes antagonism and pluralism (both terms explained below), and is suspicious of such notions as rationality and consensus. She is critical of Habermas on several grounds. Using Wittgenstein's argument that rules are integral to specific and shared forms of community life, she questions Habermas's separation of procedure from substance: the 'distinctions between "procedural" and "substantial" or between "moral" and "ethical" that are central to the Habermasian approach cannot be maintained and one must acknowledge that procedures always involve substantial ethical commitments' (1999: 749; cf. 2000: 67-9, 97). In other words, one would first have to agree on the specific 'language game' (or common world view) being used before one could agree on the rules of deliberation; as a result, any agreement on rules would already contain substantive (cultural or ethical) designs.

In the same vein, Mouffe questions Habermas's notion of consensus: as language games/community life forms are incommensurable, participants hailing from different communities would sometimes be talking at cross-purposes. Any agreement they come to would then be more the product of power politics or clever rhetoric than real consensus. She quotes Wittgenstein here to make her point: 'Where two principles really do meet which cannot be reconciled with another, then each man declares the other a fool and an heretic. I said I would "combat" the other man, but wouldn't I give him reasons? certainly; but how far do they go? At the end of reasons comes *persuasion*' (quoted in Mouffe 1999: 749-50, emphasis in original; cf. Mouffe 2000: 97-8).

Lastly, Mouffe deploys arguments by Lacan (as well as Žižek and Derrida) to criticize Habermas's notion of the ideal speech situation. The symbolic field, for her, is made up of free-floating signifiers, rendering the establishment of any discourse authoritarian: meaning can only happen by advancing a master signifier, at the expense and exclusion of other signifiers. Habermas's attempt to arrive at a coercion-free deliberative sphere is thus doomed to failure, according to her. She writes that 'far from being merely empirical, or epistemological, the obstacles to the realization of the ideal speech situation are ontological' (1999: 751).[10] The same argument is used to buttress her earlier criticism of consensus, which she believes is a distortion of the symbolic field (1999: 751), made possible only by shutting out something or someone from the deliberative process (more on this point later).

It is important to note that the Lacanian arguments just used by Mouffe against Habermas are ones that ground/frame her work (as it does for Žižek and Bhabha; cf. chapters 1 and 4). The view that the symbolic field is constituted by a chain of signifiers, and that the establishment of meaning is an interruption or distortion of it, gives way to two important Mouffean notions — 'antagonism' and 'pluralism'. Antagonisms are the limits that show up through any act of closure or when constituting any totality (e.g. 'meaning', 'discourse', 'objectivity', 'society'). For her, such limits are integral to politics, or put differently, conflict and contestation are the stuff of politics. She writes that 'antagonism is constitutive and irreducible', which is why, according to her, Habermas's attempt to banish it from deliberative democracy 'erases the dimension of the political' (1997: 25; 1999:

745).[11] Thus, for example, the formation of an identity — be it individual or collective — is an act of power requiring an I/you or us/them distinction, therein setting up an adversarial relationship to the other.

'Pluralism' refers to the fact that society is an open and discursive field, giving way to multiple social identities (although, because each social identity is an abbreviation of this discursive field, it is also non-essential, contingent, precarious). For Mouffe, this plurality of the social, this diversity of values and identities, is not just a 'fact'; it is crucial to the 'symbolic ordering of social relations': pluralism is the 'defining feature of modern democracy. . . . It is taken to be constitutive *at the conceptual level* of the very nature of modern democracy' (2000: 18-19, italics in original).

The challenge is instituting a democratic regime that allows for the expression of social plurality. 'Radical democracy', writes Mouffe, 'demands that we acknowledge difference' (1993: 13). However, she does not have in mind here a regime that sanctions unlimited incommensurability or the relativistic play of difference. Rather, she sees social antagonism as giving way to a democratic 'logic of equivalence', as a result of which the mutual contestation between different social groups changes the identity of each of these groups (Laclau & Mouffe 1985: 182-3). A pluralist democracy for her is one in which there is constant struggle and renegotiation of social identity.

Mouffe's 'agonistic pluralism' is the application of this 'logic of equivalence' to social pluralism. When democratic politics transform 'antagonistic' relations between 'enemies' into 'agonistic' relations between 'adversaries', we have 'agonistic pluralism':

> To come to accept the position of the adversary is to undergo a radical change in political identity, it has more of a quality of a conversion than of rational persuasion [*à la* Habermas] . . . compromises are possible; they are part of the process of politics. But they should be seen as tempo-rary respites in an ongoing confrontation . . . . [Hence we] could say that the aim of democratic politics is to transform an 'antagonism' into an 'agonism'.
>
> (Mouffe 1999: 755; cf. 2000: 13, 102-3)[12]

According to her, the lack of closure in politics, the 'ongoing confrontation', is to be seen not in a negative light, but as a marker of the vibrancy and pluralism of democracy.

Although in her more recent writings Mouffe does not go into the specifics of this vision of a pluralist democracy, it is clear from her earlier writings, especially *Hegemony and Socialist Strategy* (co-authored with Ernesto Laclau) (1985), that she is advocating the need for an expansion of democracy into the multiple facets of people's lives (work, home, health, education, culture, sex, etc.). She sees this trend being concretized in the rise of new social movements and their politicization of sociocultural spaces heretofore ignored or excluded by mainstream democratic regimes. The challenge, she believes, is 'the creation of a chain of equivalence among democratic demands found in a variety of groups — women, blacks, workers, gays, lesbians, environmentalists' (1988b: 24; cf. Laclau & Mouffe 1985: 149ff.).

To conclude this section, a brief reflection once again on the above debate and my treatment of it in the remainder of this chapter. As noted earlier, in many ways, the Habermas–Mouffe argument can be seen as a stand-in for the modern–postmodern argument, with Habermas defending reason, legitimacy, justice, universality, and Mouffe antagonism, pluralism, contingency. Habermas's political vision is relatively smooth, believing as he does that social complexity is manageable given legitimating procedures and communicative rationality; whereas Mouffe's is more messy, characterized by ongoing contestation between plural social groups. This is not to say that both theorists share nothing. For instance, as noted at the outset and as the next section will elaborate, they are both concerned about the failures of liberal democracy and finding ways of furthering the democratic revolution. Therefore, I would like in the remainder of the chapter to treat their debate along two parallel dimensions. On the one hand, heeding Habermas, I would like to define a few areas on which the two theorists concur, despite their ontological differences. On the other hand, heeding Mouffe, I would like to treat the areas of disagreement between the two agonally. The idea here is not to champion one theorist over the other, but to preserve and analyze their relative differences so as to bring out the strengths and limits of each.

The relevance of the debate to Third World politics

The two parallel dimensions of the debate will be specified, of course, in relation to Third World politics. Accordingly, in this section we shall begin by developing two shared areas of concern as they relate to Third World politics: (i) a non-prescriptive and critical politics; and (ii) the need to deepen liberal democracy. We shall then consider three areas of disagreement: (i) over questions of difference; (ii) over legitimacy; and (iii) over the adjudication of difference.

Non-prescriptive yet critical democratic politics

Both Mouffe and Habermas put forth a democratic politics that is non-prescriptive but critical. These are important qualities for Third World politics, given the West's history of foisting ideologies and development plans on Third World societies; and given the centralized and sometimes autocratic decision-making of state bureaucracies in many of these countries. Mouffe's democratic politics is open-ended and anti-authoritarian. As mentioned earlier, for her, democracy is by definition pluralist, decentred, and decentralized. It makes politics incumbent on as wide a participation as possible. It is thus inimical to, and critical of, any westernizing/universalizing narratives or top-down and totalizing state policies.

Arturo Escobar's views epitomize this Mouffean critique, applying it to Third World issues. Partly inspired by her work, and relying on many of the same post-structuralist sources that her work draws upon (e.g. Foucault, Derrida), Escobar, as we have already seen, carries out an anti-essentialist critique of the 'discourse of development' (1995). To briefly summarize: he argues that such a discourse, framed in a way that champions Western priorities and interests and excludes non-Western ones, furthers Western dominance over the Third World. And, in a Mouffean vein, he upholds popular/new social movements as a way to counter this authoritarian type of discourse and politics. His arguments (and those of his postdevelopment colleagues) thus bring a radical democratic bent to development issues.

Like Mouffe's, Habermas's democratic vision is open-ended. His proceduralism means that deliberative democracy refrains from limiting the public agenda or imposing blueprints upon it — be they external Western or Third World state-sponsored programmes. Power is thus decentralized. In fact, he is critical of the 'liberal' view of society centred on the state, a state which promotes market economics and embodies the 'ethical community'. His democratic theory envisions a 'decentred society', in which the political system has no centre (1996a: 26-7). As noted earlier, for him, deliberative politics happens in the formal electoral bodies and the state bureaucracy, but also in the multiple formal and informal networks of the public sphere. He entrusts all social sectors, privileging none, to dialogically make up the public agenda.

There is thus an ocean of difference between the radical democratic politics of Habermas and Mouffe and the participation programmes organized by development organizations (as discussed in Chapter 4). The former is about building and extending democracy non-prescriptively and open-endedly, the latter about imposing participation across the North–South and elite–subaltern divide. The former concerns democratic demands/movements that grow out of a particular sociohistorical context, while the latter involves artificially engineering participation from outside, thus resulting in such problems as 'transference' and 'conditionality'.[13] It is for this reason that I concluded Chapter 4 by suggesting the need for participatory development programmes to link up to broader democratic movements in order, at a minimum, to reduce the risks of external complicity and manipulation.

The limits of liberal democracy and the deepening of democracy

To the extent that liberal democracy is firmly implanted in some parts of the Third World, or is taking root in others, Habermas and Mouffe's defence and critique of it are appropriate and relevant (in this sense, the First-Third World distinction does not apply, at least not for the present: their First World democratic theories translate well in Third World contexts). Both of them believe that the democratic gains everywhere have been hard fought and hence must be valorized.

But liberal democratic institutions cannot be taken for granted. As Mouffe states, 'it is always necessary to fortify them and defend them' (2000: 4). Habermas hones in, in particular, on the fact that while such democratic institutions as parliaments are important, they can be weighted down by custom, by unquestioned procedures, and so begin to lose their legitimacy.[14] Often, he argues, governments and electoral bodies assume popular consent after the votes are cast, making important decisions (e.g. market liberalization, privatization, structural adjustment) without adequate accountability, or bowing to the power of elites and the tyranny of the majority. As noted above, moreover, state bureaucracies, while purporting to be public institutions, wield substantial power and resources, but can often dispense these in a top-down and authoritarian fashion without recourse by citizens. Thus, for Habermas and Mouffe, not only do liberal democratic institutions fail to adequately deliver on such liberal goals as participation and freedom, but sometimes they can even foreclose avenues for public contestation and redress.

One way out, as just noted, is the politicization (or the reinvigoration) of public spaces to act as a check and counterweight to state and market power. Both theorists pay particular attention to giving voice to, and overturning the subordination of, minorities and marginalized groups (e.g. 'ethnic'/cultural minorities, women, new immigrants, etc.). Habermas argues for the additional need to democratize the state administration. Opening it up to public participation, scrutiny, and contestation, he believes, is crucial to deepening democracy (1989; cf. Calhoun 1992: 28).

Questions of difference

Turning now to the issues that separate Habermas and Mouffe, there is, first, the question of representing difference/pluralism in democracy. This is the question that tops Mouffe's agenda, and which she believes is Habermas's Achilles heel. Habermas, for his part, acknowledges value pluralism and the need to arrive at outcomes despite difference. His deliberative democracy is intended precisely to allow for plural viewpoints to be heard and adjudicated. Yet, besides Mouffe, others (e.g. Seyla Benhabib, Nancy Fraser, Iris Marion Young)[15] have accused him of erasing difference. The problem, it is alleged, is that the exercise of seeking a single consensus and overcoming ethical/cultural backgrounds can silence and marginalize some community members. We have already encountered this issue in the context of participatory development programmes (cf. Chapter 4). In defining a consensus and transcending tradition, the tendency is to simplify community, to represent it in uni-dimensional ways; this makes the attainment of results easier, but also risks imposing or coercing consensus. And this is exactly Mouffe's counsel, when she argues that a morality-ethics separation and the establishment of any closure de facto entail exclusion. She thus warns Habermas 'against the illusion that a fully achieved democracy could ever be instantiated' (1999: 757).

105

The problem here can be illustrated in different ways and by way of several examples. The first concerns women, who are included in participatory development programmes, but can end up being silenced. Indeed, as does deliberative democracy, these programmes value and privilege public debate and communication. Yet, some sociopolitical environments devalue women's *public* roles, moving them to be passive to men. This is all the more the case when sensitive issues such as rape, violence, or sex are discussed publicly (cf. Mosse 1994: 509-10; Mayoux 1995). The result is that women participants either resort to letting men articulate their concerns or, if they do speak, only provide the 'official' story. This recalls the panoptic dimensions of participation, raised in Chapter 4. As David Mosse points out, relying mainly on evidence from programmes in India, women 'have to clothe their ideas and encode their desires in particular ways to make them heard and accepted as legitimate in the public domain. . . . But often, their particular concerns do not find place in the consensus' (1994: 515).

Similar feminist concerns have been raised by Western democratic theorists (e.g. Fraser 1989, 1992; Benhabib 1996a-b). And similar problems are broached in relation to disadvantaged classes or 'ethnic' and racialized groups, which may lack the sense of 'entitlement' and assertiveness in the public sphere enjoyed by privileged groups. This lacuna may be much greater for those who endure multiple sociocultural disadvantages, (e.g. lower caste and 'tribal' women in India, indigenous and mestizo people in Latin America, etc.) (cf. Young 1996: 123-4; Dhaliwal 1996: 46; Baxi 1987).

Habermas does, of course, have the ideal speech situation and communicative rationality to check against power inequalities and intimidation in the public sphere; but feminists and others doubt that his procedures and rationality *can* level 'the playing field' in a public space, especially under the panoptic gaze or the pressure of seeking consensus. Can these Habermasian measures compensate for people unable (for gender, socioeconomic, or other reasons) to sufficiently voice their opinions? Can they enable people to adequately overcome entrenched taboos and roles and arrive at universally satisfactory decisions? The examples cited above belie Habermas's confidence in procedures and rationality.

In some cases, it is not even desirable to 'transcend' cultural and ethical life. Once again, it is feminists, speaking about both First and Third World women's issues, who point out that privileging the public sphere results in undervaluing the significance of the private sphere (cf. Parpart 2000; Mayoux 1995; Fraser 1989, 1992; Benhabib 1992). This is an important consideration in societies with an unequal gender division of labour: transcendence of the ethical/personal can end up legitimizing women's oppression in the home and prevent the problem from being addressed and resolved in the political/public sphere. Thus, women's inclusion in Habermas's deliberative democracy would be no guarantee of the representation of their concerns in decision-making.

Similar problems can occur in the cultural domain. Habermas's defence of the moral over the ethical realm implies the overcoming of particularities, including one's own cultural background. Yet in countries with cultural minorities, this stance can amount to asking minorities to suppress their language or religion, which may already be under threat from the majoritarian culture. The same is true of the fate of indigenous and Third World cultures in the current global conjuncture. The rapid spread of capitalist values and Western media ('westernization') threatens these cultures, especially minoritarian ones. Under such circumstances, as Fred Dallmayr emphasizes, transcendence and proceduralism may

> conceal [the] cultural hegemony (of the West). In order for transformative learning to occur, agents have to proceed from a distinct position or background. . . . In seeking to promote 'universal' standards, including the principle of universal rights, Western culture paradoxically tends to foster monolingual conformity [e.g. the hegemony of English as a language] that is at variance with rights (or rightness). Precisely under democratic auspices, non-Western societies and people must be able to speak or 'write back' — and they must be able to do so in their native tongue, which invariably is part of their cultural fabric or tradition.
>
> (Dallmayr 1998: 211, 269)

Thus, under conditions of Western hegemony, Habermas's 'impartial' procedures and 'universally-binding' communicative rationality may not be so neutral and universal after all; in fact, they may mask both Western hegemony and non-Western cultural extinction.[16] (Similar problems were highlighted in Chapter 2 with regard to the claims to universalization made by neoclassical economics and human rights policy.)

As a way out of these Habermasian problems (of championing consensus over heterogeneity, public over private, moral over ethical), several critics have suggested 'friendly' amendments to his work (and Habermas appears to have heeded these critics on some issues).[17] Jane Mansbridge, while upholding the deliberative aspects of Habermas's democratic vision, speaks of 'informal deliberative enclaves of resistance in which those who lose in each coercive move can rework their ideas and strategies, gathering their forces and deciding in a more protected space in what way or whether to continue the battle' (1996: 47). Similarly, Nancy Fraser argues for 'subaltern counterpublics', which like Mansbridge's 'informal deliberative enclaves' are multiple deliberative spaces, but are linked deliberatively through lateral alliances and networks (1992: 123-4).

These suggestions appear to avert the problems of having a single consensus and prioritizing the moral over the ethical by not lumping marginalized or disadvantaged groups with everyone else: each group has its own sphere, in which it may decide to scrutinize its cultural/ethical norms if it so wishes, or seek to protect or strengthen them if it deems it necessary. The challenge nonetheless remains deliberatively linking the different spheres: if such linkage is accomplished through compromise, as opposed to consensus, Habermas warns the result may be an implicit or explicit endorsement of inequality. Indeed, 'mere agreement', without support of good arguments and reasons, could mean the exclusion by elites of the very disadvantaged and marginalized groups that Habermas's critics are concerned about in the first place (cf. Habermas 1985: 305). Mansbridge responds by stating that the practice of deliberative democracy must not demand absolute legitimacy, only 'rough' or 'good enough' legitimacy (1996: 54). And Seyla Benhabib adds that a lack of consensus is not necessarily negative; for, it can yield better mutual understanding among participants and the agreement to disagree (1986: 313-15).

Mouffe, it should be pointed out, while not sharing the theoretical underpinnings of these revisionist Habermasians, appears to endorse their proposal for multiple public spaces and toleration of dissensus. She writes, in this regard, that 'pluralist politics should be envisaged as a "mixed-game", that is, in part collaborative and in part conflictual and not as a wholly co-operative game as most liberals would have it' (1999: 756).

The debate over the proposal for multiple public spheres aside, there are practical implications of the proposal for Third World politics. For instance, the idea would be for (national or international) development programmes to refrain from seeking single results in favour of temporary and multiple outcomes. In turn, this would imply multi-pronged programming to meet the needs of plural audiences, rather than uni-dimensional programming that serves some and leaves the rest high and dry. Of course, such proposals are not easily realized. It is beyond the scope of this chapter to examine their practicability in any detail, but the proposals would probably require greater access to already limited resources (human, institutional, environmental) so as to cater simultaneously to multiple publics. In addition, they would necessitate new and democratic institutional forms — coordinated yet plural and flexible institutions that can represent changing and diverse audiences.[18]

Questions of legitimating procedures

The second area of disagreement sees Habermas turning the tables on Mouffe. While Habermas promotes a decentred democratic system and hence decentralized participatory politics, his legitimating procedures and communicative rationality ensure taking a critical and broad perspective of such politics.

Mouffe's agonistic pluralism, while also accentuating local and decentralized democracy, have no legitimating force and breadth of perspective. In fact, Mohan and Stokke argue that her politics have a tendency to 'essentialise and romanticise "the local"' (2000: 249). This 'localism', they point out, stems from her postmodern inclination to celebrate pluralism (especially the activities of marginalized groups), without sufficiently problematizing it (or them).

In Chapter 3, we saw that Escobar has been accused of these same tendencies (cf. Fagan 1999; Kiely 1999; Nederveen Pieterse 1998; Storey 2000). He, too, is said to homogenize and caricature the local by assuming, for example, that social movements are benign and 'progressive', despite evidence showing some can be co-opted by the state and are internally undemocratic. There is also ample evidence, as pointed out in Chapter 4, of development organizations and programmes that have the trappings of a participatory politics, but are manipulated by elites (through intimidation and power politics) at the expense of marginalized groups (cf. White 1996; Mosse 1994; Mayoux 1995).

Mouffe's politics are clearly opposed to such tendencies; as underlined earlier, she stands against the relativistic play of difference.[19] Unfortunately, she does not support her stand: she criticizes Habermas's legitimating procedures on ontological grounds, but has no alternative rule-making system to offer in their place. Instead, she resorts to her democratic 'logic of equivalence': 'But this struggle will not be one between "enemies" but among "adversaries", since all participants will recognize the positions of others in the contest as legitimate ones'; and 'What we need is a hegemony of democratic values, and this requires a multiplication of democratic practices' (2000: 74; 1993: 18). But a lot is unexplained here: Where do her imperative constructions — 'all participants will recognize' and 'we need' — come from? On what are they based? What will compel these groups to act democratically? What will guarantee or impel their legitimacy? In the absence of answers to these questions, it is difficult to interpret Mouffe's 'logic of equivalence' as anything other than voluntarism. She appears satisfied that social movements and protest groups will by themselves discover and practise democratic citizenship, in spite of evidence (noted above) to the contrary. It is no wonder, then, that Habermas insists on legitimating procedures and communicative action. Their absence in Mouffe's agonistic pluralism risks condoning authoritarian behaviour and decisions or practices that are participatory only in name (that is, that reflect 'mere agreement', as opposed to 'rational consensus').

Recall that Habermas insists as well on the institutionalization of legitimating procedures. According to him, the lack of such institutionalization, like the lack of the procedures themselves, may be costly. This argument is confirmed by David Mosse, who shows that when participatory development is informal and without rules, it can raise doubt and mistrust on the part of communities. Mosse points to the suspicion of participation by 'tribal' people in Madhya Pradesh, India, quoting an *adivasi* woman as saying 'today you are sitting on the ground [participating with us], tomorrow [what is to stop you from] sitting on our heads?' (1994: 505).[20] Participation often appears strange and foreign to some communities, and its informality can bolster this impression. More serious though is that the absence of institutionalized procedures in participatory politics may put the onus for legitimacy on the commitment of its practitioners: groups have to come up with the rules themselves (which is what Mouffe's 'voluntarism' implies). But such an eventuality can have gender implications. Feminist commentators have underlined that community women's working days can be very long (relative to men's), preventing them from adequately participating in local politics. Accordingly, the extra time burden implied by an informal and procedureless participatory politics could stretch their days even longer, further aggravating both the gender division of labour and women's participation rates (cf. White 1996).

Thus, the lack of procedures and the absence of their institutionalization can weaken democratic politics. As Habermas points out, the success of deliberative democracy depends 'not on a collectively acting citizenry but on the institutionalization of the corresponding procedures and conditions of communication' (1996a: 27). Such institutionalization allows citizens to deliberate in informal public spheres, or in what Habermas calls 'simple and episodic encounters' (1996b: 361). As a consequence, the formality of legitimating procedures provides deliberative democracy with an informal dimension, reflecting its embeddedness in people's daily encounters and interactions; whereas agonistic pluralism's informality and lack of procedures risks, ironically, making community life overly formal, thus encumbering and interrupting people's daily lives.[21]

Questions of adjudication of difference

A final, related area of disagreement between the two theorists concerns the task of adjudicating between 'differences'. Once again, Habermasian deliberative democracy appears particularly well suited to this task, since the prime functions of communicative rationality are to help obtain an 'enlarged' view, distinguish between differing claims, and decide which claims are 'better'. Foremost in Habermas's mind is the need to be able to differentiate between legitimate/just and illegitimate/unjust claims.

In contrast, and in spite of also being concerned about intolerant and undemocratic practice, Mouffe's politics appear ill-suited to this adjudicative task. Her tendency to value 'localism' prevents taking a broad perspective on politics and, as argued by Mohan and Stokke, risks underestimating wider political economy structures and ignoring their role in the creation of socioeconomic inequality, intolerance, etc. (Mohan & Stokke 2000: 249). Moreover, Mouffe's (postmodern) critique of reason and lack of alternative means of 'transcendence' leaves her with no way of either defending democratic practices or questioning undemocratic ones. As Seyla Benhabib submits, '[h]ow can theorists of agonistic democracy safeguard freedom and justice, respect for human rights of citizens as equal and free beings, if they are unwilling to place constraints that bind, trump, limit, and otherwise confine the will of the sovereign people?' (1996a: 8). Similarly, I ask: What enables Mouffe to critique, say, xenophobia, or adjudicate between, say, a Gandhian and a neoliberal environmentalism?

In fact, Mouffe does provide a response to the second question. She denies that there is any Archimedian point from which to adjudicate which differences (so to speak) make a difference: 'It is always possible to distinguish between the just and the unjust, the legitimate and the illegitimate, but this can only be done from within a given tradition, with the help of standards that tradition provides; in fact there is no point of view external to all traditions from which one can offer a universal judgement' (1988b: 37). However, this (Wittgensteinian) response is of little help when one has to decide between claims hailing from two or more different traditions.

Mouffe's implication is that one cannot do so and, without an adjudicative mechanism, she appears once again to only be able to retreat into a voluntaristic politics: 'certain differences are constructed as relations of subordination and should therefore be challenged by a radical democratic politics' (2000: 20).[22] As was the case earlier, it is difficult to attribute this 'should therefore be challenged' clause to much more than a kind of voluntarism, a voluntarism that is not immanent to her agonistic pluralism, but external to it: an add-on. Benhabib is less kind; she puts Mouffe's taking-democratic-behaviour-for-granted down to circular argumentation: 'antifoundationalist theories of democracy are circular in that they either posit or simply take for granted precisely those moral and political norms of citizens' equality, freedom, and democratic legitimacy for the justification of which what are dubbed "foundationalist" models were developed in the first place' (1996b: 71).

To conclude this section is a brief review of the fault lines in the Habermas–Mouffe debate. We have seen that both theorists share common concerns about liberal democracy and both advocate extending democracy to the multiple spheres of social and political life. However, we have also considered the sharp differences between the two theorists. Applying a Mouffean lens to Habermas exposes his difficulties in democratically representing sociocultural pluralism; whereas applying a Habermasian lens to Mouffe reveals the weaknesses of her democratic politics on questions of legitimacy and adjudication of difference. The primacy that Mouffe gives to pluralism shows up Habermas's depreciation of it in his theory; while the primacy that Habermas gives to legitimacy and justice shows up Mouffe's avoidance of them in hers. Thus, as noted earlier, each theorist brings out the limits of the other. The implication for Third World politics is that endorsing both Mouffe's critique of Habermas and her agonistic pluralism would mean accepting the associated risks and costs of voluntarism and relativism; and on the other side, sanctioning both Habermas's critique of poststructuralism and his deliberative democracy would mean supporting his tendency towards the erasure of difference. That is why engaging with both theorists agonally, rather than championing one or the other, is more fruitful, for it helps tease out the tensions in Third World democratic politics between such issues as consensus and difference, pluralism and justice, or universalism and particularity.

Limits, erasures, gaps

There is one final dimension that requires examination: the extent of the fit between Habermas's and Mouffe's theories and postcolonialism/Third World politics. I have argued that their democratic visions and their debate are compelling and relevant; but I would like now to explore the limits of my own argument. I propose to do so by investigating, first, the extent to which their theories are inappropriate, given their First World origins; second, their theories' neglect of the Third World and Western imperialism; and third, some of the gaps that need closing to make their theories more relevant to postcolonialism and Third World politics.

Inappropriate?

Looking into the question of appropriateness of Western democratic theory for the Third World seems important since, as touched on earlier, anything cross-cultural in the current global conjuncture is suspect for masking Western imperialist designs. This problem may be said to apply less to Mouffe than Habermas. Mouffe's is a decidedly Western-focused theory relying on Western philosophic traditions, but she refrains from championing universalism. As already underlined, her democratic theory is non-prescriptive and open; given the spread of Western liberal democracy, what she has to say about democratic regimes in the West applies equally to democracies elsewhere in the world (it is what she does *not* say that requires some comment; see below).

While I have argued that the same is true of Habermas, some qualifications are necessary (since, in contrast to Mouffe, he *does* prescribe a form of universalism). Fred Dallmayr argues that Habermas tends to have an evolutionary-teleological theory of modernization/rationalization that 'dovetail[s] too neatly with the progressive ascendancy and domination of Western science and technology around the globe' (1996: 165).[23] The implication is that Habermas's use of communicative rationality for deliberative democracy is possible only in 'modern' (presumably Western) societies, which have overcome 'theological/mythological' symbolization. Richard Bernstein and Stephen White disagree with this reading, Bernstein specifically accusing Dallmayr of misconstruing Habermas. For Bernstein, Habermas has been a vigorous critic of positivism throughout his work and has rejected any philosophy of history that stipulates a teleological narrative (1988: 584-5). Similarly, White states that

> Habermas wants his theory of social evolution to identify universal, modern structures of rationality in such a manner that they can be separated from . . . Western modernization which Weber described. His theory thus maintains a critical distance from Western societies in a way which (if the theory stands up) might lessen the suspicion that it is simply promoting conceptual imperialism under the guise of universalism.
>
> (White 1984: 32)

In my view, both readings of Habermas are possible, depending on whether one reads his earlier or later work. His later work is proceduralist and, in spite of the constraints noted in the previous section, is at least conducive to an open and non-prescriptive democracy.[24] Here, as we have seen, Habermas stipulates that only participants in deliberative democracy, no matter where they come from, can decide on the norms of the debate. However, his earlier work is more historical and, although critical of positivism/teleology, locates the development of the public sphere and rationalization in historically-specific Western institutions.[25] White may be right in arguing that Habermas is ultimately drawing out what he believes are universal rational structures, thus distancing communicative reason from 'Western reason'; it remains nonetheless that Habermas's point of reference is Western, not non-Western, history. Had Habermas supplemented his views with historical analyses of non-Western societies, and had his conception of rationalization not so neatly coincided with Western historical development, perhaps doubts about his universalist arguments would be minimized.

The erasure of the Third World and Western imperialism?

Neither Habermas nor Mouffe take the Third World or Western colonialism/imperialism into consideration in their democratic theories. It may be objected that they cannot be expected to cover everything; it is enough that they have analyzed and condemned a range of Western democratic institutions. However, given that both subscribe to a critical and anti-authoritarian politics, it is curious that neither has devoted any space in their sizeable (in the case of Habermas, voluminous) writings to the question of the West's relationship to the Third World.[26] Mouffe's critique of Western liberalism, it seems to me, would be strengthened by highlighting its complicity with colonialism and neocolonialism. Habermas's own critique of modernity would also gain from this type of analysis. Yet, his relative silence on the issue is perplexing.[27] In this regard, Edward Said wonders how the Frankfurt School (to which Habermas purportedly owes allegiance), in spite of its critique of domination in modern Western society, is 'stunningly silent on racist theory, anti-imperialist resistance, and oppositional practice in the empire' (1993: 278). And Said is exasperated that Habermas, when asked in an interview about the importance of anti-imperialist and anti-capitalist struggles to democratic socialism in the advanced capitalist world, declares that he 'would rather pass the question' even though he is 'aware of the fact that this is a eurocentrically limited view' (cf. Habermas 1992b: 183).

It is difficult to interpret this silence on the part of both theorists as anything other than erasure. It is as though, for them, the Third World and colonialism are invisible or are insignificant to the development of Western democratic institutions.[28] Habermas's advocacy of universal justice is thus made more suspect. And Mouffe appears equally incredulous (on this question). She criticizes Habermas's universalism, but the absence in her work of any meaningful treatment of First/Third World issues and Western imperialism can be read precisely as masking a type of universalism: it is as if she is claiming radical democracy can be practised unfettered by the fact that it is constructed on the ruins of Western imperial history.

Gaps

Finally, from the perspective of Third World politics, there are at least three gaps in Habermas's and Mouffe's democratic theory: insufficient attention to materiality, inadequate appreciation of the discursive barriers between elite and subaltern, and the lack of importance given to the state. In what follows, I do not claim to

113

be exhaustive; I propose only to sketch the broad outlines of these three dimensions.

(i) The importance of economic/material conditions

The inadequate emphasis given to the economic dimensions of democratic politics is more a Mouffean than a Habermasian problem. In Mouffe's case, the difficulty stems from the privileged place her work extends to the 'symbolic field'. Although she does not discount labour or economic struggles, her tendency is to valorize 'post-materialist' struggles and, as noted earlier, the need to reconfigure symbolic, ethico-cultural discourses. In the Third World context (some would argue in the First World context as well), her priority is out of kilter with the extent of socioeconomic inequality and the prevalence of inequality-related struggles.

Escobar's work deals with the Third World context, but falls prey to the same Mouffean tendencies. As already highlighted, he champions 'anti-development' resistance and emphasizes the identity/cultural politics of new social movements (1992: 431-2; 1995). But recall that critics say he fails to recognize the diversity of issues among these movements, and that, far from being 'anti-development' or cultural, many are livelihood movements fighting *for* better access to development (Nederveen Pieterse 1998). Jonathan Rigg contends, for example, that in Southeast Asia many groups have 'climbed aboard the modernization bandwagon, whether they be for or against it' (1997: 36). For some groups, development has not necessarily meant exploitation, underdevelopment, or cultural dislocation; in fact, in some cases, it has meant material enablement (better wages, access to education, etc.). Escobar may thus be said to be transposing (Mouffean) radical democratic theory to the Third World too indiscriminately and uncritically. And, as a result, to use Mohan and Stokke's words, his work (and Mouffe's) appears to require 'a more complete analysis of the relations between materiality and identity' (2000: 260).[29]

Although Habermas has tended to be relatively silent on economic issues in his recent work, they feature prominently in the rest of his writings. He is well aware of the need to link materiality to symbolization and that deliberative democracy is meaningless unless there is a modicum of socioeconomic equality among participants. He talks of the need to guarantee basic/positive rights (such as welfare rights) to protect the individual's integrity to speak and communicate (1993: 68-9). In this sense, as Bernstein notes, 'Habermas has never backed away from the Marxist legacy in arguing that a society in which undistorted communication is embodied in everyday life requires a transformation of economic, social, and political institutions' (1988: 587).

The problem, in the Third World context especially, is that such a transformation is easier said than done. Socioeconomic inequalities tend to be much bigger there than in the West. This puts a much greater onus on Habermas's ideal speech situation to level 'the playing field'. The risks that socioeconomic elites will manipulate and impose consensus are heavier and more difficult to minimize. Moreover, as so many disagreements in developing countries centre on (economic or resource) distribution questions, Habermas sets the bar unreasonably high by demanding consensual outcomes, as opposed to compromise. Indeed, when it comes to livelihood and survival issues, participants tend to be very polarized, making it extremely arduous to achieve even compromise. As it happens, Habermas has come to recognize this problem, admitting that distributional conflicts may after all require some give-and-take on both sides.[30]

(ii) Listening to the subaltern

But even if material inequities were to be addressed to some extent, there remains the question of how the Third World subaltern, in particular, can adequately participate. Here, Habermas is much more vulnerable than Mouffe. This is partly because, as Mouffe and others have already underlined, he puts his faith in the possibility of transparency in communication, as though people (whether subaltern or not) can come to an agreement as long as the dialogue between them is undistorted. He fails to adequately appreciate the power relationships that pervade speech-acts and that often show up as slips, unconscious desires, and interpretive or translational blind spots.

Habermas assumes, first, that people *can* speak, as if they can always comprehend and articulate the structures of their own oppression. So often the opposite is the case; and the problem is perhaps most marked for the subaltern, cut off as s/he is from the lines of social mobility. As Spivak reminds us: 'On the other side of the international division of labor, the subject cannot know and speak the text of female exploitation' (1988a: 288). To be sure, verbalizing oppression is a difficult task when power is so complicatedly and abstractly mediated through global socioeconomic and cultural systems.

But Habermas also assumes that, even when the subaltern does speak, s/he can be heard. His notion of intersubjectivity is so wedded to reciprocity, mutuality, and symmetry that he misses Spivak's important argument that communication is often blocked, notably across North–South and elite–subaltern lines. For Spivak, there is not just a class apartheid separating us, privileged classes, from the poor, but a discursive apartheid through which our epistemic systems filter out, deny, or suppress subaltern voices. Thus, even when there is dialogue between us, the subaltern's views are barely intelligible or audible, and our speaking 'to' all too easily slips into our speaking 'for' (Hutchings 2005: 164). Under such conditions, any agreement or consensus is an ideological fantasy.

Mouffe's radical democratic vision is much more attuned to the problems Spivak alerts us to. Questions of power, as we have seen, are front and centre to her critique, as is her sensitivity to issues of discursive mistranslation or communication gaps. She does not, however, tease out the impacts of these gaps on elite-subaltern relationships, or the ethico-political implications for subaltern democratic participation.

We must turn, therefore, to Spivak: if the subaltern is to count, then inclusive and 'transparent' dialogue (Habermas) or chains of equivalence (Mouffe) will not be enough. Attentive listening will also be crucial. For Spivak, as we have seen in Chapter 3, this involves an act of *unreciprocated* 'ethical singularity', which, practically speaking, entails such activities as unlearning elite prejudices to help decolonize one's learning; learning to speak a language of the South, which, while not averting problems of mistranslation, is nonetheless an act of affirmation of, and affiliation with, the subaltern; and a better education in the humanities, which helps train that in-built instrument of othering — our imagination (cf. Spivak 2003b).

In Chapter 3, we have already underlined the limitations of this approach: Spivak has in mind slow, careful, and one-on-one learning and listening, which is difficult to generalize. As before, the big challenge then becomes coming up with institutional forms that are flexible and responsive, capable of cross-cultural translation and much, much better listening.

(iii) The significance of the state and transnational governance

The state plays a crucial role in Third World politics. Unlike in the West, it is (and has been) by far the main source of socioeconomic investment in the developing world. It often intervenes to address inequalities and protect the rights of the subaltern or minorities against private interests and majoritarian power. And it frequently plays an important part in directing and monitoring foreign multinational investment. On the negative side, the state can also be (and has been) an obstacle to democracy, sometimes having a monopoly on power and violence and using it to impose market liberalization, 'ethnic' nationalism, or bureaucratic authoritarianism. Addressing the role of the Third World state is, therefore, important to any democratic theory.

On this issue, Habermas comes out looking better than Mouffe. As already emphasized, both theorists are critical of state bureaucratic/technocratic authoritarianism. However, unlike Mouffe, Habermas devotes a lot of attention to ways of strengthening liberal democracy's civic and political institutions and democratizing its administrative organs so that state power is made more discursive and accountable. While suspicious of state abuse and its manipulation by private and corporate elites, Habermas is a defender of state welfarism. In contrast, Mouffe offers little in terms of a positive role for the state. She advocates decentring politics and fighting state suppression of the popular sectors, but she shies away from proffering specific ways in which the state can be made more responsive. This absence only adds fuel to suspicions about the voluntarism and narrow decentralization implied by her politics.

Habermas also recognizes (unlike Mouffe) the growing importance of transnational governance (cf. Habermas 2001a; 2001b: 58ff.), although he does so from a European point of view. Perhaps, more than ever, this is a burning issue for Third World countries. Its importance is evidenced by continuing Western global hegemony and the loss of national control resulting from a host of occurrences — the extra-territorial powers of multinational corporations, the activities of transnational actors (e.g. NGOs, multilateral and international organizations), the heightened imbrication of issues (e.g. health, environment, agriculture, migration) across the globe, and the increasing commodification of myriad aspects of people's daily lives. More than ever, Western hegemony and the loss of national control in some parts of the world point to a need for transnational democratic governance. This entails the democratization and greater accountability of existing global governance institutions (e.g. the Bretton Woods institutions)[31] and the establishment of new and democratic ones (e.g. a world environmental organization).

In a Habermasian vein, one can therefore make an argument for the enlargement of the public sphere to accommodate for such transnationalism: this would mean, for example, instituting civic participation in the drafting of international rules for, and the monitoring of, multinational corporate investment *and* NGO activities (which, as pointed out earlier, can also be undemocratic, although arguably less so than corporate activities). But, in a Mouffean vein, one would need to quickly warn against the tendency towards the totalization of transnational governance that such a Habermasian enlargement would involve, and against the corresponding risk of excluding pluralism within the global public sphere(s).

Conclusion

What emerges from the above discussion is that while the Habermas–Mouffe debate on radical democracy translates well into the Third World context, there are important differences between First and Third World democracies that constrain any automatic translation. These differences — the extent of socioeconomic inequality, the pivotal position of the state, continuing patterns of subjugation to the West — are what make the First World–Third World distinction necessary. In other words, given the current spread of Western models of democracy throughout the globe, Mouffe's and Habermas's First World democratic theories, despite their open and non-prescriptive qualities, can be projected onto other parts of the world only up to a point.

What emerges as well is that it is necessary not just to introduce these important Third World 'differences' in polite conversation with Habermas's and Mouffe's democratic theories and then identify or bridge the relevant gaps/absences. Rather, I have found it necessary to also *confront* (in as it were an 'agonal hermeneutic' manner) Habermas and Mouffe with these differences so as to unearth the existence of erasures in their work, notably their (complicit) silence on the Third World/subaltern and on Western imperialism/colonialism.[32] To do so is not to devalue the importance and relevance of their work to postcolonialism and Third World politics, but to recognize some limits to it and, perhaps more importantly, to begin the task of writing the Third World into it, opening it up, prodding it to listen to the Third World 'Other'.

7

ACTING IN A TIGHT SPOT
Homi Bhabha's postcolonial politics

Poststructuralism faults modern, emancipatory politics for positing a stable and rational agent that can free itself from necessity/constraint. Pointing to the historical and socio-linguistic webs in which the agent is inescapably caught and positioned, and to the subject's unconscious slips and blind spots, poststructuralism tends to paint the picture of an unstable and not always rational agent. But in eschewing emancipatory politics, an important problem has been poststructuralism's propensity to reduce politics to critique and 'resistance'. The decentring of power, the deconstruction of the subject, tend to provide a weak and limited basis or justification for agency.

Bhabha's work on postcolonial agency, as we have briefly touched upon in Chapter 1, averts many of these problems, even as it relies on poststructuralism. It foregrounds discursive colonial authority and subjection, yet retrieves subaltern subterfuge. It reconstructs a critical politics despite and *because* of hegemonic and orientalist representational systems. And it demonstrates the (im)possibility of a stable, sovereign subject — thus problematizing the subject, at least in the Enlightenment sense of the term — but still manages to assert creative and performative agency.

In this chapter, I shall analyze these feats and paradoxes, relying both on Bhabha's writing and on a number of criticisms and controversies surrounding it.[1] The latter will help identify the strengths of his notion of agency — especially its movement beyond resistance towards creativity — but also some of its limits and vulnerabilities — in particular its privileging of semiotics over materiality, and its relatively localized politics.

Hybridity and agency

Applying the Lacanian notion of 'lack' and the Derridean idea of *différance* to the colonial context, Bhabha shows how colonial authority is hybrid (1995a: 114). As noted in Chapter 1, while colonial power presents itself as muscular and incontrovertible, it simultaneously betrays its instabilities, fractures, or contradictions. Thus, racist stereotypes such as 'the lying Indian' or 'the lazy African', which Bhabha sees as part of the cultural armoury of colonial authority, need to appear fixed to be taken as 'true'. Yet, they are often ambivalent (e.g. Indians are also constructed as 'wily', and Africans as hyperactively 'sexual') and have to be constantly repeated and confirmed (to become stereotypic*al*), thus betraying an anxiety that their appeal may unravel at any instant. This repetition and doubling, these psychic fears and insecurities, expose the instability and lack within colonial power. And the crux of Bhabha's reasoning is that such undecidability is grounds for agency: for, the native or subaltern can attempt to 'disarticulate the voice of authority at the point of splitting' (1995a: 82). The ruptures in discursive power become windows of opportunity.

To illustrate the argument, Chapter 1 referred to the colonial creation of 'mimic men' (whose unintended consequence is mockery) and the Women Against Fundamentalism (who use the Rushdie affair to call public attention to women's issues). I want, however, to mention a couple of other important Bhabhaian instances of agency. In one, the British view the 'quaint' act of villagers passing a *chapati* (flat bread) from hand to hand as a warning signal of the impending 1857 'Indian Mutiny'. But the story is subsequently transformed by the villagers from whisper into exaggerated and uncontrollable rumour, to the point of panic within the British ranks: 'The iterative action of rumour, its *circulation* and *contagion*, links it with panic — as one of the *affects* of insurgency' (Bhabha 1994: 200, italics in original).

Probably the most famous Bhabhaian instance of 'spectacular resistance' (1994: 121)[2] though is to be found in the essay entitled 'Signs taken for wonders'. Relying on missionary records of the early nineteenth century, the essay discloses how an Indian catechist's bid to convert a group of villagers outside Delhi is subverted: the villagers refuse the sacrament and resist conversion on the grounds that the word of God comes from the mouth of a meat-eater, not a vegetarian. As Bhabha explains, 'When the natives demand an Indianized Gospel [or a 'vegetarian Bible'!], they are using the powers of hybridity to resist baptism and to put the project of conversion in an impossible position' (1994: 118). They contaminate the dominant discourse with their own suppressed knowledge (i.e. vegetarianism), and in so doing undermine colonial authority. In this sense, as Bhabha emphasizes, the episode is not just 'an exchange between a muscular colonial Christianity that was keen to convert and an indigenous tradition that resisted conversion' but a 'colonial antagonism' that produces a 'supplementary' or 'incommensurable' discourse as a site of 'resistance and negotiation' (1995a: 114).

Agency with subjection

I want to reflect upon, and tease out several implications of, an important argument in Bhabha's thinking — that agency is possible only with subjection. The idea here is that we do not act under conditions of our own choosing; we act *within* a given discursive context. Speaking of agency as a kind of 'translation', Bhabha says that 'there must be a text for it to be translated. It may be a priority that is internally liminal or displaced, but there is something there that endows a particular kind of authorization and authentication' (1995a: 83). There is no question of effecting change from somewhere 'outside the text' (to echo Derrida); agency can happen no matter whether the given text is interdictive, repressive, stereotypical, or orientalist. All of Bhabha's instances of agency arise precisely from the challenge of imperial authority, each instance a specific response, but also an impediment, to such authority. Hence, without discursive subjection, no agency is possible. Or, to quote Judith Butler, to whose work Bhabha sometimes refers (more on this point later): 'There is only a taking up of the tools where they lie, where the very "taking up" is enabled by the tool lying there' (1990: 145).[3]

Key to the notion of acting only with(in) a given discursive terrain is the idea of repetition. It is Derrida who points out that all utterances (or 'speech acts') are repetitions (or 'citational doubling'), so that when one articulates, one is actually re-articulating (1982: 307ff.). Each iteration is never the same, moreover, because it is always marked by *différance* (contained in the very structure of language). This means that discourse is always already iterative, and each discursive iteration is differently articulated in different contexts. Bhabha says as much when he writes: 'To recognize the *différance* of the colonial presence is to realize that the colonial text occupies that space of double inscription, hallowed — no, hollowed — by Jacques Derrida' (1994: 108). The implication for politics is that agency is precisely the performance, the acting out, of this repetition. So it is not by accident that Bhabha refers to 'mimicry' as a strategy of *both* colonial subjection and subterfuge.[4] 'The *menace* of mimicry', he writes, 'is its *double* vision which in disclosing the ambivalence of colonial discourse also disrupts its authority' (1994: 88). Thus, the idea of 'repetition' is a re-statement of the idea of 'discursive instability', which, as discussed earlier and as Bhabha just confirms, creates the opportunity for postcolonial agency. From the perspective of politics though, the notion of 'repetition' adds to the earlier notion of 'discursive instability' the important point that agency is restricted to only those openings and opportunities presented by discursive subjection.

But if discourse is always already repetition, and agency is the acting out of such repetition, then what difference does agency make?[5] In other words, what is agency's particular distinction? I think at least two such distinctions can be found in Bhabha's work. The first is agency's role precisely in exposing repetition, its 'staging' of the ambivalence and contingency of authority. Bhabha calls this 'desacraliz[ing] the transparent assumptions of cultural supremacy', 'introduc[ing] a lack' or 'exposing the limits of any claim to a singular or autonomous sign of difference — be it class, gender or race' (1994: 228, 119, 219). When the villagers transfigure the quaint and stereotypical *chapati* story into uncontrollable rumour (through repetition), they are revealing the fear upon which their master's authority is founded but is attempting to hide, pushing this fear to the point of panic; they are disarticulating and de-naturalizing the story or stereotype by exaggerating it to its absurd limits.

Critics such as Robert Young (1995) and Brett Nicholls (1997) appear to neglect this important feature of Bhabha's politics when they argue that his notion of agency can be easily co-opted by the hegemonic power. Nicholls, for example, complains that the 'problematics of communication — the slippage of signs — is a general condition that "is no respecter of persons", slaves or masters. Moreover, if this is the case it is difficult to see how this problematic benefits the native yet at the same time thwarts the process of domination' (1997: 19). Bhabha would agree that repetition or discursive instability is 'no respecter of persons' for, as just noted, iteration is part and parcel of both dominant discourse and subaltern agency. The crucial difference, however, is that subaltern agency is about exposing the doubling and constructedness of discourse/power, while domination, to *be* domination, is about fixing or hiding them. (It is difficult to see how prejudice, for example, can maintain itself if its artifice and contingency are exposed, no matter who does the exposing.)

Agency's second distinction is that, while 'repeating the lessons of the masters', it 'changes their inflections' (Bhabha 1995b: 54). Bhabhaian politics are a kind of variation on a (discursive) theme: mimicry is not just returned, it is returned as mockery; colonial Christianity is not just reappropriated and reinterpreted, it is misappropriated, misinterpreted, mistranslated, estranged. Often, as the 'Delhi villagers' example shows, politics involves only minor tinkering. Bhabha speaks of 'small differences' and 'slight alterations and displacements' as 'often the most significant elements in a process of subversion or transformation' (1995b: 82).[6] These alterations are 'most significant' because they produce supplemental positions: the villagers' 'vegetarian Bible' is not simply a new variation, it is an incommensurable position, an irresolvable riddle that flummoxes colonial authority. Bhabha calls this a 'Third Space' (1994: 37), that is, a position that is made possible by discursive subjection, but cannot be directly derived from it. It is a non-dialectical space standing in-between the binary structures of orientalist representations and imperial power. In this sense, agency's 'difference' is about negotiating 'polarizations without acceding to their foundational claims' (1995a: 83), 'both challenging the boundaries of discourse and subtly changing its terms' (1994: 119).

I think it is important to note that by retrieving these creative possibilities in agency, Bhabha is innovating Foucauldian politics. To Foucault's 'there are no relations of power without resistance' (1980: 142), Bhabha appears to be responding with 'there are no relations of power without agency'. This slight inflection — true to Bhabhaian style — provides a significant positive dimension to Foucauldian politics, making it more than just the 'effect' of discourse. For Bhabha, as for Foucault, power is productive, but whereas for the latter the political response to subjection is a negative and restricted 'resistance', for the former, the response is a more positive and creative agency. Not surprisingly, Bhabha states that power is about '*incitement* and interdiction' (1994: 72, italics mine), 'making possible *and making trouble*, both at once' (1995a: 110, italics mine). The 'mimic men' and the Women Against Fundamentalism are not only resisting, they are also engaging in subterfuge and mis-recognition that produce a Third Space.

Implications for 'native' representation and historiography

The notion that agency happens only within discourse is a conundrum for identity politics, since it implies that the identity you call upon for agency is restricted to an imposed script: you can construct it exclusively from the signification system of the colonizer or hegemon. This is a difficult position to defend in the face of many nationalist[7] or decolonization movements, which aim at mitigating the native's estrangement from her/his own culture by recovering a 'pure' or 'indigenous' history and regaining a sense of national pride. But like Fanon and Spivak, from whom he often draws on this question (e.g. Bhabha 1994: 40ff., 183-4), Bhabha is critical of these types of attempts. He argues that the nationalist, the politician, and the cultural critic alike can neither extricate themselves from their position in post-colonial history, nor resort to a language uncontaminated by Orientalism or imperialism: they have no 'immediate access to an originary identity or a "received" tradition' (1994: 2).

This argument about the (im)possibility of a 'nativist' position is controversial for some historiographers (O'Hanlon & Washbrook 1992; Vaughan 1994; Thomas 1994). These critics question the extent to which postcolonial theorists such as Bhabha can maintain that native identity is tied to colonial discourse. Nicholas Thomas, for example, declares that Bhabha 'excludes the possibility that "natives" often had relatively autonomous representations and agendas, that might have been deaf to the enunciations of colonialism, or not so captive to them that mimicry seemed a necessary capitulation' (1994: 57; cf. Comaroff & Comaroff 1991). He concludes that Bhabha's position ends up 'diminish[ing] or deny[ing] difference' (1994: 51). Similarly, O'Hanlon and Washbrook invoke Jameson and Huyssen to argue for a 'labour of remembrance', a historical understanding that allows agents to 'orient themselves' (1992: 153; cf. Vaughan 1994: 5). Summarizing these arguments, Meagan Vaughan writes that 'colonial discourse theory completely neglects and negates the pre-colonial' (1994: 7).

Although Bhabha does not directly respond to these criticisms, it is possible to draw out answers from his work. To start, there is an important passage to consider in *The Location of Culture*:

> [T]he text of transparency inscribes a double vision: the field of the 'true' emerges as a visible sign of authority only after the regulatory and displacing division of the true and the false. From this point of view, discursive 'transparency' is best read in the photographic sense in which a transparency is also always a negative, processed into visibility through the technologies of reversal, enlargement, lighting, editing, projection, not a source but a re-source of light. Such a bringing to light

is a question of the provision of visibility as a capacity, a strategy, an agency.

(Bhabha 1994: 110)

Colonial discourse is thus a kind of 'negative transparency' through which identity and agency are constructed. To wit: the Delhi villagers assert a 'native' identity (e.g. vegetarianism) but only through the imposed transparency of colonial Christianity. Far from neglecting or ignoring the pre-colonial, then, Bhabha is validating or 'tracing' it (in the Derridean sense); his idea of agency is decidedly about the possibility of suppressed knowledges coming to the fore, but only within — or more accurately, between — the contours of hegemonic representations. The native *can* and *does* have a degree of autonomy and a labour of remembrance, but only in the liminal spaces opened up from inside the dominant discourse.

The historiographers affirm the 'relative autonomy' of identity and remembrance vis-à-vis the hegemonic discourse, but in so doing they appear not to be taking 'hegemony' seriously enough. The encounter between colonizer and colonized is not one of equals; it is not a contest of multiple discourses on a 'level playing field' (so to speak). Indigenous identity *must* be mediated through colonial representational systems *because* the latter are dominant. Of course, for Bhabha the latter are not fully dominant, and it is because they aren't that agency is possible: 'agency requires a grounding', he writes, 'but it does not require a totalization of those grounds' (1994: 185). Moreover, native identity or remembrance cannot avoid, or be 'deaf to', hegemonic discourse. After all, it is when the hegemon flexes his muscle that a response is needed. As Bhabha says, power forces you to 'put yourself elsewhere', or 'be pushed into another space or time from which to revise or review the problem' (1995a: 83). Thus, it is precisely when the native is faced with a challenge that s/he must construct and assert her/his memory or identity; and, perforce, s/he can do so only in relation to, and in *the* terms of, the hegemonic discourse.

Implications for politics

I would like now to draw out three of the specifically political implications of tying agency to discursive subjection. The first is Bhabha's implied note of caution to those whose response to subjection is direct opposition. He warns that overcoming domination, far from getting rid of it, often occasions its mere reversal (1995b: 55). The ensuing message to revolutionaries (Marxist or otherwise), for example, is that a violent counter-force to imperialism is likely to result in the perpetuation of violence and the replacement of one domination by another. The message to nationalists (like those mentioned earlier) is that harkening back to a 'pure' native identity or 'true' national history yields a reverse ethnocentrism or racism; it buys into and reproduces in another form the very oppressor's binary structure of signification (us/them, White/Black, civilized/uncivilized) that it is trying to avert (recall that the same argument was applied to the human rights 'cultural relativist' position in Chapter 2). Bhabha endorses the views of Fanon, whom he believes is cognizant of the need for a national culture, but is 'far too aware of the dangers of the fixity and fetishism of identities within the calcification of colonial cultures to recommend that "roots" be struck in the celebratory romance of the past or by homogenizing the history of the present' (1994: 9; cf. 152-3, 157). Given, then, that the eradication of one disciplinarity produces another, and granted the hazards of direct opposition to power (supposedly) 'from without', it is not surprising to find Bhabha advocating an agency that displaces, interrupts, and estranges power only from within.

A second implication, following especially from the notion of agency as a form of repetition, is that Bhabha does away with a 'pro-active' conception of politics. He does away with it, that is, at least in the Enlightenment sense of positing a sovereign or calculating agent who can plan ahead autonomously and *ex nihilo*. For Bhabha, politics cannot happen 'ahead', as it is always already an 'after', an iteration of the discourse that has both preceded it and made it possible. Bhabha is merely reinforcing here the poststructuralist critique of any illusion of politics as a 'total break', of action taking place in a vacuum.

A final implication, which Bhabha emphasizes often, is that agency is a form of 'negotiation' (1994: 25, 38, 185, 191). That action happens iteratively and within the hegemonic discursive field means there is a degree of mutuality and complicity between the agent and the hegemon, even if each may want to deny it. The agent must play with the cards s/he is dealt, and the hegemon, despite the appearance of absolute strength, needs or desires the subaltern.[8]

What is compelling about Bhabha's argument here is the idea that, in the semiotic/discursive realm, the oppressed can act subversively in spite of the master's dominance. The negotiative aspect of the encounter, even in the face of unfavourable odds, is what allows for subaltern agency. Hence Bhabha notes 'Forms of popular rebellion and mobilization are often *most* subversive and transgressive when they are created through . . . *cultural* practices' (1994: 20, italics mine). The problem, however, is that he does not support this claim. As I have argued in Chapter 1, to say that cultural practices are 'most subversive' — presumably relative to material ones — he would need to supply a comparative political economy analysis. Not only does he not do so, he tends to omit the material realm in his analysis of agency. His instances of agency are restricted to semiotic transactions (i.e. resistance to imitation, stereotypes, religious conversion), for the most part disregarding material ones (e.g. anti-capitalist subversion, protests against unequal pay or inhuman working conditions). Even in his analysis of semiotic transactions, he makes no mention of the differential socioeconomic positioning of his interlocutors, ignoring how the power inequality between them may affect their negotiating abilities.

It seems to me that Bhabha's argument is not necessarily undermined by this neglect, since even social/material status must be semiotically represented in any political encounter, thus being subject to discursive instabilities and subterfuge.

But as Benita Parry points out, what is missing is an analysis of the relationship between materiality and agency and the limits material inequality impose on subaltern 'negotiation' (1996: 21). For example, will the hegemon's threat of economic retaliation, or the subaltern's *relative* lack of access to education or health, not weaken to some extent the latter's ability to engage in semiotic subterfuge? Unfortunately, as I have underlined in Chapter 1, Bhabha leaves these types of questions unanswered. He also says little about the negotiative possibilities *among* colonized subjects. In the Delhi incident, for example, the villagers' action could be read as privileged, since vegetarianism in many parts of India is often practised by the dominant castes (some lower castes and many non-Hindus, especially the minority Muslim communities, are meat-eating). As Bhabha neither provides us with a social context nor takes it into account in his theorizing on the incident, it is impossible to tell whether such political action is reserved for colonized elites or open to all colonized subjects/subalterns, or indeed whether or not the former are likely to be more effective than the latter in semiotic challenges to the colonizer.

Agency without a subject?

Several critics have taken Bhabha to task for making agency impersonal, involuntary, and robotic (Young, R. 1990: 152; Moore-Gilbert 1997: 130ff.; Parry 1996: 16ff.). They suggest, in fact, that he 'vacillates', at times positing a 'transitive' and at others an 'intransitive' mode of agency. Certainly, Bhabha's use of terms such as 'indeterminacy' and 'deliberate' (1994: 205, 209) when referring to subaltern politics can leave one with this impression. Hence Moore-Gilbert *et al*. state that he 'fudges the question of whether the kinds of "active" resistance he outlines are actually (self)conscious or not, so that it remains unclear whether the agency of the colonized/postcolonial subject can be consciously purposive and programmatic' (1997: 38). Moreover, Robert Young (1990: 152) and Benita Parry (1996: 15) wonder why Bhabha's subject, in the absence of self-consciousness, would want to act, and on the basis of what normative or moral horizon s/he would be moved to act.[9] Young asks: 'what political status can be accorded the subversive strategies that Bhabha articulates?' (1990: 152). Thus, if we are to take these critics at their word, not only is Bhabha's notion of agency possible despite or because of subjection, but it also takes place without a definable grounding or subject.

I would like to suggest that, indeed, these critics are right, but they miss the *performative* dimension of Bhabha's position. They appear to be in search of what may be called an 'expressive' agency (Butler 1990: 141; cf. Honig 1992; Kulynych 1997: 321), one that reveals an ontological subject with intentions, morals, and consciousness, as opposed to a 'performative' agency, in which these subjective qualities are 'acted out' by the agent, not given cut-and-dried before hand. Judith Butler and Hannah Arendt are the main proponents of this notion of performativity, and it is helpful to consider briefly what they have to say about it before returning to Bhabha.

Butler speaks of the gendered body as performative, in the sense of a 'forced reiteration of norms' (1993: 94; cf. 225). Invoking the concept of 'repetition' (which, as mentioned earlier, Bhabha also invokes), she shows how gender is a socially imposed or discursive code that is responded to and performed. Drawing on drag, she also shows how performative agency includes (although is not to be equated with) perform*ance*, in this case a parody of the idea of a 'fixed' or 'original' female or male identity (1990: 138).[10] Her overall point though is that, in acting, the subject 'has no ontological status apart from the various acts which constitute its reality' (1990: 136). Like the stage actor performing a scripted role, the agent is subjectivized in the very performance of the (socially interpellated) act.

While Arendt does not, of course, share the same intellectual horizons as Butler (Arendt's performativity is indebted, in particular, to Greek/Aristotelian political thought, Butler's to Foucauldian and Derridian thought through discursivity and speech-act theory), Arendt puts forth a similar conception of the subject/agent. For her, agency and subjectivity are only palpable in the public realm. The self is multiple and fragmented — a private self, labouring to meet survival needs, working to provide for life's luxuries, carrying out innocuous conversations with itself — before it enters the public arena; but it coheres once it engages in public performance and debate, that is, once it transforms itself from individual into citizen (Arendt 1958a: 7-9, 175-81; cf. Honig 1992: 219). According to Arendt, to act in public is of prime importance: it is 'to begin' (1958a: 177), to start the process of forming an identity and a persona. As Bonnie Honig writes, 'There is no "being" behind this [Arendtian] doing. The doing, the performance, is everything' (1992: 217).

Bhabha has many affinities with both Butler and Arendt. He refers to their work several times (1994: 188-90, 219; 1995a: 110), and especially to Arendt on the relationship between subjectivity and agency. His writing is strewn with the words 'performance' or the 'performative', speaking for example about the 'postcolonial performance of repetition' (1995b: 52) or the 'performative nature of differential identities' (1994: 219). But it is in 'DissemiNation' that he elaborates what he means. In the essay, he distinguishes between the 'pedagogical' and the 'performative', the former denoting the nation's narrative authority 'signifying the people as an a priori historical presence, a pedagogical object', and the latter the 'people constructed in the performance of a narrative, its enunciatory "present" marked in the repetition and pulsation of the national sign' (1994: 147). The distinction is similar to the one we broached earlier between the iterative, hegemonic discourse that attempts to fix subaltern identity, and (performative) agency that acts out the discourse but exposes its doubling and contingency. The important point for our present purposes though is that, like Butler and Arendt, Bhabha conceives of the subject as being performed in the 'enunciatory present marked in the repetition'. As emphasized in Chapter 5, the people-as-subject, for him, only emerge out of the nation when they act as political agents, parading the heterogeneity and ambivalence (as opposed to the static 'pedagogical object') that is the nation.

As is the case with Butler and Arendt, there is an unmistakable theatricality attendant in Bhabha's performativity. He refers to the agency of the Delhi villagers as 'spectacular resistance' (as noted earlier), and in other instances directs our attention to a *'spectatorial distance'* or how 'the contingency of the subject as agent is articulated in a double dimension, a dramatic action' (1994: 244, 186). Frequently, his notion of agency is both a 'show' and a 'showing up' (Kulynych 1997: 323), as witnessed by the mischief-making, 'messing around', and meddling in which his agents engage. The comedic and parodic elements of his narrative help demonstrate to the audience — and draws them into — the agent's campaign to scrutinize, mock, and/or interrupt the hegemonic discourse. Like all (political) theatre, the comedic is mixed in with the dramatic: as Arendt underlines (1958a: 180, 191) and Bhabha rehearses (1994: 12-13), a performance is always risky and unpredictable, with the protagonists never sure of the impact of their words and actions — 'will I succeed?', 'will s/he respond?', 'will the audience care?'. Thus, the native and British circulation of the *chapati* story has no control over how, or even if, the story turns into rumour or panic. What such unpredictability reveals once again though, as Jessica Kulynych points out, is 'the contingency of both subjectivity and subjection' (1997: 324).

We are now in a position to better answer Bhabha's critics: his alleged vacillation over whether agency is transitive or intransitive is to be understood in the context of performativity. For Bhabha, the subject is interpellated in action: there is no subject before or after but only *when* s/he becomes an agent. It is no wonder, then, that on the very pages that he is accused of wavering between 'indeterminate' and 'deliberate' agency, he repeatedly refers to the 'performative' (compare 1994: 200, 202, 204, 209). The critics are in search of a *pre*-formed rather than a *per*formed subject; they seek either a transitive or intransitive subject, but miss that s/he is always already *in transit*. The existence of an onto-logical subject is an illusion[11] which performative agency helps expose and disrupt. Implicit here again is Bhabha's critique of the modern conception of a sovereign and transcendent politics: 'Despite all the talk about fragmented subjects, floating signifiers, structural totalities, and post-Modern "space"', he says, 'there is an interesting paradoxical return to traditional articulations of consciousness-intention-action' (1995b: 118). Moreover, when the critics ask about the normative basis of Bhabhaian agency, they appear to have in mind an oppositional or argumentative politics, in which the subject expresses an already formed 'ethics' or imports it from 'outside', something which we have already noted Bhabha is trying to resist. Kulynych explains and summarizes it well:

[T]he performative protestor does not argue against the state, he mocks it. The protestor works at the margins of the discourse, utilizing puns and jokes and caricature to 'expose' the limits of what is being said. Thus, performative resistance, when considered as critique, does not need to tell us what is wrong, rather it reveals the existence of subjection where we had not previously seen it. . . . [P]erformativity is not about normative distinctions. We bring normativity to our performances as ethical principles that are themselves subject to resistance. By unearthing the contingency of the 'self-evident', performative resistance enables politics. Thus, the question is not should we resist (since resistance is always, already present), but rather what and how we should resist.

(Kulynych 1997: 323)

Of course, Bhabha's performativity does more than 'resist'. It produces a Third Space. In this, it must be mentioned, he appears to push performativity further than Butler (or Kulynych). Although he shares much with Butler[12] (more perhaps than with Arendt, who does not have a notion of discursivity), his postcolonial lens helps him open up the creative possibilities of a performative agency. Several analysts (cf. Benhabib 1995; Fraser 2002; Lloyd 2002; McNay 1999, 2000) have warned against the Butlerian tendency to view agency mainly as a negative and constrained act of resignification. The reason, according to them, is that Butler too narrowly conceives of the symbolic sphere, restricting her analysis principally to gender identity and representations of sexuality. According to Lois McNay, Butler thus 'fails to draw out fully . . . the ways in which the symbolic realm is composed of conflicting values and resources which may be actively, and sometimes creatively, appropriated by actors to institute new value systems and new forms of collective identity' (1999: 187). As the previous sections in this chapter have underlined, Bhabha does precisely what critics like McNay say Butler should — he conceives of discursive instability in such a way that it becomes possible for agents not only to re-cast the hegemonic discourse (e.g. mimicry/mockery) but to estrange it in multifarious ways by retrieving from within it suppressed and 'foreign' meanings that yield supplemental representations (e.g. the vegetarian Bible).

Agonisitic difference

Bhabha's conception of politics as performative allows him to do a number of things, one of which is to valorize heterogeneity. *Différance*, as we have seen, is integral to the very hybridity and iterability of discourse, and agency's role is to help reveal it. Like Arendt, who sees the public arena as both thriving on difference and holding it together agonistically (1958a: 57, 176), Bhabha aims at an agonistic cultural pluralism, that is, a (Third) space that preserves 'the enunciative boundaries of a range of other dissonant, even dissident histories and voices — women, the colonized, minority groups, the bearers of policed sexualities' (1994: 5). This objective is particularly important to him (and to postcolonialism), given imperialism's past and continuing attempts to suppress heterogeneity in the name of 'modernity', 'civilization', 'development', or 'revolution'. The creation of an agonistic Third Space is not about trying to sublate or transcend imperialism (i.e. it is not a 'third term' or synthesis); it is a non-dialectical location created in the interstices of imperialism, where the 'stubborn chunks' and the 'incommensurable' and 'untranslatable' elements are articulated (1994: 219, 227).

One of the notable ways in which Bhabha marks *différance*, as briefly touched on in Chapter 1, is by deploying the notion of the 'time-lag'. Partly, he is making us critically aware here of the temporal disjunctures within modernity, so that, for example, at the same time that nineteenth-century Britain was laying the groundwork for democracy and citizenship at home, it was engaging in economic exploitation, authoritarianism, and human rights abuse in its colonies (something similar may be said of the current neocolonial relationships between the First and Third Worlds). And partly, Bhabha is attempting to deconstruct teleological time, so that Western modernity[13] does not pose as History, and non-Western 'tradition(s)' are encountered on their own terms and time(s). Always reading the world in binary terms (First/Third World, developed/underdeveloped), ignores the existence of Third Worlds in the First (e.g. the colonial conditions of current North American native communities, the existence of substantial non-European migrant communities in Europe, significant regional economic disparities within Western countries) and First Worlds in the Third (e.g. 'global' and cosmopolitan cities in the South, the development of cutting-edge technologies in India, the availability of universal health care in Cuba). It also ignores the different temporalities of decolonization: for instance, the fact that Latin America has experienced a longer period of formal independence compared to Africa.

'Time-lag' thus acts as a kind of critique of the universalization of Euro-North American cultural priorities, as well as a validation of those political attempts to articulate differential and post-orientalist knowledges. Let me quote Bhabha here:

> The power of the postcolonial translation of modernity rests in its *performative, deformative* structure that does not simply revalue the contents of a cultural tradition, or transpose values 'cross culturally'. The cultural inheritance of slavery or colonialism is brought *before* modernity *not* to resolve its historic differences into a new totality, nor to forego its traditions. It is to introduce another locus of inscription and intervention, another hybrid, 'inappropriate' enunciative site, through temporal split — or time-lag — that I have opened up . . . for the signification of postcolonial agency.
>
> (Bhabha 1994: 241-2, italics in original)

Democratizing politics

Following Foucault, Bhabha's examination of the strategies of power leads him to identify them not just at macro/global levels (in the form of imperialism or Orientalism), but most especially at local levels. He sees the techniques and strategies of power at work in the far-flung corners of the globe. But on the other side of power's sweeping reach lie multiple local responses and acts of resistance — which is what his notion of performative politics aims at recognizing. Kulynych notes that performativity is not 'intentional, rational, and planned; it may be accidental, impulsive, and spontaneous' (1997: 325). Indeed, for Bhabha it is: his instances of agency capture people's everyday encounters with, and challenges to, power. Most often, the acts happen in spaces hidden from view, spaces that would usually be considered 'marginal', 'vulgar', or 'banal'. Most often, too, the acts are performed by the subaltern, the displaced, marginals, minorities. For Bhabha, it is they who are (and have been) at the forefront of cultural struggles, since it is they who must act to survive and 'negotiate' between past and present, East and West. He writes that their struggles and histories 'speak of the reality of survival and negotiation that constitutes the lived moment of resistance, its sorrow and its salvation — the moment that is rarely spoken in the stories of heroism that are enshrined in the histories we choose to remember and recount' (1995b: 60; cf. 1994: 172).

Bhabha's performative politics are thus an implied critique of the 'grand politics' carried out by, and viewed from the perspective of, elites and the state. His is an attempt[14] to democratize politics. In part, the goal is to widen the political terrain by capturing the myriad and daily forms of subjection, as well as the concomitant, 'ordinary' acts of resistance. And, in part, the goal is to 'lower the sites' of politics, showing the 'ordinary' to be extraordinary — nay, 'spectacular' — as it reveals hegemonic or imperial power to be fractured and not as effective and totalizing as all that.

But what Bhabha leaves unclear is the extent to which localized agency can and does bring about meaningful change at the macro-levels of power (this is a problem he shares with the poststructuralist politics of Foucault, Mouffe, and Escobar, as this and previous chapters have mentioned). Although his work makes visible global or national power in the local, it is difficult to see how local agency, in turn, affects broader structures. His everyday and relatively informal and unorganized politics, coupled with his critique and comparative neglect of the nation-state and formal transnational structures, offer nothing in the way of coordinating mechanisms needed for sustained political transformation. Localized resistance may be multiple and widespread, but this does not necessarily translate into expansive change in hegemonic structures, or if it does then Bhabha does not demonstrate how. At a time of rapidly advancing and changing socioeconomic globalization, the need for such coordinated political responses (whether through coalitional politics, community networking, or intersubjective deliberation) appears ever more pressing. I am not saying that Bhabha's performative politics are not amenable to a more complex politics, only that they appear incomplete in this respect (which the next chapter will attempt to address). In fact, as Kulynych argues, they are not only amenable to, but can throw new light on, mainstream politics: performativity is 'important not only for understanding the potential for innovation in the micro-politics of identity, but also for understanding the potential for innovation in an inter-subjective politics of deliberation. . . . Performative resistance is evident in intimate and personal relationships, in the deliberations of civil society, and in the problem-solving institutions of the constitutional state' (1997: 324, 327).

Conclusion: an innovative and radical politics

Meagan Vaughan declares that 'To be "discursively formulated" seems bad enough, but to be unstably discursively formulated looks like an impossible position from which to act' (1994: 5). It *does* look like an impossible position, and yet, as I have tried to show, Bhabha manages to negotiate it (for the most part). In many ways, his politics are captured by the two moments implied in Vaughan's remark: (i) an unstable discursive subjection which produces fractured identities and representations; and (ii) the interpellation of a subject-as-agent who not only resists or responds to subjection but also exploits its discursive instabilities in favour of a supplemental, Third Space. Bhabha's gloss is innovative for showing that, despite being hegemonic, discourse's power precludes neither resistance/agency nor the (critical) retrieval of indigenous representations. In this sense, his postcolonial examination of power reveals it to be more pervasive but also more vulnerable than we are accustomed to thinking. His gloss is innovative as well for demonstrating that the instability and multiplicity of the subject never impedes, and in fact enables, political action. Thus, he suggests that the deconstructive critique of the (Enlightenment) subject need not get mired in political defeatism and, verily, can be recast to empower the subject. Notwithstanding its limits (i.e. its relative neglect of materiality, and its privileging of informal over formal politics, which the next chapter will tackle head-on), this positive and creative Bhabhaian turn on agency, as I have underlined above, is an important advance on the poststructuralist politics of 'resistance'.

As for his radicality: there is, curiously enough, what may appear as a deeply *conservative* strain in Bhabha — his notion that politics can avoid revolutionary breaks, involve only slight alterations, and happen only within discursive subjection looks decidedly traditionalist. Perhaps it is this strain that some of his critics are responding to. And yet, his politics are critical, subversive, and transgressive. The paradox is compelling, without being just a Bhabhaian device: as we have registered, there are important reasons for having to work within discourse, which have principally to do with the dangers of opposing, reversing, or cancelling power lest it be reproduced in new forms. That is why I must admit finding the paradox of acting within an imposed discourse or tradition, but still subverting its representational codes and producing new and unanticipated sites, compelling — and yes, radical.

BEND IT LIKE BHABHA

Hybridity and political strategy

As discussed in the last chapter, rather than shying away from an emancipatory project or equating politics with localized 'resistance', Bhabha offers a refreshingly optimistic political vision that opens up possibilities for creative and transgressive change. In this chapter, I would like to draw attention to the compellingly political character of his project, demonstrating its relevance and applicability to a wider, contemporary politics of change (i.e. a 'postcolonial politics'). But in order to do so, I will need to twist and stretch his argument. Indeed, his deconstructive approach appears to make him disinclined to transform the notion of hybridization into a more explicit political strategy; and, as just discussed, his reliance on semiotics causes him to restrict his analysis to the sphere of cultural politics. By extending the political and semiotic possibilities of hybridization, and in particular by making hybridization into political strategy, I want to argue that we can move beyond his relatively restricted agency towards a postcolonial politics that effects broader, structural change, and that includes materialist or anti-capitalist challenges. I will use workers' and social movement case studies to help me make this argument, but also to assess the limits of a 'strategy of hybridization'.

Bending Bhabha

Bhabha's notion of hybridity, as we have seen, disrupts the view of domination and imperialism as all-encompassing and impenetrable by exposing their vulnerabilities and blind spots. This is a rejoinder both to the triumphalism of the oppressor and the acquiescence of the oppressed, pointing to the potential for instability and the opportunity for insurgency at any moment. This is a rejoinder as well to all those who see the Third World as passive bystander under (neo) colonialism. Bhabha maintains not only that colonialism faced countless daily acts of resistance — which throws some doubt on the idea of colonial power's effectivity — but also that colonial subjects were active and creative agents despite their subjugation. Finally, this is a rejoinder to the relatively negative Foucauldian view of politics as 'resistance'. For Bhabha, power produces much more than a resistant subject. It can bring forth a creative agent, capable of subverting authority in positive and unanticipated ways. The Delhi villagers and the Women Against Fundamentalism are not merely stubborn antagonists; they stymie their adversaries by contriving an unexpected hybrid — a vegetarian Bible, immigrant gender politics, a Third Space.

Recall as well that a significant feature of Bhabha's politics is its 'performativity'. The term encompasses the perform*ance* of his actors, the surprising spontaneity of their actions, their meddling and mischievousness. It is as if his agents are playing to a public, sometimes comedically (e.g. humouring the missionary, mimicking and mocking the colonial master), sometimes dramatically (e.g. when the underdog outsmarts the master). More importantly, Bhabhaian 'performativity' refers to being able to act only *within* a discursive context: the (social or political) script to which you respond is given to you; it is your inheritance whether you like or want it or not. How you act it out, however, is up to you. The discursive text *enables* you to act, no matter whether it is relatively benign or repressive; but, on the other hand, you cannot act from somewhere 'outside'. There is, of course, a significant rationale to this line of thinking: meeting one discourse/power with another ends up reproducing power, not vanquishing or replacing it. This is why Bhabha insists that, rather than trying to negate, obliterate, or counter a hegemony (purportedly from the outside), the agent can critique and displace it from the inside.

But while there are important strengths to the notion of performativity, there are also significant *political* problems tied to making both hybridity and the political subject performative or 'enunciatory'. Indeed, Bhabha speaks of hybridity occurring 'in the very practice of domination' and the agent as a 'discursive event' arising only 'in a moment of displacement' or 'emergency' (1994: 33, 23, 185; 1999: 39, 19). Politics for him is thus a spontaneous burst, a crisis situation in which the subject-as-agent instantaneously grasps what hybridity is about and creatively negotiates it. He writes about this process as a 'pulsional incident' and a 'split-second movement' (1994: 185).

The main reasons for positing an enunciatory subject is that Bhabha is skeptical (with good reason, in my view) of the Enlightenment subject. He shares with poststructuralism the critique of the subject/agent as autonomous, transparent, and transcendent. For him, the Enlightenment view is epistemologically and onto-logically wrong-headed (the subject is always positioned discursively, historically, socioeconomically, linguistically, etc., and therefore cannot claim sovereignty) and politically dangerous (much havoc — from colonialism to gender oppression — has been wreaked in the name of the mostly male and Western-centric Enlightenment subject).

Similarly, Bhabha stands firmly against ontologizing hybridity. To say that hybridity is everywhere and anywhere is to trivialize it and render it meaningless. Of concern, too, is making hybridity into a 'thing'. This is exemplified in Western multiculturalism's uncritical celebration of the 'hybrid' and the 'migrant', wherein ethnoculture is portrayed not as the outcome of change and contestation, but as discrete product that is essentialized and museumized (Bhabha 1999: 16;

cf. 1994: 34). Such a policy not only depoliticizes minority cultures, making them 'manageable' for the majoritarian one, but also helps advance late capitalism by enabling the commodification, niche-marketing, and consumption of ethnicity (visible, for example, in the current ascendancy of 'fusion' and 'world music'). The enunciatory nature of Bhabhaian hybridity renders it difficult to capture or co-opt the hybrid, thus averting these types of dangers.

But while there are solid reasons for arguing for the performativity of hybridity and subjectivity, the difficulty is that Bhabha's position sidelines, if not denies, the prospect of any explicit political strategy. Without an agent bearing norms and intentionality, without coordination, plans, and expectations, 'strategy' becomes both meaningless and impossible. The absence of reflexivity means that it is unclear whether Bhabha's agent even has any advanced notion that s/he will resist.

To be certain, Bhabha expressly refuses to reduce agency to consciousness and intention: 'My use of the concept of enunciation . . . has led me to want to understand not only . . . agency in times and places where it is least acknowledged, but also to try and understand forms of agency that do not emanate from individual intention' (1999: 33; cf. 1994: 185).[1] It is not surprising, then, that his texts provide only scant information to the reader about the historical context or identity of the agent. The incident about the Delhi villagers, for example, provides no details about the social standing or purposiveness of the villagers. Bhabha prefers, as indicated earlier, the notion of the individuation of the subject-as-agent only at the moment of confrontation with the hegemonic power.

Yet, surely there is middle ground between (Bhabha's construction of) the straw man of the transcendent Enlightenment subject and the radically performative agent? Bhabha so wishes to avoid reducing subjectivity to consciousness and hybridity to 'thing' that he ends up reducing politics to crisis management. He over-fixates on the contingency of identity, with the result that knowledge of hybridity is only last minute and fleeting, and agency does not extend beyond spontaneous guerilla tactics.[2] An agent, it seems to me, can plausibly be seen to have a degree of foresight, without denying either contingency or limited consciousness. S/he can be tactical and strategic without claiming autonomy or transparency. I am trying to argue, in other words, for an in-between position between Bhabha's performativity and those who seek an ontological and fully intentional subject (cf. Young, Parry, and Moore-Gilbert, as discussed in the previous chapter).

Thus, I believe that Bhabha's agents are more calculating than he represents them, in particular because he does not grant them what he in fact grants himself: *a greater awareness of hybridity*. If he can claim that hybridity is constitutive of discourse, as indeed he does, then why not extend the knowledge of this claim to his protagonists, thereby making possible a more explicit strategy of hybridization? Bhabha would of course be worried about the essentializing tendencies of this maneuver. But there is no reason to have to posit perfect knowledge or transparent strategy. Rather, I would like to suggest these take a more limited and contingent form: call it a 'vigilance' or 'tactical predisposition' towards hybridity. Here, hybridity is not made into formula or ontology but into rule. A rule has no meaningful content by itself and must be applied and implemented according to a specific context. The rule in this case is that 'there is no kingdom of hybridity, but hybridity instigates the subversion of every kingdom'.[3] Strategy then, in the diluted sense in which I mean it, is putting this rule to work. It is about being watchful that wherever there is hegemony, there is slippage, and so devising the appropriate subterfuge. It is about seeing how this authority is constructed or that discourse is enunciated, so as to check for cracks and contradictions in each case.

To skew Bhabha in this way, to walk his work down a path indicated but not taken (in the fashion that he recommends his protagonists do), is to extend the strategic possibilities of hybridity. It is to admit a degree of foresight and planning, without claiming transparency or transcendency, thus allowing for a more interventionist politics.

Indeed, the political implications of a strategy of hybridization are worth pondering. A vigilant and tactical approach is likely to have greater reach and impact than Bhabha's radical performativity. His politics may be an advance on Foucauldian resistance, but its momentariness and emergency-driven character render it just as localized and microscopic. With Bhabha, one has to make a quantum leap of faith that local agency, or a series of unconnected acts of resistance, will somehow add up to structural or global change. A more calculated and coordinated response, on the other hand, is conducive to realizing longer-term, macroscopic transformation in the form of, say, institutional change or corporate accountability. Making hybridity into a rule, moreover, gives it relevance and applicability, not just to colonial and post-colonial authority as in Bhabha's case, but to *any* hegemonic formation — be it local, state, or transnational, public, non-governmental, or corporate.

Finally, a strategy of hybridization can unhinge itself from Bhabha's unmistakable culturalism. Most of his instances of agency, as we have already noted, involve cultural transactions (religious conversion, education, cultural stereotypes), and notably absent from his writings is any significant treatment of socioeconomic strife. True, Bhabhaian struggles are semiotic ones, in which agents take advantage of cultural hybridization. But just because these struggles are semiotically and culturally *mediated* is no reason to privilege the domain of culture as *object* of struggle. Socioeconomic domination must also be semiotically represented in any political contest, thus being subject to hybridization and possible subterfuge. There is no reason, therefore, to restrict a strategy of hybridization to the realm of culture.

A 'strategy of hybridization'

In what follows, I want to illustrate my above arguments with the help of examples drawn from contemporary social/workers' movements. I do not purport to do justice to the sociopolitical histories of these movements or the range of issues they have espoused; I have chosen them to focus on their *political campaigns*. My point is to examine how these campaigns operationalize what I have called a 'strategy of hybridization', even though the movements themselves may not call it by that name. My purpose is to demonstrate the political forms and consequences of such a strategy.[4] And to this end, I will distinguish between (1) a 'hybridizing strategy', and (2) a 'Third Space strategy', both of which I see as making up a strategy of hybridization.

A hybridizing strategy

This type of strategy hybridizes power by exposing and exploiting its instabilities. It seeks to explicitly unravel what is, in a sense, always already unravelling. Two well-known Indian environmental campaigns will help demonstrate what I mean.

(i) Chipko Andolan

This is the movement (mentioned only fleetingly in Chapter 3) that pioneered environmental resistance in India, and has now achieved almost mythical status both in the country and in environmental/social movement circles (Rangan 2000). It began in response to the pauperization and ecological destruction of the North Indian Himalayan region, wreaked by decades of logging, road construction, and mining. The struggle pitted private lumber companies, which were aided and abetted by state authorities (the forest department, the police), against Chipko's alliance of community leaders, students, and peasants, many of whom were women (Kapoor 1993: 218-23).

Although the movement had a history of resistance stretching back to British rule (Guha 1989), its campaign climaxed during the period between the early-1970s and mid-1980s. The campaign involved a series of major and minor struggles, including tree-hugging (from which the movement derives its vernacular name), vigils, rallies, spontaneous demonstrations, court litigation, blockades of lumber auctions and mining sites, and Gandhian-inspired cross-country marches that galvanized public attention.

Many of the campaigns, it should be mentioned, made use of the symbolic and the spectacular. Apart from tree-hugging, which often meant defying loggers to cut through activists' bodies to fell trees, protestors sung songs, recited poetry, and organized street theatre. Women protestors also symbolically tied *rakhees* to trees (the former are decorative silk bracelets lovingly given by women to their brothers and male friends during the Hindu festival of *Raksha Bandhan*). Such simple yet dramatic performances attracted media interest; Chipko activists consciously deployed popular and religious symbols, thus reinterpreting the familiar and colourful for political purposes to help advance their campaign.

An important part of Chipko's political strategy was exploiting various contradictions within the state (Guha 1989: 177; Basu 1987). For a start, Chipko publicized the tensions between the state's unfettered pursuit of economic growth and those legislative instruments (in particular, provisions in both the Directive Principles of the Constitution and the national Forest Policy) that urged environmental protection. Much was made of the fact that the Forest Policy recommended conserving national forest cover to a minimum of 33 percent, but that the state had allowed such cover to slip well below that level (about 14 percent in the 1980s) (Kapoor 1993: 195-6). Chipko's activities also helped drive a wedge between the state government, whose responsibility it was to regulate forests, and the central government, which had to meet international environmental commitments and needed to be seen as safeguarding the country's long-term interests. In part, this caused the central government to gradually, albeit reluctantly, become a champion of forest protection. Eventually, a nationwide environmental regulatory framework was established in 1986 that acted, and continues to act, as a check on state government environmental activities.

The most direct outcome of Chipko's struggle was to force the state government, first to investigate the movement's ecological claims, then gradually to declare a series of local moratoria on timber felling and mining, and eventually to institute a fifteen-year moratorium on deforestation in the entire region (which still holds today). The more indirect political or symbolic outcome was to contribute to a national awareness of, and debate on, such issues as the place of environmental conservation in economic development, the social and gender costs of ecological degradation, and the state's accountability to those communities located in the 'hinterland'.

(ii) Narmada Bachao Andolan (NBA)

The NBA ('Save the Narmada Movement') is a regional, national, and international coalition of environmental and human rights groups, community organizations, citizens, scientists, celebrities, and even government policymakers. Its transnational links extend to more than 20 countries. The movement was formed in the late 1980s to oppose a giant dam project of over 30 major and 3,000 minor dams being constructed along the Narmada river in Western India. One of the largest of these dams is the Sardar Sarovar: the project is meant to provide drinking water, irrigation, and power generation, but it will also submerge substantial areas of land and forests, and displace about 300,000 people/farmers living in 250 villages (Fisher 1995: 12-15; Baviskar 1995: 199-202; Friends of River Narmada 2007). Some sources estimate that over a million people will be directly or indirectly affected by this dam alone (e.g. Friends of River Narmada 2007).

Like Chipko, the NBA's strategy has been to take advantage of institutional tensions, and nowhere is this more visible than in its late 1980s to early 1990s campaign against international funders of the project, notably the World Bank. The NBA understood early on in the campaign that the Bank was neither a monolithic organization nor immune to outside pressure and persuasion (Fisher 1995; Udall 1995: 204-5). Accordingly, NBA leaders began by meeting with senior

Bank staff in Washington to try and bring them on side. They then lobbied the Bank's president and organized information meetings with the executive directors, who sit on the board and represent the Bank's funders. This provided the executive directors with information about the project that was often at odds with reports they were receiving from Bank staff.

The NBA also spent a lot of effort publicizing its cause (e.g. open letters in newspapers) and lobbying finance ministers and legislators in the countries of the Bank's five main funders (US, Japan, France, UK and Germany). Significant in this regard was the dramatic testimony in 1989 of Medha Patkar, a charismatic and articulate NBA leader, before the US congressional Appropriations Committee, which approves US funding for the Bank (Udall 1995: 210-11). Her testimony generated important international media attention and led some American legislators to ask the Bank's president to suspend assistance for the dam. The result was for the president to call for an unprecedented independent review of the project. As well, Japan, one of the direct co-funders of the dam, withdrew its loan commitment.

The 1992 independent review was critical of the Bank and recommended it pull out of the project. The report underlined how Bank staff and their Indian government partners had undertaken inadequate environmental and social assessments, failed to meaningfully consult with displaced communities, and afforded insufficient resources for the rehabilitation and resettlement of oustees (Udall 1995: 214-15). The review helped heighten latent and existing divisions between and among Bank staff and board members. And, later that year, amid signs that several board members were about to withdraw their support for the project, the Bank announced a face-saving deal under which the Indian government would not seek the remaining Bank loans for the dam.

The NBA's campaign, in addition to ending international backing for the dam, is generally credited as initiating a process of policy reform within the Bank during the 1990s, notably in regards to future Bank support and funding for 'mega-dam' projects (Fisher 1995). But these successes notwithstanding, to date, construction of the dams continues in India, intermittently interrupted by government policy reviews and court injunctions provoked by the NBA. The Sardar Sarovar dam is now almost complete, and construction on some of the other major dams has begun, although state governments have had difficulty raising sufficient funding for them, in part due to the negative publicity surrounding the Sardar Sarovar.

There are perhaps several other social movement campaigns that could be cited as examples of a 'hybridizing strategy'.[5] But what emerges as important from the Chipko and NBA campaigns is the way in which they treat laws and policies, institutional practices, and ideological apparatuses as deconstructible. That is, they refuse to take dominant authority at face value, and proceed to reveal its contingencies. Sometimes, they expose what the hegemon is trying to disavow or hide (exclusion of affected communities in project design and implementation, faulty information gathering and dissemination). Sometimes, they problematize dominant or naturalized truths ('development = unlimited economic growth = capitalism', 'big is better', 'technology can save the environment'). In either case, by contesting, publicizing, and politicizing accepted or hidden truths, they hybridize power, challenging its smugness and triumphalism, revealing its impurities. They show power to be, literally and figuratively, a bastard.

While speaking truth to power, a hybridizing strategy also exploits the instabilities of power. In part, this involves showing up and taking advantage of the equivocations of power — conflicting laws, contradictory policies, unfulfilled promises. A lot has to do here with publicly shaming the hegemon, forcing it to remedy injustices and live up to stated commitments in a more accountable and transparent manner. And, in part, this involves nurturing or manipulating the splits and strains within institutions. Such maneuvering can take the form of cultivating allies, forging alliances, or throwing doubt on prevailing orthodoxy.

Note, lastly, the way in which a hybridizing strategy works *with* the dominant discourse. This reflects the negotiative aspect of Bhabha's performativity. The strategy may outwit the hegemon, but it does so from the interstices of the hegemony. The master may be paralyzed, but his paralysis is induced using his own poison/medicine. It is for this reason that cultivating allies in the adversarial camp is possible: when you speak their language and appeal to their own ethical horizons, you are building a modicum of common ground. It is for this reason also that the master cannot easily dismiss or crush you. Observing his rules and playing his game makes it difficult for him not to take you seriously or grant you a certain legitimacy. The use of non-violent tactics may be crucial in this regard: state repression is easily justified against violent adversaries, but it is vulnerable to public criticism when used against non-violence. Thus, the fact that Chipko and the NBA deployed civil disobedience — pioneered, it must be pointed out, by the 'father of the nation' (i.e. Gandhi) — made it difficult for the state to quash them or deflect their claims.

A Third Space strategy

A 'Third Space strategy' also splits power, but unlike a hybridizing strategy, returns it in an altered, and often unexpected, form. This is a strategy that most obviously grows out of Bhabha's work (see the discussion of his notion of Third Space in Chapter 7), although the intent here is to extend it to different territory and, as the examples below indicate, particularly to struggles against corporate capitalism.

(i) Women workers in free trade zones

Kumudhini Rosa's work (1994) on Sri Lanka's free trade zones (FTZs) shows how women workers in mainly textile industries have organized against inhuman working and living conditions (low wages, workplace harassment, substandard housing, state/corporate restrictions on unionization). The women have used part of their own meagre wages, and allied themselves with local women's and community organizations, to set up several activities: a food cooperative, which helps keep the prices of basic food items low; a legal aid centre that assists in fighting workplace sexual harassment; the publication and distribution of a newspaper; and a women's centre that provides legal education, medical assistance, small credit, and alternative skills training to enable women to move out of the FTZs (Rosa 1994: 91-4; cf. Rowbotham & Mitter 1994: 8) (comparable actions in FTZs in Nicaragua, the Philippines, and Thailand are detailed in Bandy & Mendez 2003: 179; McKay 2006: 45; and Mills 2005: 119ff.).

Bandy and Mendez (2003) analyze similar strategies by the Coalition for Justice in the Maquiladoras (CJM) on the US/Mexico border. The CJM is a binational and bilingual coalition of some 120 member organizations that militates against a range of corporate and state-abetted activities relating to labour rights and health and safety conditions in the FTZs. It pressures corporations to adhere to codes of conduct on fair wages and collective bargaining. It also litigates against those corporations that violate local labour laws, and uses NAFTA trade provisions and institutions to demand better working conditions (Bandy & Mendez 2003: 176).

One of the key CJM campaigns that Bandy and Mendez analyze involves women labour organizers, who struggle for the protection of gender rights, not just in the maquilas, but *within* the member organizations of the CJM itself. Indeed, while some CJM male union leaders have reportedly been sympathetic to advancing women's issues, most have not, resulting in long-standing frustrations by women members. As a result, women organizers have been increasingly speaking out against the masculine culture of the unions, hierarchical and gendered forms of union participation and activism, and the inadequate attention paid to women workers' demands (Bandy & Mendez 2003: 177-8). Of late, they have been pushing for a range of reforms. Some involve community education programmes about domestic violence and workplace harassment; others include awareness campaigns that explicitly link sexual violence/exploitation at the workplace and the home. Female activists have also been pressing the unions to better attend to women's issues (e.g. maternity leave, homework, wage discrimination, workplace sexual harassment) and to pursue less 'macho' and confrontational collective bargaining tactics in favour of more dialogical and negotiative ones (Bandy & Mendez 2003: 178).

All of these actions defy the view that women workers necessarily succumb to sweatshop production under current economic globalization. They demonstrate that women can employ their wage-labour, not just to reproduce capital (continuing to sell their labour cheaply, engaging in consumerism), but to resist capital (fighting working conditions and gender discrimination, creating alternative forms of economic organization through co-ops) and lift themselves out of sweatshop conditions (by retraining). They are using capitalism to rework and rewrite its script.

What is more, as the CJM example illustrates, women workers are also engaging in a 'borderlands politics' reminiscent of the Women Against

Fundamentalism: they are not merely doing anti-corporate union activism, but opening a productive supplementary political site which, to paraphrase Bhabha, 'reconjugates' and 'translates' cross-border unionism into a self-reflexive politics about gender discrimination in the home, community, and workplace. The women organizers are contriving a Third Space that highlights how transnational union activism is itself gendered. Their agency helps link spaces usually kept separate — the personal and the political; home, workplace, and activism; reproductive labour, productive labour, and labour organizing. As a consequence, as Bandy and Mendez suggest, they foreground how 'gendered power structures both affect and are reflected in the spatial workings of transnational politics' (2003: 185).

(ii) Rumour and spirits

Paralleling Bhabha's valorization of rumour mongering during the Indian 'mutiny', Patricia Turner (1993) analyzes how rumour undermines US corporate power during the 1970s and 1980s. In one instance, Church's Fried Chicken, a company selling its product to mainly inner-city African-Americans across the country, is the target of a rumour campaign according to which the franchise is owned by the Ku Klux Klan (KKK) and its chicken recipe has been tainted to sterilize Black men. Thus, one of Turner's interviewees declares: 'I heard that the Klan owns Church's chicken and has been lacing the batter with a spermicide' (1993: 139). In another instance, Troop Smart, an American corporation with operations in Korea that markets military clothing almost exclusively to young Black and Latino men, struggles against widespread rumours. These allege the company is secretly run by the KKK and its name stands for 'To Rule Over Our Oppressed People'. In some versions of the rumour, the message is reportedly printed in the lining of the company's bomber jackets or hidden somewhere on its boots.

Both companies suffer significant financial losses as a result of the rumours. In the latter case, despite a concerted counter public relations campaign, the corporation is bankrupted, in part due to the rumours. Thus, Turner concludes, 'African-Americans are willing to abandon any commodity tainted by the Klan, whether in fact or in fiction' (1993: 98).

Turner offers a historically sensitive argument, showing how the rumour campaigns, typically engineered through word-of-mouth and leaflet distribution, stir African-American sensitivities to slavery and racism. They subversively associate corporate trademarks with overt or unconscious memories of such events as church burning in the Deep South, White supremacist vilification of Black bodies and sexuality, and the targeted recruitment of young Black men for front-line combat in Vietnam. Rumours that evoke fears of biological or physical contamination, as well as those that construct racists such as the Klan as intent on inhibiting the growth of minority groups, appear to be particularly damaging (Turner 1993: 142, 144). The rumours thus mimic but divert the operation of trademarks: they circulate endlessly and anonymously, much like corporate logos are meant to do under late capitalism; yet they manage to endow these logos with a specific, and in this case nefarious, identity (Coombe 1997: 268; Turner 1993: 84-8, 92-8).

Aiwa Ong (1987) examines circulation of a different kind — that of the *hantu* (evil spirits), which reportedly stalk the shop floors of corporations in the FTZs of Malaysia. The women workers who toil there hail from rural areas, where belief in animal and ancestral spirits is quite prevalent. In response to their harsh, disciplinary working conditions in the FTZs, the women reportedly become possessed by angry spirits, screaming abuse and acting violently. Thus, during the mid-to-late 1970s, several spirit possession episodes occur across the FTZs, stalling production and causing close-downs (Ong 1987: 204). Spirit visitations happen on factory floors and in toilets, yielding mass hysteria and making some women workers damage equipment, allegedly against their own will.

Ong's research and interviews reveal that, while a few spirit possession episodes are sporadic and reported (at least publicly) as 'involuntary', many are deliberate collective acts of defiance. The women appear to be protesting against inhumane working conditions: 'The *hantu* symbolism, shifting in and out of their consciousness, spoke not of an ideology of class struggle but of the right to be treated *as human beings*' (Ong 1987: 220, italics in original). The result is confusion, consternation, and disbelief in the ranks of factory owners and the broader public alike.

This example brings to mind Derrida's *Specters of Marx* (1994), in which he argues that, while the spectre is something that is not present, it nonetheless interrogates what is self-present (namely neoliberal capitalism) in unexpected ways. The FTZs may well stand as triumph of the modern market over 'tradition', yet they cannot exorcise the ghosts of the toiling female Malaysian bodies. As Medley and Carroll write, 'In effect, the IMF [whose policies result in increased creation of FTZs] recites the brutal conditions of nineteenth-century European capitalism and, ironically, resuscitates images invoked by Marx to condemn capital's voracious consumption of workers' bodies to satisfy its lust for profit' (2004: 162-3). Capitalism's disciplinary regimes come back to haunt it through the spirited agency of the Malaysian women workers, whose actions re-articulate rural 'tradition' in baffling ways and render capitalism's global triumph impossible.

As before, there may be several other examples worth citing,[6] but what appears important about a 'Third Space strategy' is how power is displaced through its creative estrangement. Political intervention here involves inflections of the dominant discourse, producing surprising and sometimes mysterious hybrids. Bhabha describes this as 'adding to without adding up' (1999: 26).[7] In the above examples, it is because the logics of capitalism are hybridized that they can be 'added to': wage-labour and trademarks alike function as circulating signs, which, made faceless and abstract under capitalism, can be hijacked: they can be put to other uses, as in the case of the Sri Lankan women workers, or ascribed strange new meanings, as in the case of the African-American rumour campaigns. The border politics of the CJM women workers, for its part, support but 'mess around' with union activism, infusing it with gender-related demands; while the collective agency of the Malaysian women splits open the universalizing time of modern capital to yield the return of repressed tradition in the form of ghostly bodily possessions. Such creative semiotic politics, it must be stated, defies the pessimism of the likes of Baudrillard (1995), according to whom people under late capitalism are indifferent consumers of signs and simulations.

To conclude this section are a few brief reflections on both 'hybridizing' and 'Third Space' strategies. Although I have illustrated them through environmental and socioeconomic struggles, there is no reason to restrict their scope, since as pointed out earlier, their character as a rule makes them relevant and specific to every hegemony. They also need not be seen as separate: they are distinct tactics, and can presumably be deployed individually or in tandem, depending on the constellation of power.

A Third Space strategy is perhaps more creative than a hybridizing one, in that the latter exposes hybridity, while the former yields a new hybrid. But this may be just an outward appearance, as the organization and planning behind either strategy may also have to be highly creative to be effective. A hybridizing strategy, for its part, may be more appropriate for legal or institutional policy-related struggles, but here again, there is no a priori reason to think that a Third Space strategy could not be used to create new law or reorient standing policy.

What can perhaps be stated more firmly of both strategies is that they can be deployed by small numbers of people requiring minimal-to-moderate organization and planning: this is the particular distinction of semiotic politics under late capitalism, where communications and media may catapult into public view the claims and struggles of small groups, sometimes helping to outwit large and powerful institutions. Whereas the power politics of, say, the large unions of yesteryear used to rely on the strength of their numbers, in today's mediatized world, the informational politics of social/workers' movements, drawing on small but credible media and Internet campaigns, is crucial. (Such campaigns need, after all, to move as quickly and flexibly as mobile transnational capital.) Here, the linking of politics and the spectacular has perhaps never been deployed more effectively. Live performance, symbolic acts, and parody have all become key ingredients of the activist's repertoire. Seemingly spontaneous, yet carefully planned and choreographed, guerilla spectacles galvanize media attention and help invigorate marginalized counterpublics.

Indeed, a degree of organization and planning is crucial for either (Third Space or hybridizing) strategy. It is not enough that hybridity serve as grounds for manipulation, as Bhabha suggests. There must also be a tactical vigilance towards hybridity, which leads to assessing the adversary and putting in place specific plans and resources to take advantage of expected faults and tensions. The NBA's example is particularly apt here for not only manipulating but also *embodying* hybridity with the help of a strategy that straddles the local, national, and global, and that coordinates an impressive spectrum of people, organizations, and resources.

In fact, coordination and transversal alliance-making may well be the hallmark of a strategy of hybridization, all the more so in an era of transnationalism. Centralized planning and strategy easily coerce consensus and stymie creativity; in contradistinction, a coordinated and decentralized alliance, while more loose and untidy, appears better suited to harnessing the enthusiasm and initiative of diverse groups. These groups may all identify a common adversary (e.g. the World Bank, the state, the market), but they do not have to always agree to the same political analysis or approach. It is for this reason that, befitting a global postcolonial politics, a local environmental problem such as that faced by the NBA succeeded in bringing together not just environmentalists, but also scientists, academicians, indigenous people, human rights organizations, and the like, from both North and South.

Limits

A strategy based on hybridity cannot be assumed to be necessarily progressive or successful. Knowledge about power's hybridization belongs to everyone and no one, and hence can be, and often has been, put to use by the hegemon. 'Divide and rule' is an old colonial tactic deployed against many anti-imperialist and nationalist struggles. Similarly, state and corporate cooptation of the opposition continues to be a common and pervasive practice. And post-Fordist capitalism, as emphasized earlier, relies on product differentiation and the commodification of hybridity. As *strategy*, then, hybridity can be put to regressive as much as progressive use.

Nonetheless, the specific 'strategy of hybridization' that I have tried to sketch here does have a critical and democratic intent and logic: both its objectives and effectivity depend on politicizing and questioning the operations and contingencies of power. Indeed, the subversion of state laws thrives or founders on publicly revealing their lacuna and contradictions. By contrast, hegemonic power cannot abide public scrutiny and challenge. Cultural stereotypes or socioeconomic inequality may divide and rule, but they are maintained precisely by the foreclosure of contestation.

As to the success of a strategy of hybridization, there can of course be no guarantees. The strategy may be more successful than Bhabha's radical performativity in terms of reach and impact, but much depends on the degree and quality of organizational resources and planning. And even with these ingredients, there is a lot of unpredictability — from possible infiltration and cooptation by the dominant power to a counter-public relations or rumour campaign. To wit, one reason for the NBA's relative lack of success in stopping dam construction has been the backing by state governments of a counter-movement, bringing together supporters of the dam.

Such unpredictability, it must be emphasized, involves not only how the adversary acts, but also how you, in turn, learn and adapt. Chipko's campaign, for example, was developed over many years, through a process of trial and error, and with a hardening of position on some issues (e.g. a ban on logging) and a spirit of compromise on others (e.g. the shift from a rejection of technological solutions for forest regeneration to the adoption of intermediate technological ones, encouraged by some quarters of government). Similarly, the CJM organizations have gradually had to face up to the gendered dimensions of unionism, brought to the fore by female organizers. All of this only points up earlier arguments about the dangers of positing a stable subject or transparent strategy.

Bhabha vs. Habermas vs. Mouffe

Before concluding, it is important to contextualize the above Bhabhaian approach to political strategy in relation to other contemporary approaches: given our analysis of the politics of Habermas and Mouffe in Chapter 6, it seems apropos to use them as a reference point.

I am struck by the contrast between all three. Habermasian strategy, like the Bhabhaian one, advocates for multiple points of intervention (informal and formal public spheres, civil society, state, market) to effect change, but it requires overarching communicative procedures to ensure equitable and democratic outcomes. From Bhabha's point of view, the problem is that the Habermasian vision is ultimately integrationist. Radical activists or minorities are welcomed into the Habermasian fold, but they must eventually adapt to, and play by the rules of, liberal democratic institutions. This is because Habermas underestimates the role of power: he ignores that, despite theoretical or legal communicative guarantees, power tends to be biased in favour of the hegemon. Communicative action does not, then, adequately account for those differences (cultural, socioeconomic) that play a significant role in people's deliberative capacities, resulting in the dominance of some claims to the exclusion of others.

Mouffe's political strategy has more in common with Bhabha's, although there are some important differences, too. Like Bhabha, she favours the expansion of public discourse in multiple spheres, principally by way of social movement mobilization. Working to deepen liberal democratic institutions, she abandons revolutionary change (e.g. a proletarian takeover of the state) in favour of radical reform. She advocates a self-limiting radicalism that implies acting, not according to some a priori procedures *à la* Habermas, but in relation to a 'logic of equivalence' which sees social movements adjusting their respective claims through a process of agonistic learning and conflict.

The Bhabhaian approach is both more conservative and more radical than Mouffe's. It is more conservative because of its greater insistence on discursive repetition. Here, Bhabha may be said to be working with, but also departing from, the Mouffean/Gramscian notion of hegemony. He accepts the idea of the coercion and pervasiveness of hegemony, but he does not espouse a 'counterhegemony' that somehow stands apart.[8] Rather, the breadth and power of a hegemony for him means that you cannot act from outside it; you are always situated within it. Nonetheless, because hegemony is unstable and fractured, you can interrupt it from within. Thus, the (neo)colonized subject may have an 'indigenous tradition', but faced with the power of the hegemon, s/he can draw upon it only in *the* terms of the hegemony. The 'vegetarian Bible', for example, may be a Third Space negotiated with the help of indigenous knowledge, but it must still be uttered in the master's language and contain the trace of the master's Bible.

Thus, Bhabha takes the reformist agenda more seriously than Mouffe, arguing for agonistic cooperation and conflict, but always within the interstices of hegemonic power. And yet, his strategy is in many ways more radical than Mouffe's because of its creative possibilities. The subaltern can simultaneously make possible and make trouble (Bhabha 1995a: 110), seizing the opportunity to stun and transgress the hegemon.

Conclusion

Bhabha's work has helped me arrive at a broader understanding of what many social or workers' movements already know and practise — the idea that the slippages of power are politically exploitable. This understanding, however contingent, enables a strategic vigilance that where there is fullness and triumphalism, there is simultaneous lack and inadequacy; where constraint, possible diversion; and where taken-for-grantedness, plausible contestation. It is a vigilance that rests, ultimately, on an optimism that even widespread domination can be undone.

The political campaigns I have highlighted help us *learn* about the specific, creative, and democratic operationalization of this vigilance. The problem with Bhabha's radical performativity is its inattention precisely to learning: its immediacy and instantaneousness cause knowledge to have to be incessantly reinvented. The strategies of hybridization (i.e. the 'hybridizing' and 'Third Space' strategies) that social movements deploy may have limited generalizability, but at the very least they help us discover that a tactical predisposition to the operations of power *can* be translated into political change, and, to this end, there may be ways of splitting, exposing, or diverting power.

Such strategies also help tease out the democratic potential of Bhabhaian hybridity. Bhabha may well be emphasizing the importance of the everyday, spontaneous struggles, and he may well be drawing our attention to their spectacularity and drama. But it is only with a more explicit strategy of hybridization that these struggles can magnify their political impact and spectacularity and thus pretend to a broader, structural politics. Indeed, such magnification turns out to be crucial: it publicizes the contestatory character of power, be it hidden or naturalized, small or grand; and, in so doing, it calls hegemonic power to account.

CONCLUSION

Postcolonialism offers an important perspective on cultural politics, seeing it as a dynamic process of meaning-making that engenders the construction, as well as the contestation, of power relationships. Such a perspective, I have argued, enables a significant critique of mainstream development practices. Partly, it helps uncover the unequal cultural, socioeconomic, and political relationships between West and Third World or elite and subaltern, relationships often rooted in colonial domination. This is witnessed, for example, by continuing North–South inequalities and the further marginalization of many parts of Sub-Saharan Africa.

But partly, postcolonialism also provides us with a much greater awareness of the ever-changing forms of neocolonial hegemony. This is evident in the new disciplinary regimes of such global institutions as the IMF and World Bank, through which governments, civil servants, or women workers in free trade zones are subjected to micro forms of surveillance and bodily engineering. It is also visible in the imposition of new economic policy prescriptions, under the guise of loan conditions, 'good' governance, or 'objective science'. It can be gleaned from development's tendency towards depoliticized cultural explanations, that divert attention away from such broader issues as inequality, transnational corporate power, or discriminatory state practices (towards women, minorities, indigenous people). And it is implied in the do-gooder politics of foreign aid, human rights, and participatory development, that hides significant ideological prejudice and institutional violence.

I have dwelled quite a bit on the elite/intellectual complicities of development, which are also part of the armoury of neocolonial power. These range from the 'progressive' academic's valorization of the subaltern — which can essentialize marginality — to our narcissistic demand to have the subaltern mimic our values, habits, or institutions. I have also drawn particular attention to institutionalized complicities. These can take the guise of defending organizational or geopolitical turf, or needing to produce a generous and benevolent nation. Finally, I have foregrounded several of development's psychoanalytic complicities, which frequently point to the desire for voyeuristic pleasure and/or panoptic control.

The considerable problem with these tactics and disguises of power, of course, is that they (further) subjugate the Third World and, most especially, they silence the subaltern. In speaking about the Third World, our ruse or mistake may be to actually speak *for* it. And in including or even 'enabling' the subaltern, our conscious or subconscious intention may be to control or appropriate it. The result is the treatment of the Third World/subaltern as object, as socioeconomic or cultural resource.

But if development's hegemony is both old and new, both expansive and multi-directional, then transforming it requires multi-pronged tactics and multiple points of intervention. I have attempted to spell out a few of these, although in no way can I claim to have done so systematically or comprehensively. I have offered some specific, albeit tentative, remedies. To name a few: radically self-reflexive fieldwork; democratization of the powerful transnational development institutions; extension of participation to the economy; and construction of non-national forms of gift-giving.

The deepening of liberal democracy is also key to transforming development. In this regard, Habermas and Mouffe offer convincing (although differing) arguments for the greater democratization of state, civil society, and/or market. Habermas posits communicative mechanisms that help in adjudicating between validity claims, although, as pointed out in Chapter 6, the inherent danger is coercing consensus. Mouffe advocates the agonistic coexistence of plural claims, but she thereby risks sanctioning injustice and intolerance.

A significant postcolonial critique of both democratic theorists is their inadequate attention to elite–subaltern relationships. Habermas, in particular, fails to recognize that, in an international context especially, the asymmetries of power can never be bracketed out: the subaltern speech-act is severely compromised across the North–South and elite–subordinate divide, even when the subaltern is included in the conversation and procedures are in place to promote reciprocity and dialogue. In such a situation, elites and intellectuals have a significant added responsibility. As Kimberly Hutchings, drawing on Spivak, suggests:

> it is a responsibility, in the context of opacity of meaning and radically inegalitarian power relations, to put your own assumptions into question and strain to imagine what it might mean to be and think differently. This is a responsibility forced on many through the moral teachings of modernity, but it is something which the metropolitan feminist [or development practitioner] is not obliged to do, and therefore has a greater responsibility for doing.
>
> (Hutchings 2005: 165)

The challenge, as I have argued, is politicizing such a Spivakian ethic: personal commitment will not nearly be enough; tremendous institutional imagination will be needed to ensure that the subaltern *is* heard.

Bhabha has a different take on this issue. He suggests that hegemony may well be disabling for the subaltern, but it can also be made into resource. Its multidimensionality and hybridity can be creatively exploited by the subaltern. I have attempted to extend this argument by indicating that social and labour movements have indeed quite deliberately and successfully deployed strategies of hybridization to advance their claims.

The question that arises at this juncture though is whether Bhabha's view should be taken as critique of Spivak. To be sure, while Spivak's argument has a definite political intent, she can be seen to focus much less than Bhabha on questions of agency, perhaps because her argument that there is no discursive space from which the subaltern can be heard makes it difficult for her to retrieve or represent subaltern agency. Bhabha's position — that politics, while always contaminated by hegemonic representations and institutions, can nonetheless be undertaken from within (the margins of) the hegemony — can be construed as helping him retrieve subaltern agency, thus averting some of Spivak's problems.[1]

But a Spivakian counter-critique lurks not far. For, just like Habermas, can Bhabha not be accused of inadequately grappling with the discursive obstacles to the subaltern speech-act? Recall that he pays scant attention to questions of socioeconomic position and hence to the subaltern's relative ability to be heard, even if it does speak. Of course, Bhabha places substantial weight on the subaltern's political creativity to pry open the hegemony. But this still begs the question of the relationship of social position to political creativity (and may imply the de facto exclusion of 'uncreative' political subjects).

Nonetheless, it seems to me that the Spivakian and Bhabhaian positions are not necessarily antagonistic; indeed they may well be complementary. *Both* are required for the success of the subaltern speech-act. Spivak is emphasizing what needs to happen at one end of the North–South, elite–subaltern spectrum — the clearing of discursive spaces so that the subaltern can be heard; and Bhabha is emphasizing what needs to happen at the other end — the activation of subaltern speech. The Bhabhaian and Spivakian maneuvers are thus interdependent: for subaltern politics to register, elite discourses must be open and responsive; and for the discursive clearing to be successful, the subaltern must speak.

Thus, if we are to listen to Spivak and Bhabha, the onus for transforming development lies with *both* elites and subaltern (and West and Third World). Meaningful change depends on the ethico-political actions of the former and the (creative) agency of the latter. As always though, there are many dangers: communication always risks failing; elite 'enablement' risks transfiguring into paternalism; and subaltern political success risks turning into new elite orthodoxy. This once again underlines that the postcolonial politics of development is never complete and always in need of critical interrogation.

NOTES

INTRODUCTION

1 See Chapter 3 for a more layered definition of the subaltern.

2 I have edited and revised all the essays for the purposes of this book, in part to make some links between themes and chapters, but in part also to raise new questions and arguments, many of which have occurred as I have placed the essays side by side. New contexts and constellations throw a different light, introduce new relationships, pose new queries. I have attempted to address as many of these as I can, but of course may not have done so adequately; and by raising new questions I will likely have implied even further ones and left quite a few unanswered.

3 Several critics (e.g. Shohat 1992; McClintock 1992) have warned against the linear chronology that the term 'postcolonial' may connote: it can be interpreted as conveying a universalized condition beyond or 'after' colonialism, thus ironically denying the continuing processes of colonization, and eliding the enormously different historical and geopolitical positionings of nations and communities. For example, Canada's white-settler colonial heritage makes it postcolonial in quite a different way than its erstwhile colonizers, Britain and France; and its indigenous communities still endure colonial relationships with the state, which the term postcolonial obscures. Yet, shifting one's attention to the 'colonial' in 'postcolonial' does the opposite — it emphasizes how the legacies of colonialism persist in our 'post' condition. Thus, Stuart Hall argues that the term, because of its ambiguities, reflects well the tensions within the field. He suggests that, despite the dangers Shohat and McClintock alert us to, the postcolonial also offers 'an alternative narrative, highlighting key conjunctures to those embedded in the classical narrative of Modernity' (1996: 249).

4 I will nonetheless use the term Third World throughout this book. As will be seen, my argument attempts to complicate the term by underlining the pluralism within and between Third World countries; and by pointing out the artificiality of the First/Third World distinction in some instances and yet its necessity in others. Of course, the discourse of development has infused all terms denoting this part of the world (South, developing countries, etc.) with a pejorative meaning. But I much prefer the term Third World to, say, 'developing countries', mainly because of its anti-hegemonic connotations and origins (it became popular after the 1955 Bandung meeting of non-aligned countries, at which Third World leaders attempted to chart an alternative course to either the capitalist West or the communist Soviet Bloc).

I will also distinguish between 'post-colonial' and 'postcolonial' (i.e. no hyphen), the former being used to denote the period after Third World countries obtained political independence, the latter to denote the critical cultural field.

5 There are also several problems with postcolonialism's tendency to privilege localized subaltern agency, missing the importance of a broader politics necessary to change mainstream development. Several of my essays (especially chapters 1, 7, and 8) will address this issue.

1 CAPITALISM, CULTURE, AGENCY: DEPENDENCY VERSUS POSTCOLONIAL THEORY

1 I do not purport to represent the gamut of arguments and positions of these Marxist critics of postcolonial theory, only those arguments relating to important dependency themes (e.g. the role of history, the status of capitalism, etc.). I do not endorse, for example, the (implicit or explicit) argument by some of these critics that postcolonial theorists such as Said, Spivak, or Bhabha are nothing but Western-based academic apologists for the current ascendancy of global capitalism (Dirlik 1994: 329, 356; Ahmad 1992: 6; Miyoshi 1993: 728). Not only are such arguments reductionist (the postcolonial theorists are highly critical of Western modernity; and Spivak, for instance, explicitly and repeatedly addresses her location as a 'privileged' intellectual in the academy, which is more than one can say for Dirlik, Ahmad, or Miyoshi), but they are also anti-intellectual for suggesting that one's intellectual activity is straightforwardly determined by one's socioeconomic or geographic location (on this issue, see Hall 1996: 258-9; Gandhi 1998; Sylvester 1999: 715). Moreover, it should be noted that not all dependency theorists are 'Marxist', although the vast majority of their work is Marxist inspired. Similarly, not all dependency theorists are Marxist in the same way (as will be seen later in this chapter). Frank is a often labelled a 'neomarxist', inspired by Paul Baran's idea of the 'development of underdevelopment'. He does not make use of classical Marxist 'modes of production' analysis, and he tends to see the national bourgeoisie as a puppet of imperialism. Cardoso/Faletto, although Marxist inspired, tend to draw from non-Marxist sources as well, in particular from the idea of a possible progressive role being played by non-class groups and ideologies (i.e. urban groups, the military, populism, nationalism, etc.). They are thus neither 'neomarxists' nor 'classical Marxists'. They believe in examining the structural relations between imperialism and social classes and groups, and see a possible (but not necessarily) progressive role being played by the national bourgeoisie (which is a 'classical Marxist' argument) (cf. Blomström & Hettne 1984: 34-5, 61-3, 89; Foster-Carter 1973).

2 The notion of the 'internalization of imperialism' is one that features prominently in the work of so-called 'postdependency' theorists such as Peter Evans (1979).

3 See also the 1995 'Afterword' of *Orientalism* (1978: 348-9, 352).

4 However, it should be noted that, in *Orientalism*, Said does recognize the agency of individual authors, believing them to not always be an 'effect' of discourse. Here, he is forging a more 'humanist' approach than Foucault, who he takes to task over this issue (1978: 23-4, 27).

5 Bhabha draws on the Lacanian argument that we are inherently linguistic beings, and because language is an unstable/arbitrary string of differentiated signs, any attempt at closure or homogeneity (e.g. a fixed or monolithic discourse, a racist/orientalist stereotype) is doomed to failure and/or instability (cf. Bhabha 1994: 124-5, 191; 1995b: 51). See Chapter 7 for details.

6 See Chapter 7 for further elaboration.

7 Bhabha, in particular, is critical of this kind of view of culture (which he calls 'cultural diversity'), where 'culture is made an object of empirical knowledge' and hence tends towards orientalist and fixed notions of tradition or custom. Instead, he points towards 'cultural difference', which is more about examining the 'enunciation of culture', its hybrid location, its production from the margins (1994: 34).

8 In many ways, the Laclau–Frank debate further brings out the totalizing character of Frank's view of power. Laclau (1971) argues that Frank's view of capitalism does not adequately consider the 'mode of production'. This causes Frank to incorrectly identify Latin America as having only one mode (a capitalist one), and to assert that it has never even been 'feudal' (Frank 1967: 115). For Laclau, this argument misses that any given economic system can have mixed/coexisting modes of production, although he agrees with Frank that these modes are non-dual and intimately linked. The upshot, as Randall and Theobold point out, is that 'Laclau finds himself, paradoxically, in agreement with Frank that development does indeed generate underdevelopment, except that Laclau is arguing that exploitation is between two modes of production rather than within one capitalist mode of production' (1985: 134). However, in the 'Indian mode of production debate', Banaji and Alavi counter Laclau, and side more (although not entirely) with Frank. They argue that Laclau cannot have it both ways: a feudal mode cannot both coexist with a capitalist mode and be linked to it: either the two modes would coexist and hence be in contradiction with one another, or the feudal mode would be in the service of imperialism, which is what Frank argues in the first place (Blomström & Hettne 1994: 129-30; Alavi 1975).

9 I am not arguing that Said, Spivak, or Bhabha completely negate materiality or that theirs is a naive postmodern politics of representation. After all, discursivity, along with its concern for material, bodily, and institutional power, is an important theme of their work. It is the lack of materiality's *adequate* foregrounding in their work (most notably in the work of Bhabha; cf. chapters 7 and 8) that I am drawing attention to here.

10 Spivak is famous for her advocacy of 'strategic essentialism', which she defines as 'a strategic use of positivist essentialism in a scrupulously visible political interest' (1996: 214). But this still begs the question of how a strategically essentialist position is arrived at, and on the basis of what different positions can be adjudicated. This is one of Habermas's main critiques of Mouffe, whose argument is not dissimilar to Spivak's on this issue (cf. Chapter 6).

11 Sometimes, Spivak attributes these gaps to her being a 'bricoleur' and using 'what comes to hand' (1988a: 281; 1990a: 55), as though issues of adjudication and political/epistemological prioritization can be left to whim or chance.

2 THE CULTURE OF DEVELOPMENT POLICY: BASIC NEEDS, STRUCTURAL ADJUSTMENT, GOOD GOVERNANCE, AND HUMAN RIGHTS

1 Huntington is actually critical of the 'multicultural' emphasis on ethnic separateness, which he believes weakens the US (1996: 307). Yet, his argument about the clash of civilizations is precisely a multiculturalist one, positing distinct and fundamentally different world civilizations.

2 That is, the tendency to reduce politics to the polite interplay between diverse cultural groups.

3 I say 'rough' historical order because there is no neat sequence to these policy regimes and much overlap between them. It is difficult to pinpoint a precise historical 'origin' to each regime: for example, governance and human rights both arose roughly at the same time in the 1990s. Moreover, as will be seen later in this chapter, there is much complicity and continuity between structural adjustment and governance.

Note that I have chosen these four regimes partly because of their continuing impact on current development policy, as will be emphasized in the rest of the chapter. Of course, several other policy regimes could also be included here — e.g. women in development (WID), participatory development, etc. Chapter 3 deals with WID to some extent, and Chapter 4 with participatory development. But in any case, I am not trying to be comprehensive, but only to draw attention to the cultural underpinnings of development policy-making.

4 I am not identifying or advocating a systematic or comprehensive semiotic method or discursive analysis here (I do not believe there is one, on philosophic grounds). I am merely suggesting some of the types of discursive strategies I see being played out some of the time in the aforementioned policy regimes. In other words, I will not systematically or mechanistically examine all of the listed discursive strategies in all of the policy regimes under consideration in this chapter, only those that appear (to me) to be pertinent to each.

5 Streeten speaks of his book as an attempt to 'distill some of the results' of the World Bank's work programme in the late 1970s (1981: 3).

6 Such positions cast doubt on statements by Streeten about the need for participation by the poor themselves in anti-poverty projects, which are mentioned but left sorely undeveloped (cf. 1981: 27).

7 He adds that BN is not a 'call to revolution' and that socialism is not 'a prerequisite' (Streeten 1981: 55, 182).

8 I take a Žižekian view of ideology, which eschews the classical Marxist view of a neutral point from which to distinguish false consciousness from reality; it looks instead for evidence of omissions, gaps, disavowals, contradictions to trip up ideological arguments about perfection, smoothness, naturalness, idealism. See Chapter 4 for an elaboration.

9 Cf. Hansen-Kuhn (1993), who makes a direct link between Costa Rica's adjustment programmes and the opening up of maquilas, showing that the number of maquilas tripled over the period of adjustment that she examines. See Alarcon-Gonzalez & McKinley (1999) for a similar pattern in Mexico during the 1990s.

10 I mean this especially in terms of the number of countries covered and programmes administered in the region, which has resulted in the disciplining and surveillance of governments and civil servants as just described. Apart from South Africa, there are not many FTZs in Sub-Saharan Africa, so my arguments about the disciplining of workers do not really apply there.

11 The classic political formula — create trouble, identify it, address it, and come away looking good — is relevant in this case, although here it is less a question of conspiracy or perfect foresight than a case of transforming each situation (good or bad) into an opportunity.

12 Presumably, such dialogue would entail that particular demands of groups around the world (e.g. the right to life, health, work, gender equity, cultural autonomy) are cross-culturally understood and recognized as *universal*; and simultaneously, universal rights (e.g. equality, justice) are cross-culturally particularized. No easy task. More on this in Chapter 6.

3 HYPER-SELF-REFLEXIVE DEVELOPMENT?: SPIVAK ON REPRESENTING THE THIRD WORLD 'OTHER'

1 The controversy turns mainly on Spivak's statement, towards the end of her article, that the 'subaltern cannot speak' (1988a: 308), which some have interpreted as saying that the subaltern has no agency or is doomed to silence. Spivak has often had to defend against such interpretations, and has more recently revised both the article and the statement (cf. 1999: 246ff.). This controversy will be dealt with later in this chapter.

2 The term 'subaltern' is a Gramscian one, central to the work of the Subaltern Studies Group (of which Spivak is part). It refers to groups subordinated and marginalized based on 'class, caste, age, gender and office or in any other way' (Guha 1988: 35). What Spivak means by the term is 'subsistence farmers, unorganized labor, the tribals, and the communities of zero workers on the street or in the countryside' (1988a: 288), emphasizing the marginalization of the women members of these groups.

3 See my biography on the book cover for (a few) details of my own involvement in this field.

4 I use the term 'hyper' as a prefix, suggesting a vigilance above-and-beyond conventional self-reflexivity, a radical self-reflexivity (hence my hyphenation, namely 'hyper-self-reflexivity'); and not as the slang 'hyper', short for 'hyperactive' or 'overstimulated' (which would not be hyphenated, namely 'hyper self-reflexivity').

5 Said's work shows how Orientalism pervades the writings of such icons of Western literature as Dickens, Austen, James, and Hardy, as well as present-day Western media reports about the Third World, particularly the Islamic world. Cf. Chapter 1.

6 Spivak often refers to herself as a 'Marxist-feminist-deconstructivist' (e.g. 1990a: 133), by which she indicates that her analyses are informed by all three perspectives, recognizing that each one has its limits and problems, and that each can sometimes complement, but also be discontinuous with, the other two (i.e. a critical interdisciplinarity). Note here, for example, how she complements her Marxist political-economy reading of imperialism with a feminist one (i.e. the condition of subaltern women under globalization) and a semiotic/culturalist interpretation of Marx's 'commodity fetishism'.

7 The term is problematic for Spivak because it derives from a field (ethnography) in which the power relationship between the Western ethnographer and the native informant, that situates the former in a dominant role and the latter in a subordinate one, has until only recently been left unquestioned (1999: 6). Note that in *A Critique of Postcolonial Reason* (1999), Spivak uses the figure of the native informant in several ways: as the West's Other, as collaborator in Western ethnographic work on the Third World, but also as Spivak's implied reader (i.e. she exhorts the reader to put her/himself in the difficult position of the native informant).

8 Note that Spivak tars both diasporic and Third World native informants with the same brush here, arguing that all — intellectuals, researchers, professionals — are privileged and complicit in capitalism and Western(ized) education. Thus, an Indian academic has no credible claim to being 'purer' or having a more 'authentic' ethnic identity or experience than his/her Western diasporic counterpart. Spivak is adamant that intellectuals and elites cannot claim a space uncontaminated by capitalism and imperialism (cf. 1990a: 67-70; 1988a: 291).

9 Of course, as is implicit here, there is much overlap and slippage between 'who represents' and 'why we represent', since our geopolitical positioning intersects with our institutional positioning, thus confounding the 'who' and 'why' of representation. Or, to put it another way, who represents and why we represent are part and parcel of the same process of discursive framing. I have only formally separated the two in this chapter for the sake of (my own) organization of arguments; their interrelationship is at the very least implied throughout.

10 Spivak does not really delve into the microtechnics of fieldwork, but there is a rich ethnographic literature that generally supports her line of thinking (e.g. Crewe & Harrison 1998; Khan 2001; Lal 1996; Sylvester 1995; Visweswaran 1994; Wolf 1996). Lal, for example, shows how the researcher's voice is often used to support his/her arguments and interests: the 'narrative serves to whet the readers' or audiences' desire to know, and the narrator's need to prove that one really was "There!". . .there is thus always a danger that "the people one studies are treated as garnishes and condiments, tasty only in relationship to the main course, the sociologist"' (1996: 201).

11 Note that the fact that every 70 cents on the aid dollar is spent on Canadian goods and services does not necessarily mean that 70 percent of Canadian aid is tied: a portion of it is officially tied (at present, this figure stands at 43 percent; cf. Chapter 5 for details), and the balance of it is spent in Canada by the aid recipients, presumably of their own volition (although, as Chapter 5 points out, this may be less a case of volition than the logical result of Canada's privileged position in the international division of labour).

12 One of the problems with Kamat's book (2002) is precisely its tendency to overgeneralize, making out as though all NGOs reproduce development discourse all of the time.

13 Shiva provides a more nuanced and less essentialist argument on this issue in her later work with Maria Mies (compare Mies & Shiva 1993: 20).

14 Escobar's more recent work on 'cultural hybridity' and 'place' has come to recognize the greater complexity and plurality of the local (cf. Escobar 2001).

15 As pointed out in Chapter 1, Spivak thinks catachresis can also serve a political function, as when it is misused or misplaced creatively by those who seek to re-code/displace hegemonic representations.

16 Cf. note 1 above.

4 PARTICIPATORY DEVELOPMENT, COMPLICITY, AND DESIRE

1 There are undoubtedly several variants and hybrids of both institutional forms. But, in any case, part of my argument here is to problematize the differences between them: for, if complicity and desire are integral to each, then they are all equally 'engineered'. As a result, a claim that, say, the PRA approach is bottom-up, while the 'country ownership' approach is top-down, appears unconvincing. The same is true, in my view, about more politicized forms of participation such as Freirian pedagogy or Participatory Action Research: while perhaps more 'critical', they, too, depend on a convenor/facilitator, and hence are accompanied by the attendant complicities and desires.

2 I mention Mouffe because, like Žižek, she draws on Lacanian psychoanalytic theory to criticize liberal democracy. She is highly skeptical of 'consensus', taking Habermas to task over the notion (cf. Mouffe 2000), as Chapter 6 will explicate.

3 This is Habermas's answer to the problem: he advocates an 'ideal speech situation', that is, a set of fair, intersubjective rules and procedures governing public deliberation. See Chapter 6 for details.

4 Žižek is referring in this passage to 'postmodernism', but it applies well to PD.

5 I am inspired here by Hardt and Negri's historically specific definition of empire, which they distinguish from imperialism: 'Imperialism was really an extension of the sovereignty of the European nation-states beyond their own boundaries. . . . In contrast to imperialism, Empire establishes no territorial center of power and does not rely on fixed boundaries or barriers. It is a decentered and deterritorialising apparatus of rule that progressively incorporates the entire global realm within its open, expanding frontiers' (2000: xii). On the relationship between participation and colonialism, see Cooke (2003). His genealogical analysis links Action Research to colonial forms of indirect rule.

6 I am twisting Arundhati Roy's line about democracy becoming a 'euphemism for neo-liberal capitalism' (2004b: 56).

7 Although, as the next section argues, regarding them as pawns does not necessarily mean they will conform to our expectations.

8 I refer here to 'us' as change agents within academic or development institutions. It is, in many ways, these change agents to whom this chapter is primarily addressed. It is we who can exploit the institutional possibilities that I refer to in the concluding sections of this chapter. If so, we may be able to take advantage of PD's instabilities and contradictions (perhaps in collaboration with PD's subjects). For example, we could push for our own institutions to face up to such contradictions and call for the extension and deepening of participation in decision-making both 'inside' and 'outside' these institutions.

5 FOREIGN AID AS G(R)IFT

1 This means that I will not really treat the topic of aid recipients, or that I will treat them only indirectly through their representation by donor/development discourse, which is to say that, more often than not, aid recipients will be portrayed as homogenous and passive. But of course, recipients do not necessarily conform to such representations, and much of my effort in subsequent chapters is about showing why. My point in this chapter and the previous one is to underline once again how development/foreign aid regimes say more about donors than recipients.

2 The DAC is made up of key Western donor nations, and is the main body of the OECD that deals with cooperation with developing countries.

3 I am being cautious here because there could well be additional explanations for these findings (e.g. the public believes the government spends too much) and also because I tend to be suspicious of public surveys (due to their mostly positivist methodologies and lack of critical dialogical engagement with respondents).

4 Of note are project-related conditionalities, which in addition to tying aid, have required user fees for services in such areas as water, health, education, power, irrigation or transport (cf. Colclough 1998).

5 To clarify: the US is the largest aid donor in terms of total annual aid allocations, but one of the smallest in terms of aid as a percentage of GNI. DAC sees the latter measurement as a more appropriate one for comparing donors.

6 All members are North American or Western European, except for Japan, Australia, and New Zealand.

7 Most of this aid was directed to Arab countries involved in the Israel-Arab conflict during that time.

8 Bilateral aid may well be differently pleasurable to the various constituencies that make up the aid machinery (governmental or non-governmental), but my point is that all derive pleasure from the dispensation of aid, while at the same time pleasuring the nation through their perpetuation of nationalist discourse.

9 For example, nationalism did serve an important, although not necessarily benign, purpose during decolonization (cf. Fanon 1963).

10 Of course, these transnational affiliations bring with them their own symbolic returns and seductions, which may be liberating (weaning us out of our nationalist tendencies), but perhaps also equally as contaminating (e.g. leading to the search for an expanded and globalized recognition or reward).

6 DELIBERATIVE DEMOCRACY OR AGONISTIC PLURALISM?: THE RELEVANCE OF THE HABERMAS–MOUFFE DEBATE FOR THIRD WORLD POLITICS

1 Strictly speaking, Habermas's standpoint is 'de-ontological' as evidenced by its proceduralism. Note as well that the title of this chapter is taken in part from the title of one of Mouffe's articles (cf. Mouffe 1999).

2 Bernstein, inspired by Adorno and Benjamin, treats the Habermas–Derrida debate as a 'constellation', much as I propose to do with the Habermas–Mouffe debate.

3 The works of Pantham (1987) and Sundara Rajan (1986, 1987, 1991), two Indian political philosophers, are notable exceptions. But while important, the arguments of these theorists are not directly relevant to the issues raised by the Habermas–Mouffe debate, which is the focus of this chapter.

4 Cf. Escobar (1995, 2000).

5 For an excellent engagement with Third World political theory, and encouragement of what may be called a cross-cultural hermeneutics, see Fred Dallmayr's work (e.g. 1996, 1998, 1999). I see this chapter, in its encounter with the work of two First World theorists,

but also in its critique and qualifications of their work from a postcolonial perspective, as part of such critical cross-cultural dialogue.

6 Note that, for Habermas, state power and economic/monetary exchange are non-dialogical and non-discursive modes of coordination; hence his defence of a dialogical and discursive public sphere.

7 Note that, for Habermas, the ideal speech situation is anticipated in the very structure of human communication (1990: 86-7). Note, as well, that of late, Habermas appears to prefer to use the terms 'norms of discourse' or 'procedures of discourse' than 'ideal speech situation'.

8 'Quasi-transcendental' because, as pointed out earlier, deliberative democracy does not impose an outside agenda on public deliberations; the agenda is specific to, and dependent on, participatory politics. As well, Habermas has in mind quasi-transcendence of ethical/cultural background, believing that rationalization requires self-reflexivity and transcendence regarding one's own traditions and beliefs. Thus, for him, culture is both the backdrop of communicative reason and its object. However, as shall be seen later, he ends up championing the 'moral' over the 'ethical', which amounts to prioritizing transcendence/universality over particularity/culture/the personal. This is the point at which he runs into feminist and other criticisms.

9 In more recent writings (e.g. 1996a: 23-5), Habermas appears to soften his stance on the absolute priority of morality over ethics, most likely because he is heeding the strong criticisms of feminists and others of this stance. These criticisms will be dealt with later in the chapter.

10 Elsewhere, Mouffe writes that the ideal speech situation is a '*conceptual* impossibility' (2000: 33). On this issue, see the excellent article by Kieran Keohane (1993), written well in advance of Mouffe's more recent work and announcing many of the themes she has later taken up.

11 Mouffe's characterization of Habermas as seeking to eliminate conflict altogether from the deliberative sphere is debatable; as implied earlier, I am of the view that Habermas wishes to minimize (not eliminate) power inequalities and conflict to the extent possible.

12 Note that Mouffe's discussion around friend/enemy, enemy/adversary is based on her reading of Carl Schmitt's work (cf. Mouffe 2000: 36ff.).

13 Cf. Chapter 4, sections on 'Transference' and 'Conditionality'.

14 See *Legitimation Crisis* (1976: 61-75) for Habermas's analysis of liberal democratic institutions and crises.

15 Cf. Benhabib (1996a-b), Fraser (1989, 1992), Young, I.M. (1990, 1996).

16 In *The Postnational Constellation*, Habermas appears to suggest that multicultural-ism needs to be the result not of the consent of minority groups, but of the accommo-dation and magnanimity of majority groups: 'The majority culture, supposing itself to be identical with national culture as such, has to free itself from its historical iden-tification with a *general* political culture, if all citizens are to be able to identify on equal terms with the political culture of their own country' (2001b: 74, italics in original).

17 See, for example, his recognition of feminist concerns about the public sphere in his 'Further reflections on the public sphere' (1992a: 428); and his somewhat softened stance on the hierarchy between moral and ethical in *The Inclusion of the Other* (1998) (whose very title is indicative of his sensitivity to this issue) and 'Three normative models of democracy' (1996a).

18 There is a rich literature in planning and policy studies on these issues (cf. Forester 1985; Healy 1993; Tewdwr-Jones and Allemendinger 1998; Dryzek 1990).

19 In this regard, Mouffe writes: 'these struggles are not necessarily socialist or even progressive. . . . They can, therefore, be as easily assimilated by the discourses of the anti-status quo Right as by those of the Left' (1988a: 98).

20 I put the word 'tribal' in quotation marks to symbolize my discomfort in using (and of the construction of) the term (as I have done with other words, e.g. 'ethnic'). In fact, in India, 'tribal' or indigenous people prefer to use the term *adivasi*.

21 Habermas's argument about the institutionalization of democratic rules and procedures is also a recognition that, in large, plural, and complex societies, not everyone can participate in all decisions all of the time.

22 Mouffe makes almost identical statements, with similar subjunctive clauses, in 'Decision, deliberation, and democratic ethos' (1997: 25), 'Radical democracy: modern or postmodern?' (1988b: 24), and 'Deliberative democracy or agonistic pluralism?' (1999: 754).

23 For a brief explanation of what Habermas means by 'rationalization', see note 8 above.

24 Craig Calhoun argues that Habermas's later work seeks a 'less historical, more transcendental basis for democracy' (1992: 31-2, 40).

25 This is particularly true of *Structural Transformation of the Public Sphere* (1989), *Legitimation Crisis* (1976), and *The Theory of Communicative Action* (1985).

26 Mouffe's colleague, Ernesto Laclau, has devoted much of his writing to Third World (especially Latin American) politics. But this does not excuse Mouffe for not doing the same, or at least touching on Third World issues in her work, if only to advance her critique of Western liberalism.

27 The one possible exception is Habermas's recent reflections on terrorism and the 'war on terror' (cf. Borradori 2003), wherein he refers (although in no real depth) to the socioeconomic inequities between North and South and the colonization of lifeworlds in the Middle East and the Islamic regions of the world.

28 Let me be clear: I am not arguing that Habermas and Mouffe should cover Third World politics in their democratic theories (that would be presumptuous of me). I argue, instead, that given their critique of Western liberal democracy, their failure to look into Western liberalism's complicity with colonialism is conspicuous by its absence and, moreover, that a discussion of this complicity would enhance their critique.

29 In fact, Mohan and Stokke are speaking about Laclau and Mouffe here, although they also see Escobar as wanting in this respect. The implied argument here is that Escobar's critique of development and construction of local resistance are too sweeping. He assumes there is a single logic to development discourse (i.e. development only destroys and never enables), as well as to resistance (e.g. all local resistance is anti-development).

30 Habermas writes: 'After all, the majority of conflicts have their sources in the collision of group interests and concern distributive problems that can be resolved only by means of compromise' (1992a: 448).

31 On this argument, see David Held (1995) and Ian Shapiro and Casiano Hacker-Cordon (1999).

32 Of course, such a hermeneutical approach warrants my declaring my own prejudices (which underlie this chapter) as an Indo-Canadian academic, living and working in the West and partial to a critical cross-cultural dialogue (with all its pitfalls) and the project of extending democracy.

7 ACTING IN A TIGHT SPOT: HOMI BHABHA'S POSTCOLONIAL POLITICS

1 To date, I am unaware of any systematic analysis of Bhabha's politics: while there is a growing literature within postcolonial studies analyzing his place in the literary critical field and some of the political dimensions of his work, there appears not to be any examination of his work done with regard to a politics; as for the field of political science, apart from Jeffrey T. Nealon's brief mention of Bhabha in *Alterity Politics* (see note 12),

I am unaware of any consideration of Bhabha's contributions to political theory. This essay is an attempt to fill these gaps, emphasizing, in general, the importance of post-colonial theory to political science/development studies, and in particular, the performative dimensions of Bhabha's work and its innovations over the poststructuralist politics of Foucault and Butler.

2 Presumably, Bhabha uses 'spectacular' to validate the subversive act, but also to draw attention to the act as 'spectacle'. I develop this idea later in the chapter.

3 In many ways, both Bhabha and Butler are echoing (but also innovating, as I will point out later) Michel Foucault's assertion that the practices of the self are 'not something that the individual invents by himself. They are patterns that he finds in his culture and which are proposed, suggested and imposed on him by his culture, his society, and his social group' (1988: 11).

4 Bhabha actually borrows the notion of mimicry from Lacan (cf. Bhabha 1994: 90), but its parallels with Derrida's notion of repetition are unmistakable.

5 Or, more precisely, if discourse is always already repetition with a difference (since each iteration is different), and agency is the performance of this repetition, then what *particular* difference does agency make?

6 Hannah Arendt points out, in this regard, that 'action, though it may proceed from nowhere, so to speak, acts into a medium where every reaction becomes a chain reaction . . . the smallest act in the most limited circumstances bears the seed of the same boundlessness, because one deed, and sometimes one word, suffices to change every constellation' (1958a: 190-1).

7 Bhabha has in mind right-wing religious nationalist movements.

8 Note that the master's 'desire' need not be merely for recognition (by the colonial subject); it can also be sexual, and is most often gendered. Bhabha implies this, although his work does not dwell upon it. For readings of sexualized colonial desire (gendered, eroticized/exoticized, repressed, homoerotic), see Frantz Fanon (1967); Anne McClintock (1995); Grant Parsons (1997); and Irvin Cemil Schick (1999).

9 See also O'Hanlon and Washbrook (1992: 152-3); and Vaughan (1994: 5).

10 Butler distinguishes 'ironic performance', where the actor can choose a role at will, from performativity, which is about responding to social norms (1993: 3, 24; cf. Nealon 1998: 23).

11 An illusion that Butler says we construct because of a *'stylized repetition of acts'* (1990: 140, italics in original).

12 In *Alterity Politics*, Jeffrey Nealon dismisses Bhabha's notion of performativity (and champions Butler's) because (puzzlingly) he believes it to be 'predicated on the possibility of some kind of wholeness or plenitude' (1998: 10) that results in resentment and impedes a politics of alterity. Nealon argues that Butler's performativity, derived from Foucault/Derrida, is more conducive to alterity politics because of the implied idea of repetition/response. I think Nealon misrepresents Bhabha, in part because he relies on the reading of only one essay ('DissemiNation'). As I argue, Bhabha is close to Butler (closer than Nealon suggests), with the idea of repetition/response very explicitly (and repeatedly!) invoked in his work (i.e. Nealon sees only the Lacanian and misses the Derridean and Foucauldian in Bhabha).

13 It should be noted that Bhabha is skeptical not only of modern time, but postmodern time/space as well. For example, he takes Foucault to task for privileging time over location or space in his historiography (cf. Nicholls 1997: 5ff.). That is, according to Bhabha, even as Foucault espouses a discontinuous and multi-perspectival view of history, his view of space — European space — is single and continuous. Foucault's time, no matter its discontinuity, is thus constructed in terms of fixed European space. Bhabha takes issue, in particular, with Foucault's reading of the French Revolution, and asks: 'what if the "distance" that constitutes the meaning of the "Revolution" as sign,

the *signifying lag* between event and enunciation, stretches not across the Place de la Bastille or the rue des Blancs-Monteaux, but spans the temporal difference of the colonial space . . . The Eurocentricity of Foucault's theory of cultural difference is revealed in his insistent spatialization of the time of modernity' (1994: 244, 243). For an elaboration of this issue, see Nicholls (1997).

14 Of course, he is building here on the pioneering work of the Subaltern Studies Group.

8 BEND IT LIKE BHABHA: HYBRIDITY AND POLITICAL STRATEGY

1 Bhabha recognizes that the agent has a past: 'the *pre* is not a givenness, but an anteriority' (1999: 24). Yet, he provides no clue as to what the content, form, or even trace of such anteriority might be.

2 Bhabha's position appears quite unlayered on this question, which is ironic given his notoriety as a theorist of hybridity.

3 I am modifying Derrida's phrase, 'there is no kingdom of *différance*, but *différance* instigates the subversion of every kingdom' (1982: 22). In many ways, Bhabha's work can be seen as teasing out the specifically postcolonial and political implications of this rule. And, in many ways, my argument here is that an *awareness* of this rule is crucial to expanding the political and strategic possibilities of Bhabhaian hybridity.

4 For the sake of clarity, I am taking 'strategy' to mean a plan of action resulting from a degree of foresight and/or coordination.

5 Campaigns that come to mind are those that challenge social mores and/or the unequal application of laws/policies (for example, campaigns carried out by feminist, queer, and civil/human rights groups).

6 To this end, see for instance, Diana Taylor's analysis (1994) of the performative politics of Argentina's 'Mothers', and the work of the group Women Living Under Muslim Laws (2006), which reinterprets Islamic laws and texts in a feminist light.

7 Note that the Third Space hybrid, although 'new', is not a 'thing' or an ontological claim. 'Vegetarian Bible' or rumour are senseless by themselves; they 'are' only insofar as they are a supplement or witness to ongoing political contestation.

8 Richard Day would probably call Bhabha's political strategy 'non-hegemonic', as opposed to 'counter-hegemonic' (2005: 8). But while I like this distinction, I cannot agree with Day's implications. He champions the 'newest' social movements because of their anarchist tendencies, arguing that they 'seek radical change, but not through taking or influencing state power, and in so doing they challenge the logic of hegemony at its very core' (p. 8). One of the key reasons he labels them 'non-hegemonic' is because, in opposing the hegemon, they are not reproducing hegemonic power. Yet, his championing of these 'newest' social movements too neatly and conveniently coincides with those movements that happen to be cutting-edge and vanguardist (by comparison, he tends to dismiss the 'new' social movements of the 1970s and 1980s as being 'counter-hegemonic'). And this itself is a reproduction of a progressive and avant-gardist notion of history and politics. In other words, I am suspicious of what appears in Day as a 'newest is best' approach to politics: *plus ça change, plus c'est la même chose . . .*?

CONCLUSION

1 I used to take such a view (cf. Kapoor 2003: 562, n. 7), but have since reconsidered.

BIBLIOGRAPHY

Aaltola, M. (1999) 'Emergency food aid as a means of political persuasion in the North Korean famine', *Third World Quarterly*, 20(2): 371-86.

Adcroft, A. and Willis, R. (2005) 'The (un)intended outcome of public sector performance measurement', *International Journal of Public Sector Management*, 18(5): 386-400.

Ahluwalia, P. (2001) *Politics and Post-Colonial Theory: African inflections*, London and New York: Routledge.

—— (2003) 'The wonder of the African market: post-colonial inflections', *Pretexts: Literary and Cultural Studies*, 12(2): 133-44.

Ahmad, A. (1992) *In Theory*, London: Verso.

—— (1997) 'Postcolonial theory and the "post-" condition', *Socialist Register 1997*, London: Merlin Press: 353-81.

Alarcon-Gonzalez, D. and McKinley, T. (1999) 'The adverse effects of structural adjustment on working women in Mexico', *Latin American Perspectives*, 26(3): 103-17.

Alavi, H. (1975) 'India and the colonial mode of production', *Socialist Register 1975*, London: Merlin Press: 160-85.

Alcoff, L. (1991) 'The problem of speaking for others', *Cultural Critique*, 20: 5-32.

Anderson, B. (1983) *Imagined Communities: reflections on the origin and spread of nationalism*, London: Verso.

Appadurai, A. (1996) *Modernity at Large: cultural dimensions of globalization*, Minneapolis: University of Minnesota Press.

Arendt, H. (1958a) *The Human Condition*, Chicago, IL: University of Chicago Press.

—— (1958b) *The Origins of Totalitarianism*, New York: Meridian.

Arvin, B.M. (ed.) (2002) *New Perspectives on Foreign Aid and Economic Development*, Westport, CT: Praeger.

AusAID (1997) 'One clear objective: poverty reduction through sustainable development', Report of the Committee of Review, Canberra: AusAID. Available at: http://www.ausaid.gov.au/publications/pdf/simons/simons.pdf (accessed 22 March 2007).

—— (2006) 'About Australia's overseas aid program', Canberra: AusAID. Available at: http://www.ausaid.gov.au/makediff/whatis.cfm (accessed 17 February 2006).

Balfour, I. and Cadava, E. (2004) 'The claims of human rights: an introduction', *South Atlantic Quarterly*, 103(2/3): 277-96.

Bandy, J. and Mendez, J.B. (2003) 'A place of their own? Women organizers in the maquilas of Nicaragua and Mexico', *Mobilization: An International Journal*, 8(2): 173-88.

Basu, A. (1987) 'Grass roots movements and the state', *Theory and Society*, 16: 647-74.

Baudrillard, J. (1981) *For a Critique of the Political Economy of the Sign*, trans. C. Levin, St Louis, MO: Telos.

—— (1995) *Simulacra and Simulation*, trans. S. Glaser, Ann Arbor: University of Michigan Press.

Baviskar, A. (1995) *In the Belly of the River*, Delhi: Oxford University Press.

Baxi, U. (1987) 'What is wrong with sycophancy? A caveat on overrationalized notions of political communication', in B. Parekh and T. Pantham (eds) *Political Discourse: explorations in Indian and Western political thought*, New Delhi: Sage.

BBC News (2005) 'G8 reaches deal for world's poor', 11 June. Available at: http://news.bbc.co.uk/2/hi/business/4083676.stm (accessed 17 February 2006).

Benhabib, S. (1986) *Critique, Norm and Utopia*, New York: Columbia University Press.

—— (1992) 'Models of public space: Hannah Arendt, the liberal tradition, and Jürgen Habermas', in C. Calhoun (ed.) *Habermas and the Public Sphere*, Cambridge, MA: MIT Press.

—— (1995) 'Subjectivity, historiography and politics', in S. Benhabib, J. Butler, D. Cornell, and N. Fraser (eds) *Feminist Contentions: a philosophical exchange*, London and New York: Routledge.

—— (1996a) 'Introduction: The democratic moment and the problem of difference', in S. Benhabib (ed.) *Democracy and Difference*, Princeton, NJ: Princeton University Press.

—— (1996b) 'Toward a deliberative model of democratic legitimacy', in S. Benhabib (ed.) *Democracy and Difference*, Princeton, NJ: Princeton University Press.

Bernstein, R. (1988) 'Fred Dallmayr's critique of Habermas', *Political Theory*, 16(4): 580-93.

—— (1993) *The New Constellation*, Cambridge, MA: MIT Press.

Bérubé, M. and Nelson, C. (1995) *Higher Education Under Fire: politics, economics, and the crisis of the humanities*, London and New York: Routledge.

Best, B. (1999) 'Postcolonialism and the deconstructive scenario: representing Gayatri Spivak', *Environment and Planning D: Society and Space*, 17: 475-94.

Beverly, J. (1999) *Subalternity and Representation*, Durham, NC: Duke University Press.

Bhabha, H.K. (ed.) (1990) *Nation and Narration*, London and New York: Routledge.

—— (1994) *The Location of Culture*, London and New York: Routledge.

—— (1995a) 'Translator translated: W.J.T. Mitchell talks to Homi Bhabha', *Artforum*, 33(7): 80-4, 110, 114, 118-19.

—— (1995b) 'Freedom's basis in the indeterminate', and 'Discussion', in J. Rajchman (ed.) *The Identity in Question*, London and New York: Routledge.

—— (1999) 'Staging the politics of difference: Homi Bhabha's critical literacy', in G.A. Olson and L. Worsham (eds) *Race, Rhetoric, and the Postcolonial*, Albany, NY: SUNY Press.

Blomström, M. and Hettne, B. (1984) *Development Theory in Transition: the dependency debate and beyond*, London: Zed.

Borradori, G. (ed.) (2003) *Philosophy in a Time of Terror: dialogues with Jürgen Habermas and Jacques Derrida*, Chicago, IL: University of Chicago Press.

Bourdieu, P. (1997) 'Selections from *The Logic of Practice*', in A.D. Schrift (ed.) *The Logic of the Gift: toward an ethic of generosity*, London and New York: Routledge.

Boyce, J.K. (2002) 'Unpacking aid', *Development and Change*, 33(2): 239-46.

Bretton Woods Project (2006) 'World Bank weeds out corruption: will it touch the roots?' Available at: http://www.brettonwoodsproject.org/art.shtml?x=531789 (accessed 24 March 2007).

Brohman, J. (1995) 'Universalism, Eurocentrism, and ideological bias in development studies: from modernisation to neoliberalism', *Third World Quarterly*, 16(1): 121-40.

Bukovansky, M. (2006) 'The hollowness of the anti-corruption discourse', *Review of International Political Economy*, 13(2): 181-209.

Butler, J. (1990) *Gender Trouble: feminism and the subversion of identity*, London and New York: Routledge.

—— (1993) *Bodies that Matter: on the discursive limits of 'sex'*, London and New York: Routledge.

Calhoun, C. (1992) 'Introduction: Habermas and the public sphere', in C. Calhoun (ed.) *Habermas and the Public Sphere*, Cambridge, MA: MIT Press.

Callari, A. (2004) 'Economics and the postcolonial other', in E.O. Zein-Elabdin and S. Charusheela (eds) *Postcolonialism Meets Economics*, London and New York: Routledge.

Cardoso, F.H. (1972) 'Dependent capitalist development in Latin America', *New Left Review*, 74: 83-95.

—— (1973) 'Associated-dependent development: theoretical and practical implications', in A. Stepan (ed.) *Authoritarian Brazil: origins, policies, and future*, New Haven, CT: Yale University Press.

Cardoso, F.H. and Faletto, E. (1971, reprinted 1979) *Dependency and Development in Latin America*, Berkeley: University of California Press.

CBC News (2005) 'Geldof deserves Nobel prize: legislator', 7 July. Available at: http://cbcca/story/arts/national/2005/07/07/Arts/geldof050707.html (accessed 15 August 2005).

CCFR (Chicago Council on Foreign Relations) (2002) 'Worldviews 2002: foreign aid', Chicago. Available at: http://www.worldviews.org/detailreports/usreport/html/ch5s8.html (accessed 20 March 2006).

CEDAW (1979) Convention on the Elimination of all Forms of Discrimination against Women, Geneva: United Nations Office of the High Commissioner for Human Rights. Available at: http://www.unhchr.ch/html/menu3/b/e1cedaw.htm (accessed 14 March 2007).

Chakrabarty, D. (1992) 'Postcoloniality and the artifice of history: who speaks for "Indian" pasts?', *Representations*, 37: 1-26.

Chambers, R. (1994a) 'The origins and practice of Participatory Rural Appraisal', *World Development*, 22(7): 953-69.

—— (1994b) 'Participatory Rural Appraisal (PRA): analysis of experience', *World Development*, 22(9): 1253-68.

—— (1997) *Whose Reality Counts? Putting the first last*, London: Intermediate Technology Publications.

Chatterjee, P. (1986) *Nationalist Thought and the Colonial World: a derivative discourse?*, London: Zed.

CIDA (2003) 'Our partners in development'. Available at: http: //www.acdi-cida.gc.ca/cida_ind.nsf/vLUallDocByIDEn/0F43722D8BDC15CA852568EB00694B0F?OpenDocument (accessed 15 February 2003).

—— (2006) 'What we do', Hull, Quebec. Available at: http://www.acdi-cida.gc.ca/whatwedo.htm (accessed 17 February 2006).

Clammer, J. (2005) 'Culture, development, and social theory: on cultural studies and the place of culture in development', *Asia Pacific Journal of Anthropology*, 6(2): 100-19.

Clifford, B. (2006) 'Marketing humanitarian crises', *YaleGlobal Online*. Available at: http://yaleglobal.yale.edu/display.article?id=7010 (accessed 20 July 2006).

Colclough, C. (ed.) (1998) *Marketizing Education and Health in Developing Countries*, Oxford: Oxford University Press.

Collingwood, V. (2003) 'Assistance with fewer strings attached', *Ethics and International Affairs*, 17(1): 55-67.

Comaroff, J. and Comaroff, J. (1991) *Of Revelation and Revolution: Christianity, colonialism and consciousness in South Africa*, Chicago, IL: University of Chicago Press.

Cooke, B. (2003) 'A new continuity with colonial administration: participation in development management', *Third World Quarterly*, 24(1): 47-61.

Cooke, B. and Kothari, U. (eds) (2001) *Participation: the new tyranny?*, London: Zed.

Coombe, R.J. (1997) 'The demotic place of the "not there": trademark rumors in the postindustrial imaginary', in A. Gupta and J. Ferguson (eds) *Culture, Power, Place: explorations in critical anthropology*, Durham, NC: Duke University Press.

Cornwall, A. and Nyamu-Musembi, C. (2004) 'Putting the "rights-based" approach to development into perspective', *Third World Quarterly*, 25(8): 1415-37.

Crewe, E. and Harrison, E. (1998) *Whose Development? An ethnography of aid*, London: Zed.

CRS (Congressional Research Service) (2004) 'Foreign aid: an introductory overview of US programs and policy', Washington, DC: CRS Report for Congress. Available at: http://usinfo.state.gov/usa/infousa/trade/files/98-916.pdf (accessed 20 March 2006).

DAC (1993) 'DAC orientations on participatory development and good governance', OECD Working Papers, Paris: OECD.

—— (2001a) *Development Co-operation, 2001*, Paris: OECD.

—— (2001b) 'Is it ODA?', Paris: OECD. Available at: http://www.oecd.org/dataoecd/ 21/21/34086975.pdf (accessed 17 February 2006).

—— (2005) 'Statistical annex of the 2005 Development Co-operation Report', Paris: OECD. Available at: http://www.oecd.org/document/9/0,2340,en_2649_33721_ 1893129_1_1_1_1,00.html (accessed 16 February 2006).

—— (2006) 'DAC members and date of membership', Paris: OECD. Available at: http://www.oecd.org/document/38/0,2340,en_2649_33721_1893350_1_1_1_1,00.html (accessed 16 February 2006).

Dallmayr, F. (1996) *Beyond Orientalism: essays in cross-cultural encounter*, Albany, NY: SUNY Press.

—— (1998) *Alternative Visions: paths in the global village*, New York: Rowman and Littlefield.

—— (1999) *Border Crossings: toward a comparative political theory*, Lanham, MD: Lexington Books.

—— (2002) '"Asian values" and global human rights', *Philosophy East and West*, 52(2): 173-89.

Danby, C. (2004) 'Contested states, transnational subjects: toward a post-Keynesianism without modernity', in E.O. Zein-Elabdin and S. Charusheela (eds) *Postcolonialism Meets Economics*, London and New York: Routledge.

DANIDA (2006) 'Danish development policy', Copenhagen. Available at: http://www.um.dk/en/menu/DevelopmentPolicy/DanishDevelopmentPolicy/ DanishDevelopmentPolicy (accessed 17 February 2006).

Day, R.J.F. (2005) *Gramsci is Dead: anarchist currents in the newest social movements*, London: Pluto Press; Toronto: Between the Lines.

Deen, T. (2005) 'Development: rich nations again falter in aid pledges', Inter Press Service News Agency. 29 June. Available at: http://www.ipsnews.net/interna.asp?idnews=29270 (accessed 20 June, 2006).

Derrida, J. (1982) *Margins of Philosophy*, trans. A. Bass, Chicago. IL: University of Chicago Press.

—— (1992) *Given Time: i. Counterfeit Money*, trans. P. Kamuf, Chicago, IL: University of Chicago Press.

—— (1994) *Specters of Marx: the state of the debt, the work of mourning and the New International*, trans. P. Kamuf, London and New York: Routledge.

—— (1997) *Politics of Friendship*, trans. G. Collins, London: Verso.

—— (1999) *Adieu to Emmanuel Lévinas*, trans. P-A. Brault and M. Naas, Stanford, CA: Stanford University Press.

—— (2002) 'Force of law: on the mystical foundation of authority', in G. Anidjar (ed.) *Acts of Religion*, London and New York: Routledge.

—— (2003) 'Autoimmunity: real and symbolic suicides: a dialogue with Jacques Derrida', in G. Borradori (ed.) *Philosophy in a Time of Terror: dialogues with Jürgen Habermas and Jacques Derrida*, Chicago, IL: University of Chicago Press.

Devarajan, S., Dollar, D., and Holmgren, T. (2001) 'Aid and reform in Africa: lessons from ten case studies', Washington, D.C.: World Bank. Available at: http://www.worldbank. org/research/aid/africa/release/aid.htm (accessed 20 March 2006).

DFID (2000a) 'Human rights for poor people', Strategy Paper, London: DFID.

—— (2000b) *Eliminating World Poverty: making globalisation work for the poor*, White Paper on international development, Cm 5006, London: FID.

Dhaliwal, A.K. (1996) 'Can the subaltern vote? Radical democracy, discourse of representation and rights, and questions of race', in D. Trend (ed.) *Radical Democracy: identity, citizenship, and state*, London and New York: Routledge.

Diawara, M. (1998) *In Search of Africa*, Cambridge, MA: Harvard University Press.

Dirlik, A. (1994) 'The postcolonial aura: Third World criticism in the age of global capitalism', *Critical Inquiry*, 22: 328-56.

Dryzek, J. (1990) *Discursive Democracy: politics, policy and Political Science*, New York: Cambridge University Press.

Edgren, G. (2002) 'Aid is an unreliable joystick', *Development and Change*, 33(2): 261-7.

Escobar, A. (1984) 'Discourse and power in development: Michel Foucault and the relevance of his work to the Third World', *Alternatives*, 10(10): 377-400.

—— (1991) 'Anthropology and the development encounter: the making and marketing of development anthropology', *American Ethnologist*, 18(4): 658-82.

—— (1992) 'Reflections on "development": grassroots approaches and alternative politics in the Third World', *Futures* 24(5): 411-36.

—— (1995) *Encountering Development: the making and unmaking of the Third World*, Princeton, NJ: Princeton University Press.

—— (2000) 'Beyond the search for a paradigm? Post-development and beyond', *Development*, 43(4): 11-14.

—— (2001) 'Culture sits in places: reflections on globalism and subaltern strategies of localization', *Political Geography*, 20: 139-74.

Eurodad (European Network on Debt and Development) (2005a) 'French ODA and the politics of development cooperation'. Available at: http://www.eurodad.org/articles/ default.aspx?id=664 (accessed 17 February 2006).

—— (2005b) 'Devilish details: implications of the G7 debt deal'. Available at: http://www.eurodad.org/uploadstore/cms/docs/Overview_G7_debt_deal.pdf (accessed 17 February 2006).

—— (2006) 'World Bank and IMF conditionality: a development injustice'. Available at: http://www.eurodad.org/uploadstore/cms/docs/Microsoft_Word__Eurodad_World_Bank_ and_IMF_Conditionality_Report_Final_Version.pdf (accessed 3 February 2007).

Evans, P. (1979) *Dependent Development: the alliance of multinational, state, and local capital in Brazil*, Princeton, NJ: Princeton University Press.

Fagan, G.H. (1999) 'Cultural politics and (post) development paradigms', in R. Munck and D. O'Hearn (eds) *Critical Development Theory: contributions to a new paradigm*, London: Zed.

Fanon, F. (1963) *The Wretched of the Earth*, C. Farrington (ed.), New York: Grove Press.

—— (1967, reprinted 1982) *Black Skin, White Masks*, New York: Grove Press

Ferguson, J. (1990) *The Anti-Politics Machine: development, depoliticization and bureaucratic power in Lesotho*, Cambridge: Cambridge University Press.

—— (1998) 'Transnational topographies of power: beyond "the state" and "civil society" in the study of African politics', mimeo, Irvine: University of California, Irvine.

Fisher, W.F. (1995) 'Development and resistance in the Narmada Valley', in W.F. Fisher (ed.) *Toward Sustainable Development: struggling over India's Narmada river*, New York: M.E. Sharpe.

Forester, J. (ed.) (1985) *Critical Theory and Public Life*, Cambridge, MA: MIT Press.

Foster-Carter, A. (1973) 'Neomarxist approaches to development and underdevelopment', *Journal of Contemporary Asia*, 3(1): 7-33.

Foucault, M. (1979) *The History of Sexuality*, vol. 1, New York: Vintage.

—— (1980) *Power/Knowledge*, C. Gordon (ed.), New York: Pantheon.

—— (1984) *The Foucault Reader*, P. Rainbow (ed.), New York: Pantheon.

—— (1988) *The Final Foucault*, J. Bernauer and D. Rasmussen (eds), Cambridge, MA: MIT Press.

Francis, P. (2001) 'Participatory development and the World Bank', in B. Cooke and U. Kothari (eds) *Participation: the new tyranny?*, London: Zed.

Frank, A.G. (1967) *Capitalism and Underdevelopment in Latin America*, New York: Monthly Review Press.

—— (1969) *Latin America: underdevelopment or revolution*, New York: Monthly Review Press.

—— (1972) *Lumpenbourgeoisie-Lumpendevelopment*, New York: Monthly Review Press.

—— (1977) 'Dependence is dead, long live dependence and class struggle: an answer to critics', *World Development*, 5(4): 355-70.

—— (1998) *ReOrient*, Berkeley: University of California Press.

Frank, A.G. and Gills, B.K. (eds) (1993) *The World System, Five Hundred Years or Five Thousand?*, London and New York: Routledge.

Fraser, N. (1989) *Unruly Practices: power, discourse and gender in contemporary social theory*, Minneapolis: University of Minnesota Press.

—— (1992) 'Rethinking the public sphere: a contribution to the critique of actually existing democracy', in C. Calhoun (ed.) *Habermas and the Public Sphere*, Cambridge, MA: MIT Press.

—— (2002) 'False antitheses', and 'Pragmatism, feminism, and the linguistic turn', in S. Benhabib, J. Butler, D. Cornell, and N. Fraser (eds) *Feminist Contentions: a philosophical exchange*, London and New York: Routledge.

Friends of River Narmada (2007) 'The Saradar Sarovar dam: a brief introduction'. Available at: http://www.narmada.org/sardarsarovar.html (accessed 3 May 2007).

Furtado, C. (1970) *Economic Development of Latin America*, Cambridge: Cambridge University Press.

Gandhi, L. (1998) *Postcolonial Theory: a critical introduction*, New York: Columbia University Press.

Geertz, C. (1973) *The Interpretation of Cultures*, New York: Basic Books.

Gideon, J. (2006) 'Accessing economic and social rights under neoliberalism: gender and rights in Chile', *Third World Quarterly*, 27(7): 1269-83.

Globe and Mail (2006) 'UN report deems China third-largest food donor', 20 July.

Godbout, J.T. with Caillé, A. (1998) *The World of the Gift*, trans. D. Winkler, Montreal: McGill-Queen's University Press.

Griffith-Jones, S. (2002) 'Governance of the World Bank', Sussex: IDS. Available at: http://www.stephanygj.com/_documents/Governance_of_the_World_Bank._Paper_prepared_for_DFID.pdf (accessed 22 March 2006).

Guha, R. (1988) 'Preface', in R. Guha and G. Spivak (eds) *Selected Subaltern Studies*, New York: Oxford University Press.

Guha, R. (1989) *The Unquiet Woods*, New Delhi: Oxford University Press.

Gupta, A. (1998) *Postcolonial Developments*, Durham, NC: Duke University Press.

Habermas, J. (1976) *Legitimation Crisis*, trans. T. McCarthy, London: Heinemann.

—— (1985) *The Theory of Communicative Action*, vol. I, trans. T. McCarthy, Boston, MA: Beacon.

—— (1989) *Structural Transformation of the Public Sphere*, trans. T. Burger, Cambridge, MA: MIT Press.

—— (1990) *Moral Consciousness and Communicative Action*, trans. C. Lenhardt and S. Weber Nicholsen, Cambridge, MA: MIT Press.

—— (1992a) 'Further reflections on the public sphere', in C. Calhoun (ed.) *Habermas and the Public Sphere*, Cambridge, MA: MIT Press.

—— (1992b) *Autonomy and Solidarity: interviews with Jürgen Habermas*, P. Dews (ed.), London: Verso.

—— (1993) *Justification and Application*, Cambridge, MA: MIT Press.

—— (1996a) 'Three normative models of democracy', in S. Benhabib (ed.) *Democracy and Difference*, Princeton, NJ: Princeton University Press.

—— (1996b) *Between Facts and Norms: contributions to a discourse theory of law and democracy*, trans. W. Rehg, Cambridge, MA: MIT Press.

—— (1998) *The Inclusion of the Other*, Cambridge, MA: MIT Press.

—— (2001a) 'Why Europe needs a constitution', *New Left Review*, 11: 5-26.

—— (2001b) *The Postnational Constellation*, trans. M. Pensky, Cambridge, MA: MIT Press.

Hall, S. (1977) 'Culture, the media and the "ideological effect"', in M. Gurevitch, J. Curran, and J. Woollacott (eds) *Mass Communication and Society*, London: Edward Arnold.

—— (1992) 'The question of cultural identity', in S. Hall, D. Held, and T. McGrew (eds) *Modernity and its Futures*, Cambridge: Polity Press.

—— (1996) 'When was "the post-colonial"? Thinking at the limit', in I. Chambers and L. Curti (eds) *The Post-Colonial Question*, London and New York: Routledge.

—— (1997) 'The local and the global: globalization and ethnicity', in A.D. King (ed.) *Culture, Globalization and the World-System*, Minneapolis: University of Minnesota Press.

Hansen-Kuhn, K. (1993) *Structural Adjustment in Central America: the case of Costa Rica*, Washington, DC: Development Gap.

Hardt, M. and Negri, A. (2000) *Empire*, Cambridge, MA: Harvard University Press.

Harrison, G. (2005) 'The World Bank, governance and theories of political action in Africa', *British Journal of Politics and International Relations*, 7(2): 240-60.

Hasty, J. (2005) 'The pleasures of corruption: desire and discipline in Ghanaian political culture', *Cultural Anthropology*, 20(2): 271-301.

Hattori, T. (2001) 'Reconceptualizing foreign aid', *Review of International Political Economy*, 8(4): 633-60.

—— (2003a) 'Giving as a mechanism of consent: international aid organizations and the ethical hegemony of capitalism', *International Relations*, 17(2): 153-73.

—— (2003b) 'The moral politics of foreign aid', *Review of International Studies*, 29(2): 229-47.

Hayes, C. (1966) *Essays on Nationalism*, New York: Russell and Russell.

Healy, P. (1993) 'The communicative work of development plans', *Environment and Planning B: Planning and Design*, 20: 83-104.

Held, D. (1995) *Democracy and the Global Order: from the modern state to cosmopolitan governance*, Stanford, CA: Stanford University Press.

Hellinger, S. (1988) *Aid for Just Development: report on the future of foreign assistance*, Boulder, CO: Lynne Rienner.

Henkel, H. and Stirrat, R. (2001) 'Participation as spiritual duty; empowerment as secular subjection', in B. Cooke and U. Kothari (eds) *Participation: the new tyranny?*, London: Zed.

Hewitt, V. (2006) 'A cautionary tale: colonial and post-colonial conceptions of good government and democratisation in Africa', *Commonwealth & Comparative Politics*, 44(1): 41-61.

Hildyard, N., Hegde, P., Wolvenkamp, P., and Reddy, S. (2001) 'Pluralism, participation and power: joint forest management in India', in B. Cooke and U. Kothari (eds) *Participation: the new tyranny?*, London: Zed.

Hindess, B. (2005) 'Investigating international anti-corruption', *Third World Quarterly*, 26(8): 1389-98.

Honig, B. (1992) 'Toward an agonistic feminism: Hannah Arendt and the politics of identity', in J. Butler and J. Scott (eds) *Feminists Theorize the Political*, London and New York: Routledge.

Hook, S.W. (1995) *National Interest and Foreign Aid*, Boulder, CO: Lynne Rienner.

Huntington, S. (1996) *The Clash of Civilizations and the Remaking of the World Order*, New York: Simon & Schuster.

Hutchings, K. (2005) 'Speaking and hearing: Habermasian discourse ethics, feminism and IR', *Review of International Studies*, 31: 155-65.

Idahosa, P. and Shenton, B. (2004) 'The Africanist's "new" clothes', *Historical Materialism*, 12(4): 67-113.

ILO (1976) *Employment, Growth and Basic Needs: a one-world problem*, Report of the Director-General of the ILO, Geneva: ILO.

Jackson, C. (1995) 'Radical environmental myths: a gender perspective', *New Left Review*, 210 (March/April): 124-40.

James, P. (1997) 'Postdependency? The Third World in an era of globalism and late-capitalism', *Alternatives*, 22: 205-26.

Jenkins, R. (2001) 'Mistaking "governance" for "politics": foreign aid, democracy, and the construction of civil society', in S. Kaviraj and S. Khilnani (eds) *Civil Society: history and possibilities*, Cambridge: Cambridge University Press.

Jenkins, R. and Goetz, A-M. (1999) 'Accounts and accountability: theoretical implications of the right-to-information movement in India', *Third World Quarterly*, 20(3): 603-22.

Jepma, C.J. (1991) *The Tying of Aid*, Paris: OECD Development Centre.

—— (1996) 'The case for untying aid in OECD countries', in O. Stokke (ed.) *Foreign Aid Towards the Year 2000: experiences and challenges*, London: Frank Cass.

Joss, J. (1996) 'Postcolonialism: subverting whose empire?', *Third World Quarterly*, 17(2): 239-50.

Kamat, S. (2002) *Development Hegemony: NGOs and the state in India*, New Delhi: Oxford University Press.

Kamel, R. and Hoffman, A. (1999) *The Maquiladora Reader: cross-border organizing since NAFTA*, Philadelphia, PA: American Friends Service Committee.

Kapoor, I. (1993) 'Abstraction as violence and the radical democratic alternative: a political-ecological critique of India's development process', unpublished PhD thesis, Department of Political Science, University of Toronto.

—— (2002a) 'Deliberative democracy or agonistic pluralism? The relevance of the Habermas–Mouffe debate for Third World politics', *Alternatives*, 27(4): 459-87.

—— (2002b) 'The devil's in the theory: a critical assessment of Robert Chambers' work on participatory development', *Third World Quarterly*, 23(1): 101-17.

—— (2003) 'Acting in a tight spot: Homi Bhabha's postcolonial politics', *New Political Science*, 25(4): 561-77.

Kelsall, T. and Mercer, C. (2003) 'Empowering people? World Vision and the "transforma-tory development" in Tanzania', *Review of African Political Economy*, 96: 293-304.

Keohane, K. (1993) 'Central problems in the philosophy of the social sciences after post-modernism: reconciling consensus and hegemonic theories of epistemology and politi-cal ethics', *Philosophy and Social Criticism*, 19(2): 145-69.

Khan, S. (2001) 'Performing the native informant: doing ethnography from the margins', *Canadian Journal of Women and the Law*, 13(2): 266-84.

Kiely, R. (1999) 'The last refuge of the noble savage? A critical assessment of post-development theory', *European Journal of Development Research*, 11(4): 30-55.

Klein, M. (2000) *No Logo: taking aim at the brand bullies*, Toronto: Vintage.

Koeberle, S. and Malesa, T. (2005) 'Experience with World Bank conditionality', back-ground paper, 'Conditionality revisited: development policy forum', Washington, DC: World Bank. Available at: http://siteresources.worldbank.org/PROJECTS/Resources/Session1dExperiencewithWorldBankConditionalityS.pdf (accessed 23 March 2007).

Kothari, R. (1988) *State Against Democracy*, Delhi: Ajanta Publications.

Kristeva, J. (1977) *About Chinese Women*, trans. A. Barrows, New York: Urizen.

Kuhn, T. (1970) *The Structure of Scientific Revolutions*, Chicago, IL: University of Chicago Press.

Kulynych, J.J. (1997) 'Performing politics: Foucault, Habermas, and postmodern partici-pation', *Polity*, 30(2): 315-47.

Laclau, E. (1971, reprinted 1986) 'Feudalism and capitalism in Latin America', in P.F. Klaren and T.J. Bossert (eds) *Promise of Development*, Boulder, CO: Westview.

Laclau, E. and Mouffe, C. (1985) *Hegemony and Socialist Strategy*, London: Verso.

Lagae, W. (1990) 'A public choice approach to the supply of official bilateral aid', Leuven: CES Research Paper in Economic Development No. 15.

Lal, J. (1996) 'Situating locations: the politics of self, identity, and "other" in living and writing the text', in D. Wolf (ed.) *Feminist Dilemmas in Fieldwork*, Boulder, CO: Westview.

Landry, D. and MacLean, G. (1996) 'Introduction: reading Spivak', in G.C. Spivak, *The Spivak Reader*, D. Landry and G. MacLean (eds), London and New York: Routledge.

Lerner, D. (1962) *The Passing of Traditional Society: modernizing the Middle East*, Glencoe, IL: Free Press.

LeVine, V. (1993) 'Administrative corruption and democratization in Africa: aspects of the theoretic agenda', *Corruption and Reform*, 7(3): 271-8.

Live8 (2005) '2005 highlights'. Available at: http://www.live8live.com/ (accessed 16 February 2006).

Lloyd, M. (2002) *A Feminist Politics of Difference*, London: Sage.

Lumsdaine, D.H. (1993) *Moral Vision in International Politics: the foreign aid regime, 1949–1989*, Princeton, NJ: Princeton University Press.

McClelland, D. (1967) *The Achieving Society*, New York: Free Press.

McClintock, A. (1992) 'The myth of progress: pitfalls of the term post-colonialism', *Social Text*, 31/32: 84-97.

—— (1995) *Imperial Leather: race, gender and sexuality in the colonial contest*, London and New York: Routledge.

McKay, S.C. (2006) 'The squeaky wheel's dilemma: new forms of labor organizing in the Philippines', *Labor Studies Journal*, 30(4): 41-63.

McNay, L. (1999) 'Subject, psyche and agency: the work of Judith Butler', *Theory, Culture and Society*, 16(2): 175-93.

—— (2000) *Gender and Agency: reconfiguring the subject in feminist and social theory*, Cambridge: Polity Press.

Makuwira, J. (2004) 'Non-governmental organizations (NGOs) and participatory development in basic education in Malawi', *Current Issues in Comparative Education*, 6(2): 1-11. Available at: http://www.tc.columbia.edu/cice/articles/jm162.htm (accessed 3 June 2005).

Mansbridge, J. (1996) 'Using power/fighting power: the polity', in S. Benhabib (ed.) *Democracy and Difference*, Princeton, NJ: Princeton University Press.

Manzo, K. (1991) 'Modernist discourse and the crisis of development theory', *Studies in Comparative International Development*, 26(2): 3-36.

Marchand, M. and Parpart, J. (eds) (1995) *Feminism, Postmodernism, Development*, London and New York: Routledge.

Mauss, M. (1950, reprinted 1990) *The Gift: the form and reasons for exchange in archaic societies*, trans. W.D. Halls, New York: W.W. Norton.

Mayoux, L. (1995) 'Beyond naivety: women, gender inequality and participatory development', *Development and Change*, 26(2): 235-58.

Mbembe, A. (2001) *On the Postcolony*, Berkeley: University of California Press.

Medevoi, L., Raman, S., and Robinson, B. (1990) 'Can the subaltern vote?', *Socialist Review*, 20(3): 133-49.

Medley, J. and Carroll, L. (2004) 'The hungry ghost: IMF policy, global capitalist transformation, and laboring bodies in Southeast Asia', in E.O. Zein-Elabdin and S. Charusheela (eds) *Postcolonialism Meets Economics*, London and New York: Routledge.

Mercer, C. (2003) 'Performing partnership: civil society and the illusions of good governance in Tanzania', *Political Geography*, 22: 741-63.

Merry, S.E. (2003) 'Human rights and the demonization of culture', *Polar: Political and Legal Anthropology Review*, 26(1): 55-77.

Mies, M. and Shiva, V. (1993) *Ecofeminism*, London: Zed.

Mills, M.B. (2005) 'From nimble fingers to raised fists: women and labor activism in globalizing Thailand', *Signs: Journal of Women in Culture and Society*, 31(1): 117-44.

Miyoshi, M. (1993) 'A borderless world? From colonialism to transnationalism and the decline of the nation-state', *Critical Inquiry*, 19: 726-51.

—— (2000) 'Ivory tower in escrow', *Boundary 2*, 27(1): 7-50.

Mohan, G. and Hickey, S. (2004) 'Relocating participation within a radical politics of development: critical modernism and citizenship', in G. Hickey and S. Mohan (eds) *Participation – From Tyranny to Transformation? Exploring new approaches to participation in development*, London: Zed.

Mohan, G. and Stokke, K. (2000) 'Participatory development and empowerment: the dangers of localism', *Third World Quarterly*, 21(2): 247-68.

Mohanty, C. (1991) 'Under Western eyes: feminist scholarship and colonial discourse', in C. Mohanty, A. Russo, and L. Torres (eds) *Third World Women and the Politics of Feminism*, Bloomington: Indiana University Press.

Moore-Gilbert, B. (1997) *Postcolonial Theory*, London: Verso.

Moore-Gilbert, B., Stanton, G., and Maley, W. (eds) (1997) *Postcolonial Criticism*, London: Longman.

Morton, S. (2003) *Gayatri Chakravorty Spivak*, London and New York: Routledge.

Mosley, P. (1985) 'The political economy of foreign aid: a model of the market for a public good', *Economic Development and Cultural Change*, 33(2): 373-93.

Mosse, D. (1994) 'Authority, gender and knowledge: theoretical reflections on the practice of Participatory Rural Appraisal', *Development and Change*, 25(4): 497-526.

—— (2001) '"People's knowledge", participation and patronage: operations and representations in rural development', in B. Cooke and U. Kothari (eds) *Participation: the new tyranny?*, London: Zed.

Mouffe, C. (1988a) 'Hegemony and new political subjects: towards a new concept of democracy', in C. Nelson and L. Grossberg (eds) *Marxism and Interpretation of Culture*, Chicago: University of Illinois Press.

—— (1988b) 'Radical democracy: modern or postmodern?', in A. Ross (ed.) *Universal Abandon? The politics of postmodernism*, Minneapolis: University of Minnesota Press.

—— (1993) *The Return of the Political*, London: Verso.

—— (1997) 'Decision, deliberation, and democratic ethos', *Philosophy Today*, Spring: 24-30.

—— (1999) 'Deliberative democracy or agonistic pluralism?', *Social Research*, 66(3): 745-58.

—— (2000) *The Democratic Paradox*, London: Verso.

Mudimbe, V.Y. (1988) *The Invention of Africa: gnosis, philosophy, and the order of knowledge*, Bloomington: Indiana University Press.

—— (1994) *The Idea of Africa*, London: James Currey.

Mutume, G. (2001) 'Africa: World Bank study says aid cannot buy economic reforms', Third World Network, 27 March. Available at: http://www.twnside.org.sg/title/cannot.htm (accessed 20 March 2006).

Narayan, U. (1997) *Dislocating Cultures: identities, traditions, and Third-World feminism*, London and New York: Routledge.

NDCP (2006) 'Dutch aid policy', The Hague: Ministry of Foreign Affairs. Available at: http://www.minbuza.nl/default.asp?CMS_ITEM=151164CE0CA6431AB867CE8C7E 36F841X1X58362X45 (accessed 17 February 2006).

Nealon, J.T. (1998) *Alterity Politics*, Durham, NC: Duke University Press.

171

Nederveen Pieterse, J. (1998) 'My paradigm or yours? Alternative development, post-development, reflexive development', *Development and Change*, 29(2): 343-73.

—— (2000) 'After postdevelopment', *Third World Quarterly*, 21(2): 175-91.

—— (2001) *Development Theory: deconstructions/reconstructions*, London: Sage.

Nederveen Pieterse, J. and Parekh, B. (eds) (1995) *The Decolonization of the Imagination: culture, knowledge and power*, London: Zed.

Nicholls, B. (1997) 'Disrupting time: post-colonial politics in Homi Bhabha's *The Location of Culture*', *Southern Review*, 30(1): 4-25.

Northover, H. (2004) 'To lend or to grant? A critical view of the IMF and the World Bank's proposed approach to debt sustainability analyses for low-income countries', CAFOD Working Paper. Available at: http://www.cafod.org.uk/var/storage/original/application/phphQhUd5.pdf (accessed 17 February 2006).

Nussbaum, M. (1995a) 'Human capabilities, female human beings' in M. Nussbaum and J. Glover (eds) *Women, Culture and Development*, Oxford: Clarendon.

—— (1995b) 'Introduction' in M. Nussbaum and J. Glover (eds) *Women, Culture and Development*, Oxford: Clarendon.

OECD (2001) 'Untying aid to the least developed countries', Paris: OECD Policy Brief. Available at: http://www.oecd.org/dataoecd/16/24/2002959.pdf (accessed 17 February 2006).

—— (2006a) 'Ratification of the Convention of the OECD', Paris: OECD. Available at: http://www.oecd.org/document/58/0,2340,en_2649_201185_1889402_1_1_1_1,00.html (accessed 17 February 2006).

—— (2006b) 'Overview of the OECD', Paris: OECD. Available at: http://www.oecd.org/document/18/0,2340,en_2649_201185_2068050_1_1_1_1,00.html (accessed 17 February 2006).

O'Hanlon, R. and Washbrook, D. (1992) 'After Orientalism: culture, criticism, and politics in the Third World', *Comparative Studies in Society and History*, 34: 141-67.

O'Neill, J. (1999) 'What gives (with Derrida)?', *European Journal of Social Theory*, 2(2): 131-45.

Ong, A. (1987) *Spirits of Resistance and Capitalist Discipline: factory women in Malaysia*, Albany, NY: SUNY Press.

Osteen, M. (2002) 'Introduction: questions of the gift', in M. Osteen (ed.) *The Question of the Gift*, London and New York: Routledge.

Oxfam (2005) 'Paying the price: why rich countries must invest now in a war on poverty', Oxford: Oxfam Publishing. Available at: http://www.oxfam.qc.ca/html/publications/PDFpublications/etudes/Payingpercent20thepercent20Pricepercent20screenpercent20version.pdf (accessed 17 February 2006).

Pantham, T. (1987) 'Habermas' practical discourse and Gandhi's *Satyagraha*', in B. Parekh and T. Pantham (eds) *Political Discourse: explorations in Indian and Western political thought*, New Delhi: Sage.

Parfitt, T. (2004) 'The ambiguity of participation: a qualified defence of participatory development', *Third World Quarterly*, 25(3): 537-56.

Parpart, J. (2000) 'Rethinking participation, empowerment, and development from a gender perspective', in J. Freedman (ed.) *Transforming Development: foreign aid for a changing world*, Toronto: University of Toronto Press.

Parry, B. (1987) 'Problems in current theories of colonial discourse', *Oxford Literary Review*, 9(1-2): 27-58.

—— (1996) 'Signs of our times', *Third Text*, 28(9): 5-24.

Parsons, G. (1997) 'Another India: imagining escape from the masculine self', in P. Darby (ed.) *At the Edge of International Relations: postcolonialism, gender and development*, London: Pinter.

Petras, J. and Veltmeyer, H. (2002) 'Age of reverse aid: neo-liberalism as catalyst of regression', *Development and Change*, 33(2): 281-93.

Pomerantz, P.R. (2004) *Aid Effectiveness in Africa: developing trust between donors and governments*, Lanham, MD: Lexington Books.

Prakash, G. (1990) 'Writing post-orientalist histories of the Third World: perspectives from Indian historiography', *Comparative Studies in Society and History*, 32(2): 383-408.

—— (1992a) 'Postcolonial criticism and Indian historiography', *Social Text*, 31/32: 8-19.

—— (1992b) 'Can the "subaltern" ride? A reply to O'Hanlon and Washbrook', *Comparative Studies in Society and History*, 34: 168-84.

—— (1999) *Another Reason*, Princeton, NJ: Princeton University Press.

Pronk, J. (2001) 'Aid as catalyst', *Development and Change*, 32(4): 611-29.

Raffer, K. and Singer, H.W. (1996) *The Foreign Aid Business*, Cheltenham: Edward Elgar.

Randall, V. and Theobold, R. (1985) *Political Change and Underdevelopment*, London: Macmillan.

Rangan, H. (2000) *Of Myths and Movements: rewriting Chipko into Himalayan history*, London: Verso.

Razack, S. (1998) *Looking White People in the Eye: gender, race, and culture in the courtrooms and classrooms*, Toronto: University of Toronto Press.

Renan, E. (1882, reprinted 1990) 'What is a nation?', in H.K. Bhabha (ed.) *Nation and Narration*, London and New York: Routledge.

Renard, R. and Molenaers, N. (2003a) 'Civil society participation in Rwanda's poverty reduction strategy', discussion paper, Antwerp: University of Antwerp, Institute of Development Policy and Management.

—— (2003b) 'The World Bank, participation and PRSP: The Bolivian case revisited', *European Journal of Development Research*, 15(2): 133-61.

Rigg, J. (1997) *Southeast Asia: the human landscape of modernization and development*, London and New York: Routledge.

Rist, G. (1997) *The History of Development: from Western origins to global faith*, trans. P. Camiller, London: Zed.

Robbins, B. and Stamatopoulou, E. (2004) 'Reflections on culture and cultural rights', *The South Atlantic Quarterly*, 103(2/3): 419-34.

Rosa, K. (1994) 'The conditions and organisational activities of women in free trade zones: Malaysia, Philippines and Sri Lanka, 1970–1990', in S. Rowbotham and S. Mitter (eds) *Dignity and Daily Bread: new forms of economic organising among poor women in the Third World and the First*, London and New York: Routledge.

Rostow, W. (1960) *The Five Stages of Economic Growth: a non-communist manifesto*, Cambridge: Cambridge University Press.

Rowbotham, S. and Mitter, S. (1994) 'Introduction', in S. Rowbotham and S. Mitter (eds) *Dignity and Daily Bread: new forms of economic organising among poor women in the Third World and the First*, London and New York: Routledge.

Roy, A. (2004a) 'Help that hinders', *Le monde diplomatique*, November. Available at: http://mondediplo.com/2004/11/16roy (accessed 22 March 2006).

—— (2004b) *An Ordinary Person's Guide to Empire*, Cambridge, MA: South End Press.

Sachs, W. (ed.) (1992) *The Development Dictionary: a guide to knowledge as power*, London: Zed.

Said, E. (1978, reprinted 1995) *Orientalism*, London: Penguin.

—— (1983) *The World, the Text and the Critic*, Cambridge, MA: Harvard University Press.

—— (1985) 'Orientalism reconsidered', in F. Barker, P. Hulme, M. Iversen, and D. Loxley (eds) *Europe and Its Others*, vol. 1, Colchester: University of Essex.

—— (1993) *Culture and Imperialism*, New York: Vintage.

Schick, I.C. (1999) *The Erotic Margin*, London: Verso.

Seminar (1987) The R. Guha and V. Shiva / J. Bandyopadhyay debate on Chipko in the February, June, August and November issues.

Shah, A. (2005) 'G8 Summit 2005 outcome'. Available at: http://www.globalissues.org/TradeRelated/Debt/g8summit2005/outcome.asp (accessed 17 February 2006).

Shapiro, I. and Hacker-Cordon, C. (eds) (1999) *Democracy's Edges*, New York: Cambridge University Press.

Shihata, I. (1997) *Complementary Reform: essays on legal, judicial, and other institutional reforms supported by the World Bank*, The Hague: Kluwer Law International.

Shiva, V. (1989) *Staying Alive: women, ecology and development*, London: Zed.

Shohat, E. (1992) 'Notes on the "post-colonial"', *Social Text*, 31/32: 99-113.

SIDA (2007) 'Human rights and democracy'. Available at: http://www.sida.se/sida/jsp/sida.jsp?d=104&language=en_US (accessed 22 March 2007).

Smillie, I. (1999) 'Public support and the politics of aid', *Development*, 42 (3): 71-6.

Spivak, G.C. (1985a) 'The Rani of Sirmur: an essay in the reading of archives', *History and Theory*, 24(3): 247-72.

—— (1985b), 'Strategies of vigilance: an interview with Gayatri Chakravorty Spivak', *Block*, 10: 5-9.

—— (1988a) 'Can the subaltern speak?', in C. Nelson and L. Grossberg (eds) *Marxism and Interpretation of Culture*, Chicago: University of Illinois Press.

—— (1988b) *In Other Worlds: essays in cultural politics*, London and New York: Routledge.

—— (1990a) *The Post-Colonial Critic: interviews, strategies, dialogues*, S. Harasym (ed.), London and New York: Routledge.

—— (1990b) 'Gayatri Spivak on the politics of the subaltern, interview by Howard Winant', *Socialist Review*, 20(3): 81-97.

—— (1990c) 'Poststructuralism, marginality, postcoloniality and value', in P. Collier and H. Greyer-Ryan (eds) *Literary Theory Today*, London: Polity Press.

—— (1993) *Outside in the Teaching Machine*, London and New York: Routledge.

—— (1995) 'Teaching for the times', in J. Nederveen Pieterse and B. Parekh (eds) *The Decolonization of Imagination: culture, knowledge and power*, London: Zed.

—— (1996) *The Spivak Reader*, D. Landry and G. MacLean (eds), London and New York: Routledge.

—— (1997) 'Pax Electronica: against crisis-driven global telecommunication, an interview with Gayatri Spivak by Geert Lovink'. Available at: http://kunstradio.at/FUTURE?/DX/EVENTS/geert-spivak.html (accessed 12 October 2002).

—— (1999) *A Critique of Postcolonial Reason: toward a critique of the vanishing present*, Cambridge, MA: Harvard University Press.

—— (2000) 'From Haverstock Hill flat to US classroom, what's left of theory?', in J. Butler, J. Guillory, and K. Thomas (eds) *What's Left of Theory?*, London and New York: Routledge.

—— (2001) 'A note on the New International', *Parallax*, 7(3): 12-16.

—— (2002) 'Righting wrongs', unpublished paper. Available at: http://www.law.columbia.edu/law_culture/Spivakpercent20Paper.doc (accessed 12 October 2002).

—— (2003a) 'A conversation with Gayatri Chakravorty Spivak: politics and the imagination, interview by Jenny Sharpe', *Signs: Journal of Women in Culture and Society*, 28(2): 609-24.

—— (2003b) *Death of a Discipline*, New York: Columbia University Press.

—— (2004) 'Righting wrongs', *South Atlantic Quarterly*, 103(2/3): 523-81.

Srinivasan, L. and Narayan, D. (1994) 'Participatory development tool kit: materials to facilitate community empowerment', Washington, DC: World Bank.

Stokke, O. (1996) *Foreign Aid Towards the Year 2000: experiences and challenges*, London: Frank Cass.

Storey, A. (2000) 'Romanticism and Pontius Pilate politics', *Development*, 43(4): 40-6.

Streeten, P. (1981) *First Things First: meeting basic human needs in developing countries*, New York: Oxford University Press for the World Bank.

Streeten, P. and Burki, S.J. (1978) 'Basic needs: some issues', *World Development*, 6(3): 11-21.

Sundara Rajan, R. (1986) *Innovative Competence and Social Change*, Ganeshkind: Poona University Press.

—— (1987) *Towards a Critique of Cultural Reason*, Delhi: Oxford University Press.

—— (1991) *The Primacy of the Political*, Delhi: Oxford University Press.

Sunder Rajan, R. (1997) 'The Third World academic in other places; or the postcolonial intellectual revisited', *Critical Inquiry*, 23(3): 610-18.

Sylvester, C. (1995) 'Africa and Western feminisms: world traveling and the tendencies and possibilities', *Signs*, 20(4): 941-76.

—— (1999) 'Development studies and postcolonial studies: disparate tales of the "Third World"', *Third World Quarterly*, 20(4): 703-21.

Tarnoff, C. and Nowels, L.Q. (1994) *U.S. Foreign Assistance: the rationale, the record, and the challenges in the post-Cold War era*, Washington, DC: National Planning Association.

Taylor, D. (1994) 'Performing gender: Las Madres de la Plaza de Mayo', in D. Taylor and J. Villegas (eds) *Negotiating Performance*, Durham, NC: Duke University Press.

Tewdwr-Jones, M. and Allemendinger, P. (1998) 'Deconstructing communicative rationality: a critique of Habermasian collaborative planning', *Environment and Planning A*, 30(10): 1975-89.

Theobold, R. (1990) *Corruption, Development and Underdevelopment*, London: Macmillan.

—— (2002) 'Can the state deliver?', *New Political Economy*, 7(3): 435-41.

Thérien, J.-P. (2002) 'Debating foreign aid', *Third World Quarterly*, 23(3): 449-66.

Thomas, N. (1994) *Colonialism's Culture*, Princeton, NJ: Princeton University Press.

Tisch, S.J. and Wallace, M.J. (1994) *Dilemmas of Development Assistance*, Boulder, CO: Westview.

Transparency International (2000) *TI Source Book. Confronting Corruption: the elements of a national integrity system*, Berlin: Transparency International.

—— (2007a) 'TI Corruption Perceptions Index'. Available at: http://www.transparency.org/policy_research/surveys_indices/global/cpi (accessed 22 March 2007).

—— (2007b) 'TI Bribe Payers Index'. Available at: http://www.transparency.org/policy_research/surveys_indices/global/bpi (accessed 22 March 2007).

Turner, P. (1993) *I Heard it Through the Grapevine: rumor in African-American culture*, Berkeley: University of California Press.

Udall, L. (1995) 'The international Narmada campaign: a case study of sustained advocacy', in W.F. Fisher (ed.) *Toward Sustainable Development: struggling over India's Narmada river*, New York: M.E. Sharpe.

UNDP (1994) *Human Development Report 1994*, New York: Oxford University Press.

—— (1997) 'Governance for sustainable human development', policy document, New York: UNDP.

—— (2006) 'Membership of the Executive Board', New York: UNDP. Available at: http://www.undp.org/execbrd/memberseng.htm (accessed 16 February 2006).

USAID (2006) 'This is USAID', Washington, DC. Available at: http://www.usaid.gov/about_usaid/ (accessed 17 February 2006).

Varadharajan, A. (1995) *Exotic Parodies: subjectivity in Adorno, Said and Spivak*, Minneapolis: University of Minnesota Press.

Vaughan, M (1994). 'Colonial discourse theory and African history, or has postmodernism passed us by?', *Social Dynamics*, 20(3): 1-23.

Visweswaran, K. (1994) *Fictions of Feminist Ethnography*, Minneapolis: University of Minnesota Press.

—— (2004) 'Gendered states: rethinking culture as a site of South Asian human rights work', *Human Rights Quarterly*, 26: 483-511.

Werbner, R. and Ranger, T. (eds) (1996) *Postcolonial Identities in Africa*, London: Zed.

White, S.C. (1996) 'Depoliticising development: the uses and abuses of participation', *Development in Practice*, 6(1): 6-15.

White, S.K. (1984) 'Habermas's communicative ethics and the development of moral consciousness', *Philosophy and Social Criticism*, 10: 25-47.

Williams, G. (2004) 'Evaluating participatory development: tyranny, power and (re)politicisation', *Third World Quarterly*, 25(3): 557-78.

Williams, R. (1979) *Politics and Letters: interviews with New Left Review*, London: NLB.

—— (1982) *The Sociology of Culture*, New York: Schocken.

Winstanley, D. and Stuart-Smith, K. (1996) 'Policing performance: the ethics of performance management', *Personnel Review*, 25(6): 66-84.

Wolf, D. (ed.) (1996) *Feminist Dilemmas in Fieldwork*, Boulder, CO: Westview.

Women Living Under Muslim Laws (2006). Available at: http://www.wluml.org (accessed 17 January 2006).

World Bank (1989) *Sub-Saharan Africa: from crisis to sustainable growth*, Washington, DC: World Bank.

—— (1992) *Governance and Development*, Washington, DC: World Bank.

—— (1994a) *Managing Development – The Governance Dimension*, Washington, DC: World Bank.

—— (1994b) *Adjustment in Africa: reform, results, and the road ahead*, New York: Oxford University Press for the World Bank.

—— (1997a) *World Development Report 1997: the state in a changing world*, Washington, DC: World Bank.

—— (1997b) *Helping Countries Combat Corruption: the World Bank role*, Poverty Reduction and Economic Management Section, Washington, DC: World Bank.

—— (2000) *PRSP Handbook*, Washington, DC: World Bank.

—— (2001) 'Adjustment lending retrospective: final report', Operations policy and country services, Washington, DC: World Bank. Available at: http://siteresources.worldbank.org/PROJECTS/Resources/ALR06_20_01.pdf (accessed 27 March 2007).

—— (2003) *The Heavily Indebted Poor Countries (HIPC) Debt Initiative: an OED review*, Washington, DC: World Bank.

—— (2006) 'About us: organization', Washington, DC. Available at: http://web.world-bank.org/WBSITE/EXTERNAL/EXTABOUTUS/0,,contentMDK:20040580~menuPK:1696997~pagePK:51123644~piPK:329829~theSitePK:29708,00.html (accessed 22 March 2006).

—— (2007) 'IBRD Articles of Agreement', Washington, DC: World Bank. Available at: http://web.worldbank.org/WBSITE/EXTERNAL/EXTABOUTUS/0,,contentMDK:20049557~menuPK:63000601~pagePK:34542~piPK:36600~theSitePK:29708,00.html (accessed 25 March 2007).

Young, I.M. (1990) *Justice and the Politics of Difference*, Princeton, NJ: Princeton University Press.

—— (1996) 'Communication and the Other: beyond deliberative democracy', in S. Benhabib (ed.) *Democracy and Difference*, Princeton, NJ: Princeton University Press.

Young, R. (1990) *White Mythologies: writing history and the West*, London and New York: Routledge.

—— (1995) *Colonial Desire: hybridity in theory, culture and race*, London and New York: Routledge.

Zein-Elabdin, E.O. (2004) 'Articulating the postcolonial (with economics in mind)', in E.O. Zein-Elabdin and S. Charusheela (eds) *Postcolonialism Meets Economics*, London and New York: Routledge.

Zein-Elabdin, E.O. and Charusheela, S. (2004) 'Introduction: economics and postcolonial thought', in E.O. Zein-Elabdin and S. Charusheela (eds) *Postcolonialism Meets Economics*, London and New York: Routledge.

Žižek, S. (1989) *The Sublime Object of Ideology*, London: Verso.

—— (1993) *Tarrying with the Negative*, Durham, NC: Duke University Press.

—— (1997) *The Plague of Fantasies*, London: Verso.

—— (1999) *The Žižek Reader*, E. Wright and E. Wright (eds), Oxford: Blackwell.

—— (2002) *Welcome to the Desert of the Real!*, London: Verso.

—— (2004) 'From politics to biopolitics . . . and back', *South Atlantic Quarterly*, 103(2/3): 501-21.

INDEX

Aaltola, M. 87
adivasi 58, 69, 109, 157n20; and
   traditional knowledge 69; *see also*
   indigenous peoples
Africa xiv, 25, 28–9, 31, 35, 83, 147; Sub-
   Saharan 31, 83, 147; and state 31-2
agency 7-8, 12-14, 17, 74-5, 118ff., 132ff.;
   see also politics
agonistic pluralism 97-9, 100-3, *see also*
   Mouffe
Ahmad, A. 16
Alcoff, L. 53
Althusser, L. 15
Arendt, H. 34, 125-8; and performativity
   126

Bandy, J. 140-1
basic needs 22-5; and poverty alleviation 22
Baudelaire, C. 76, 81
Baudrillard, J. 23-4, 143
Benhabib, S. 105, 108, 110-11
Bernstein, R. 98, 112, 114
Bhabha, H.K. 7-8, 11-15, 17, 75, 86,
   101, 118ff., 132ff., 148-9; and agency
   7-8, 75, 118ff., 132ff.; and ambivalence
   7; and cultural/semiotic approach 14-15,
   124-5, 132, 135; and colonizer-
   colonized encounters 7-8, 119; and
   creativity 118, 121, 131, 132-3, 148-9;
   critiques of 14-17, 124-5, 130, 133-4,
   149, 150n1; and democracy/politics
   123-5, 129-31, 132ff.; vs.
   Habermas/Mouffe 145-6; and
   historiography 122-3; and hybridity 7,
   86, 118-19, 132-5, 148; and localized
   resistance 17, 130, 135, 146; and
   negotiation 8, 124; and
   materiality/capitalism 14-15, 124-5,

132, 152n9; and mimicry 7-8, 119-22,
128; and nation/nationalism 122-3, 126;
and performativity 118, 120, 125-30,
133-4, 139, 144, 146; and rumour 119,
127; and stereotypes 7, 118-19; and
Third Space 8, 121-2, 128, 133, 139,
141-4, 146; and time-lag 9, 11, 129,
159n13; and 'vegetarian Bible'/Delhi
villagers episode 119, 121-2, 125,
127-8, 133-4, 146
Bono 87-8
Bourdieu, P. 89
Bukovansky, M. 32-3
Butler, J. 120, 125-8; and performativity 126

Caillé, A. 93
Callari, A. 26
Canadian International Development
   Agency (CIDA) 48, 80; and tied aid 48
capitalism 4-5, 11-12, 14-16, 43, 74, 77,
   124, 134, 139-40
Cardoso, F.H. 5-6, 10-16; and associated-
   dependent development 6; and
   dialectical approach 5, 11; and new
   dependency 5; and social alliances 5
Carroll, L. 28, 142
Chambers, R. 42, 50-1, 53, 63; and
   Participatory Rural Appraisal (PRA)
   50-1, 60, 63-4; and power relationships
   50-1, 63-4
Charusheela, S. 27
Chipko *andolan* 136-7, 139, 144-5
class 44, 66; cultures of 44; inequality
   66-7
Coalition for Justice in the Maquiladoras
   140, 142, 145
colonialism 4-7, 13, 43, 86, 98, 113,
   118-20, 125, 133, 136